2021
2022
年度実施

The United Nations Association's Test of English

国連英検
過去問題集

公益財団法人
日本国際連合協会 編著

UNA-JAPAN

A級

SANSHUSHA

はじめに
英語コミュニケーション能力の測定と国連英検

国連英検統括監修官　服部孝彦

国連英検は，英語コミュニケーション能力を測るためのテストです。ひとくちにコミュニケーション能力をテストするといっても，「コミュニケーション能力」という概念は複雑です。ここでは，コミュニケーション能力の理論的枠組みをできる限り明らかにし，コミュニケーション能力をより的確に測るためのテストとしての国連英検のあり方について論じます。

1960年代以降に言語研究に科学的な手法が求められるようになり，「コミュニケーション能力」という概念が生まれました。コミュニケーション能力の概念を最初に示したのはハイムズ（Hymes, 1972）ですが，それ以前に彼は，能力（competence）と運用（performance）の概念を提唱したチョムスキー（Chomsky, 1965）から大きな影響を受けたため，まずチョムスキーの言語理論から考察することにします。

チョムスキーは，従来の学習を習慣形成による刺激と反応の結合が発達したもの，すなわち練習と強化によって形成された習慣とみなす行動主義（behaviorism）の考え方に異論を唱えました。彼は「具体的状況における実際の言語使用」（the actual use of language in concrete situation）を運用（performance）とし，それを「話者―聴者の言語の知識」（the speaker-hearer's knowledge of his language）である能力（competence）と区別しました。

ハイムズはチョムスキーの能力（competence）の概念を発展させ，コミュニケーション能力（communicative competence）の概念を示しました。ハイムズは，文法的な意味に限定したチョムスキーの能力（competence）は不十分であるとし，能力を社会的文化的に拡張すると主張しました。ハイムズのコミュニケーション能力は次の4つに分類されます。

(1) Whether (and to what degree) something is formally possible;

(2) Whether (and to what degree) something is feasible in virtue of the means of implementation available;

(3) Whether (and to what degree) something is appropriate (adequate, happy, successful) in relation to a context in which it is used and evaluated;

(4) Whether (and to what degree) something is in fact done, actually performed, and what its doing entails.

ハイムズは，文法的に正しいのか，発話することが現実的に可能か，社会的に適切であるか，実際に遂行されているのか，といった４つの基準を示したわけです。前者２つが文法に関するもので，後者２つが発話としての容認性に関するものであるといえます。

ハイムズのコミュニケーション能力は，ウィドウソン（Widdowson, 1983），バックマン（Bachman, 1990），さらにはバックマンとパーマー（Bachman and Palmer, 1996）へと引き継がれました。「コミュニケーション能力」という用語は，communicative competence, communicative language ability, language ability と表記が変わり，定義も見直されました。コミュニケーション能力理論で最も新しいものは，バックマンの論理，およびバックマンとパーマーの理論です。バックマンとパーマー（Bachman and Palmer, 1996）の理論は，バックマン（Bachman, 1990）の理論を踏襲した改訂版で，テスティングのための理論という色彩を強めたものです。この２つの理論は現在，コミュニケーション理論の中で最も信頼のおけるものとして，言語教育で受け入れられています。

バックマンとパーマーは，コミュニケーション能力に language ability という用語を用いています。そして，その language ability の中にハイムズやカネールとスウェインなどが言う communicative competence の構成要素をすべて含んだ言語知識（language knowledge）という概念を設けました。バックマンとパーマーの言語知識は，組織的知識（organizational knowledge）と語用論的知識（pragmatic knowledge）に分けられます。組織的知識はさらに，文法的知識（grammatical knowledge）とテキスト的知識（textual knowledge）に分類されます。語用論的知識は，機能的知識

(functional knowledge) と社会言語学的知識 (sociolinguistic knowledge) に分類されます。バックマンとパーマーは，言語知識以外にトピック知識 (topical knowledge) や個人的特徴 (personal characteristics) なども language ability の中に含まれる要素としており，これらすべてを結びつける能力として方略的能力 (strategic competence) を挙げています。

バックマンとパーマーは次のように述べ，自分たちが提示したコミュニケーションのモデルはテスト開発のためのものである，としています。

> We would note that we conceive of this not as a working model of language processing, but rather as a conceptual basis for organizing our thinking about the test development process.

バックマンとパーマーは，心理的な意味での言語処理モデルではなく，テスト開発のための概念的な枠組みを設定したといえます。

バックマンとパーマーの language ability 理論の基礎になったのが，バックマン (Bachman, 1990) の communicative language ability 理論です。バックマンは，知識 (knowledge) ではなく能力 (competence) という用語を用いて，語用論的能力 (pragmatic competence) と組織的能力 (organizational competence) について，次のように述べています。

> Pragmatic competence includes the types of knowledge which, in addition to organization competence, are employed in the contexturalized performance and interpretation of socially appropriate illocutionary acts in discourse.

ここでバックマンは，語用論的能力／語用論的知識は，組織的能力／組織的知識の基盤の上にできあがるものであることを示しました。また，語用論的能力／語用論的知識は，テキストを構成しない一文単位でも発揮されるということを考えますと，組織的能力／組織的知識の中心は文法的能力／文法的知識であることがわかります。

以上のコミュニケーション能力理論に基づき，国連英検では以下のように出題されています。高等学校で学習する英語の範囲内で出題されるＣ級は，語用論的知識に先行して学習する必要のある組織的知識について問い，加えて組織的知識の基礎となる文法的知識を中心として出題しています。B 級では，組織的知識の中の文法的知識に加え，英文エッセイをテーマに沿って“書く”問題も出題され，組織的知識の中のもう 1 つの力であるテキスト的知識も問われます。さらに，国連英検の特徴である国連に対する理解についての設問も出されます。特 A 級と A 級では，1 次試験の筆記試験で文法的知識とテキスト的知識および国連に関する知識が問われ，1 次試験合格者を対象に実施される 2 次試験の面接テストでは，これらに加えて語用論的知識である機能的知識と社会言語学的知識，言語力の要素を統合させる方略的能力，さらには国際事情についての知識も問われます。

以上のように，国連英検ではコミュニケーション能力の研究成果を踏まえ，コミュニケーション能力の基盤をなす力を下の級で測定し，上の級ではそれらの基盤的な力の測定に加え，語用論的な力とメタ認知方略に関する力も測定しています。特に最上級の特 A 級では，良識ある国際人として持つべき国際常識や国際適応能力についてもテストされます。国連英検は，まさしく総合的英語コミュニケーション能力を測定する試験であるといえます。

参考文献

Bachman, L. F. (1990). *Fundamental considerations in language testing*. Oxford: Oxford University Press.

Bachman, L. F & Palmer, A. S. (1996). *Language testing in practice*. Oxford: Oxford University Press.

Canale, M. (1983). On some dimensions of language proficiency. In J. Oller (Ed.) *Issues in language testing research*. (pp. 333-387). Massachusetts: Newburry House.

Canale, M. & Swain, M. (1980). Theoretical bases of communicative approaches to second language teaching and testing. *Applied Linguistics, 1* (1), 1-47.

Chomsky, N. (1965). *Aspects of the theory of syntax*. Cambridge, M.A.: The MIT Press.

Hymes, D. (1972). On communicative competence. In J. Pride & J. Holmes (Eds.) *Sociolinguistics: Selected readings*. (pp. 269-293). Harmondsworth: Penguin.

Widdowson, H. G. (1983). *Learning purpose and language use*. Oxford: Oxford University Press.

国連英検過去問題集　A 級（2021-2022 実施）

目次

※本書は，実際の検定試験で使用された試験問題に基づいて編集されておりますが，一部修正されている場合があります。

国連英検とは

■「国連英検」（国際連合公用語英語検定試験）は，1981 年に始まり，長い歴史を持つ英語検定試験です。試験は年に 2 回，全国主要都市で実施されます。特 A 級から E 級まで全部で 6 つの級があり（注：現在 D 級・E 級は休止中），中学生から社会人，シニアエイジまでの幅広い層を対象とし，受験資格は特になく，どなたでも受験できます。

試験を主催するのは，外務省の外郭団体としてスタートした公益財団法人日本国際連合協会です。日本国際連合協会は，国連の A 級諮問民間団体である「国連協会世界連盟」（WFUNA）の有力メンバーで，国内外での国連普及活動を積極的に行っています。

国連英検も国連普及活動の一環として実施されており，国連の理念である「国際協力」「国際理解」をコンセプトに，「真に役立つグローバルコミュニケーション能力」の育成を目標としています。試験内容は国連の活動に沿って，世界平和，地球環境，世界政治，世界経済から，人権，食品，医療などの世界情勢，国際時事問題まで幅広く出題されるため，今まさに地球上で問われている問題を認識し，自分の考えや解決策を論理的に伝達する表現力が求められます。単なる語学力の判定にとどまらず，総合的な国際コミュニケーションスキルが問われます。

■ 国連英検は，資格として多角的にアピールできる検定試験です。多くの大学で推薦入試・編入試験の評価資格として認められ，B 級以上の合格を単位認定している大学もあります。

特 A 級は，成績優秀者に外務大臣賞が授与されるほか，合格者には外務省国際機関人事センターが実施している「JPO 派遣候補者選考試験」において加点が行われます。

この JPO は，国際公務員（国連職員・ユネスコ職員など）になるための登竜門と言えるもので，2 年間の海外派遣を経て国際公務員試験に挑戦できる制度です。

A 級は成績優秀者に国連協会会長賞が授与されます。

C 級以上の合格者は，文部科学省より，高等学校卒業程度認定規則において，英語資格としてレベル認定されています。

また，国際協力機構（JICA）では，C 級以上の合格者を，応募の際に必要となる語学力の評価基準をクリアしたものと認定しています。

なお，警視庁では警察官採用試験（1 次試験）に「資格経歴等の評定」を導入していますが，国連英検 C 級以上の合格者については，1 次試験の成績の一部として評価しています。

■ 国連英検は，コミュニケーションを重視した試験です。B 級～ E 級で出題されるリスニング問題のウェイトは 40％と高く，また B 級以上は国際時事問題をテーマとした英作文（ウェイト 20％）が設けられています。A 級以上は 2 次試験で面接試験を実施し，ネイティブスピーカーと国際時事問題について討論を行います。さらに特 A 級については，ネイティブスピーカーに加え，元外務省大使など外交実務経験者や国際関係を研究する大学教授を面接官として，より深い議論を行います。

●国連英検 D 級・E 級の開催休止について

国連英検では昨今の英語教育における新学習指導要領の大幅な改定に鑑み，主に中学生～高校生を受験対象としている D 級・E 級の試験実施を 2023 年度より休止しています。再開時期・受験形式等は，決定次第国連英検のホームページにて広報致します。

●国連英検受験のための指定テキストについて

国連英検は国連に関する基礎知識を学習するための教材として『新 わかりやすい国連の活動と世界』（三修社）を指定テキストとし，特 A 級～ C 級の出題にも使用しています。級により出題範囲が異なりますので，事前にホームページで確認することをお勧めします。

● A級のレベルと審査基準および問題の傾向と対策 ●

レベルと審査基準

問題の形式と内容が異なるため，他の英語検定試験との比較は困難ですが，国連英検A級は実用英語検定1級とほぼ同じ，あるいはそれより高いレベルといってよいでしょう。英字新聞や雑誌の記事を限られた時間内で理解できる，比較的高度な語句や表現を認識できる，またはあるテーマについて論理的な内容を英文で表現する，日常の身辺の出来事・時事問題などに関して，国籍や文化背景を異にする人々を交えて討議する能力も要求されます。

問題の傾向と対策

1次試験は，マークシートによる客観テスト（80点）と英作文（20点）から成り立っています（リスニングテストはありません）。

客観テストでは特A級と同じく，8題の大問が出されます。最初の大問は国連に関するものですので，指定テキストの『新 わかりやすい国連の活動と世界』*New Today's Guide to the United Nations*（三修社）を読んでおくことが課題になっています。各級の指定テキストからの出題範囲は国連英検のホームページに掲載されています。各題の英文の長さは約400～1000語程度で，速読が求められます。その他の大問のトピックも特A級と同じく，国際問題・政治・経済・歴史・文化・科学や小説などが出題されます。

英作文では，約150～200語程度の英文を作成できる知識・思考力・表現力が要求され，受験者の意見の有無も考慮されます。

2次試験は1次試験合格者が対象の面接試験で，約10分間，ネイティブスピーカーとディスカッションを行います。

面接でカバーされるトピックは主に，国連の理念と活動・時事問題・自己紹介・日常の事柄についてで，発音や文法のチェック・知識・判断力・表現力・マナーなどが審査されます。実施の詳細はp.216をご参照ください。

2021年
第1回試験
問題

A級第１次試験問題用紙

A級

外務省後援

２０２１年度第１回国際連合公用語

英語検定試験（120分）

受験上の注意

1．問題用紙は試験開始の合図があるまで開いてはいけません。その間に、この**受験上の注意を熟読しておいてください。**

2．**受験番号と氏名を解答用紙（マークシートと作文用紙）**に記入してください。

3．解答用紙の配布は１人１部のみです。複数の配布は致しません。

4．試験開始前は、答案への解答記入は禁止です。

5．マークシートの記入は、１～100までの記入箇所がありますが、この級では１～80までを使います。

6．マークシートの記入は、必ずＨＢ以上の濃い鉛筆を使って該当箇所を黒く塗りつぶしてください。書き間違いの場合は「アト」が残らないように消してください。マークシートは絶対に折ったり曲げたりしないでください。

7．受験級、受験地区、会場番号、受験番号のマークシートへの記入は監督者の指示に従い、間違いなく記入してください。**(裏表紙の「マークシート記入例」参照)**

8．作文は、⑴読みやすい文字をペン、ボールペンまたはＨＢ以上の濃い鉛筆で書いてください。⑵使用語数の150～200語を目安にしてください。

9．試験問題についての質問は、印刷が不鮮明な場合を除き、一切受けつけません。

10．中途退室の際は、マークシートと作文用紙を持って監督者に渡し、他の受験者の迷惑にならないように静かに退室してください。中途退室後の再入室はできません。

11．試験中は他の受験者の妨げとなる行動は慎んでください。また携帯電話等の電源はお切りください。

12．マークシートと作文用紙は監督者に提出し、問題用紙はご自由にお持ち帰りください。

＊試験問題の複製や転載、インターネットへのアップロード等、いかなる媒体への転用を禁止します。

試験結果について

1．第１次試験の結果は2021年６月30日㈬頃に受験申込書に記載された住所に郵送で通知します。

2．その間に住所変更をされた方は、郵便局へ住所変更の届け出を忘れずに行ってください。

3．発表前の試験結果のお問合せには応じられません。

第２次試験について

1．第１次試験合格者には、試験結果発表と同時に試験日時、会場を指定して通知します。（第１次試験を特別会場で受験した合格者には最寄りの２次試験会場が指定されます。）

2．第２次試験は2021年７月11日㈰です。Ａ級の試験地は札幌・仙台・東京・名古屋・大阪・福岡・鹿児島・沖縄のいずれかになります。（特Ａ級との併願で特Ａ級の第１次試験に合格された方の試験地は東京と大阪になります。）あらかじめご了承願います。

UNA-JAPAN
公益財団法人 日本国際連合協会
http://www.unaj.or.jp/

I. Fill in each of the following blanks with the most appropriate of the four alternatives according to the knowledge and information gained from *New Today's Guide to the United Nations*.

1. Foreword

From this vision of the role of the United Nations in the next century flow three key priorities for the future: eradicating poverty, preventing conflict, and promoting ________.

A. peace
B. human rights
C. sustainability
D. democracy

2. Address to the General Assembly

I take note of State Counsellor Aung San Suu Kyi's address today — and her intention to implement the recommendations of the Advisory Commission on ________ State that was chaired by Kofi Annan within the shortest time possible.

A. Chin
B. Kayah
C. Rakhine
D. Mon

3. Membership

The 51 original Members of the United Nations were the States that took part in the ________ Conference or had previously signed the Declaration by United Nations, and which signed and ratified the charter.

A. San Francisco
B. Cairo
C. Yalta
D. Potsdam

4. Security Council

The Security Council may investigate any dispute that could endanger international peace and security, and may recommend methods for adjusting such disputes or terms for their ________.

A. friction
B. obligation
C. settlement
D. procedure

5. Peacebuilding Commission

The Peacebuilding Commission is an intergovernmental advisory body composed of ________ Member States elected from the General Assembly, the Security Council, and the Economic and Social Council.

A. 15
B. 31
C. 47
D. 54

6. **<u>Budget of the United Nations</u>**

The regular program budget of the United Nations is approved by the General Assembly ________.

A. every six months
B. annually
C. biennially
D. every three years

7. **<u>International Atomic Energy Agency (IAEA)</u>**

In ________, the Nobel Prize for peace was awarded to the IAEA and the then Director-General Mohamed ElBaradei to honor the Agency's achievements in both fields.

A. 1969
B. 1988
C. 2001
D. 2005

8. **<u>World Health Organization (WHO)</u>**

The major organs of the WHO are the World Health ________, which is the supreme decision-making body, the Executive Board, which comprises members from 34 countries, and the Secretariat.

A. Assembly
B. Council
C. Movement
D. Institution

9. **<u>World Trade Organization (WTO)</u>**

The World Trade Organization (WTO) is an international organization with the aim to promote multilateral trade ________ and make rules on trade.

A. agreements
B. liberalization
C. cooperation
D. act

10. **<u>The End of the Cold War and the Revival of UN Diplomacy</u>**

Seeking a more influential status in the UN, since 2004, Japan aligned with Germany, ________ and India to ask for the expansion of the permanent membership of the Council.

A. Indonesia
B. Canada
C. Australia
D. Brazil

II. Choose from among the four alternatives the one that is the most appropriate form of each of the underlined verbs.

"We will never give up, we will never concede!" President Donald Trump told the crowd of supporters he **(11)** **summon** to Washington on January 6. They heard him and obeyed. Within hours, a mob of self-styled revolutionaries **(12)** **wave** Trump flags had stormed the Capitol. Scaling scaffolding and breaking windows, they filled the marble halls. Shots were fired inside the building as lawmakers and their staff scrambled for cover and tear gas filled the Rotunda. For the first time since the Civil War, America **(13)** **not have** a peaceful transfer of power.

Before the riot interrupted it, Trump's last-ditch attempt to steal the presidential election that he unambiguously lost was not going well. Vice President Mike Pence announced he would fulfill his ceremonial role of counting the states' electoral votes, **(14)** **reject** Trump's demand to throw them out. The Republican Senate leader, Mitch McConnell, gave an impassioned speech rebuking colleagues **(15)** **seek** to disrupt the process on Trump's behalf.

For four years, Trump's party had submitted to a Faustian bargain. Recognizing the loyalty he commanded from voters, officials fell in line–some gleefully, some grudgingly–behind a President who pushed America nearly to its breaking point. Republicans decided that winning elections and wielding power **(16)** **justify** ignoring Trump's authoritarian tendencies, his assaults on the political system, his attacks on the GOP's members and ideals. But two weeks before the end of his presidency, the price of enabling Trump–for the GOP and the country alike–became clear.

In his final bid to overturn the election, Trump browbeat dozens of Republican lawmakers into objecting to the certification of Joe Biden's victory on January 6, forcing partisans **(17)** **take** sides on his final challenge to democracy and the Constitution. In the process, Trump helped **(18)** **ensure** that the GOP candidates in two Georgia runoff elections would lose by slim margins, giving Democrats control of the Senate. A party that abandoned its principles to gain power has lost both.

In the final weeks of his term, Trump ran amok. He vowed to ruin the careers of GOP officials **(19)** **not go** along with his baseless election claims. He vetoed the annual military budget. He sided with Democrats by demanding $2,000 stimulus checks the GOP would not support. He painted the Georgia Senate races as rigged, prompting supporters to urge a ballot boycott. He urged "patriots" to descend on D.C. for a final showdown at the Capitol. As the chaos unfolded, Trump tweeted a limp request for nonviolence and hours later released a video **(20)** **tell** his supporters to "go home" while praising them and continuing to insist the election was stolen.

11. A. was summoning　B. had summoned
C. has summoned　D. would summon

12. A. were waving B. waved
C. who were waved D. waving

13. A. would not have B. must not have
C. has never had D. isn't having

14. A. rejecting B. to reject
C. who rejected D. rejected

15. A. were seeking B. who sought
C. to be sought D. sought

16. A. were justified B. justifying
C. that justified D. justified

17. A. were taking B. who took
C. taking D. to take

18. A. to be ensured B. ensure
C. ensuring D. ensured

19. A. were not going B. who would not go
C. that cannot go D. which did not go

20. A. tells B. told
C. telling D. that tells

Ⅲ. Fill in each of the following blanks with the most grammatically and logically appropriate of the four alternatives.

The volume of data in the world is increasing exponentially. By some estimates, 90 per cent of the data in the world has been created in the last two years, and it is projected to increase by 40 per cent annually. A large share of this output is "data exhaust," or passively collected data deriving from everyday interactions with digital products or services, including mobile phones, credit cards, and social media. This deluge of digital data is known as big data.

Data is growing because it is increasingly being gathered by inexpensive and numerous information—sensing, mobile devices and because the world's capacity for storing information has roughly doubled every 40 months since the 1980s.

The data revolution -- which encompasses the open data movement, the rise of crowdsourcing, new ICTs for data collection, and the explosion in the availability of big data, together with the emergence of artificial intelligence and the Internet of Things -- is already transforming society. Advances in computing and data **(21)** ________________ big data in real time. New insights gleaned from such data mining can complement official statistics and survey data, adding depth and nuance to information on human behaviours and experiences. The integration of this new data with **(22)** ________________ detailed, timely and relevant.

Data is the lifeblood of decision-making and the raw material for accountability. Today, in the private sector, analysis of big data is commonplace, with consumer profiling, personalised services, and predictive analysis being used for marketing, advertising and management. Similar techniques could be adopted **(23)** ________________ target aid interventions to vulnerable groups. New sources of data - such as satellite data -, new technologies, and new analytical approaches, if applied responsibly, can enable more agile, efficient and evidence-based decision-making and can better measure progress on the Sustainable Development Goals (SDGs) in a way that is both inclusive and fair.

Fundamental **(24)** ________________ the opportunities presented by big data: privacy, ethics and respect for data sovereignty require us to assess the rights of individuals along with the benefits of the collective. Much new data is collected passively – from the 'digital footprints' people leave behind and from sensor-enabled objects – or is inferred via algorithms. Because big data is **(25)** ________________, removal of explicit personal information may not fully protect privacy. Combining multiple datasets may lead to the re-identification of individuals or groups of individuals, subjecting them to potential harms. Proper data protection measures must be put in place to prevent data misuse or mishandling.

There is also a risk of growing inequality and bias. Major gaps are already opening up between the data haves and have-nots. Without action, a whole new inequality frontier will split the world between those who know, and those who do not. Many people are excluded from the new world of data and information by language, poverty, lack of education, lack of technology infrastructure, remoteness or prejudice and discrimination. There is a broad range of actions needed, including building the capacities of all countries and particularly the Least Developed Countries (LDCs), Land-locked Developing Countries (LLDCs), and Small Island Developing States (SIDS).

One of the key roles of the UN and other international or regional organisations is **(26)** ______________________________ the safe use of big data for development and humanitarian action within a global community and according to common norms. These standards seek to increase the usefulness of data through a much greater degree of openness and transparency, avoid **(27)** ______________________________ misuse of data on individuals and groups, and minimise inequality in production, access to and use of data. Achievement of the SDGs in our digital world will require recognition of the need not only to prevent misuse of data, but also to ensure that when data can be used responsibly for the public good, it is.

The Secretary-General's Independent Expert Advisory Group on a Data Revolution for Sustainable Development (IEAG) has **(28)** ______________________________, calling for a UN-led effort to mobilise the data revolution for sustainable development.

For example, every **(29)** ______________________________ of tweets [using the Twitter app] in dozens of languages. Such social conversations contain real-time information on many issues, including food costs, the availability of jobs, access to health care, quality of education, and reports of natural disasters. The partnership [between Twitter and the UN] allows UN development and humanitarian agencies to turn the public data into actionable information to aid communities around the globe.

Other examples of partnerships include the GSMA[Global System for Mobile Communications]'s "Big Data for Social Good" initiative, which leverages mobile operators' big data capabilities to address humanitarian crises, including epidemics and natural disasters; Data for Climate Action, a competition which connects **(30)** ______________________________ leading companies to enable data-driven climate solutions; and Data Collaboratives, a new form of collaboration beyond the public-private partnership model, in which participants from different sectors (and companies in particular) exchange their data to create public value.

21.
- A. make science analyze now it possible to process and
- B. to process science now analyze and make it possible
- C. now possible science make it process and analyze to
- D. science now make it possible to process and analyze

22. A. high-quality traditional produce should more data information that is
B. traditional data should produce high-quality information that is more
C. information that is more traditional should high-quality data produce
D. more that is traditional high-quality data information produce should

23. A. to gain real-time insights into people's wellbeing and to
B. people's to real-time insights and into wellbeing to gain
C. to wellbeing gain to real-time insights into people's and
D. insights into people's real-time to gain and to wellbeing

24. A. human elements must to be realize safeguarded rights of
B. safeguarded elements rights of human must be realize to
C. rights must be safeguarded to realize of human elements
D. elements of human rights must be safeguarded to realize

25. A. behavior of the product of individuals unique of patterns
B. unique the individuals of product of patterns of behavior
C. the product of unique patterns of behavior of individuals
D. individuals unique product of the behavior of patterns of

26. A. setting principles and standards to guide collective action around
B. guide principles action setting standards around to collective and
C. action standards setting principles and collective around to guide
D. around guide standards setting action to collective and principles

27. A. privacy of rights of human and from abuse invasion
B. human abuse of invasion and privacy from rights of
C. rights from human invasion of privacy of abuse and
D. invasion of privacy and abuse of human rights from

28. A. address these challenges to specific made recommendations how on
B. recommendations made specific to address challenges on how these
C. made specific recommendations on how to address these challenges
D. challenges to address these specific made recommendations on how

29. A. millions people send hundreds of day around the world
B. day people around the world send hundreds of millions
C. hundreds people around millions of day send the world
D. people millions of the world around day send hundreds

30. A. researchers around the world with data and tools from
B. from data tools and with the world around researchers
C. data the world around and with tools researchers from
D. tools around data researchers the world from and with

Ⅳ. Choose from among the four alternatives the one that best completes the following sentence.

31. Joe Biden was _________ as president of the United States on Wednesday, offering a message of unity and restoration to a deeply divided country _________ from a battered economy and a raging coronavirus pandemic that has killed more than 400,000 Americans.

A. rebuffed − stumbling　B. sworn in − reeling
C. inaugurated − recuperating　D. inducted − antagonizing

32. A Moscow judge denied Kremlin critic Alexei Navalny's appeal for release from _________ Thursday, after the opposition leader _________ the court process and thanked protesters for showing that his supporters "cannot be intimidated."

A. complicity − subverted　B. angst − mused
C. enmity − floated　D. detention − slammed

33. South Korean President Moon Jae-in said Monday that, from the standpoint of Japan-South Korea relations, it is undesirable to convert the assets seized from Japanese companies into cash _________ the ruling ordering these firms to pay compensation to former wartime _________ workers.

A. at the behest of − stationed　B. in accordance with − requisitioned
C. in retaliation for − conscripted　D. in light of − lethargic

34. Pope Francis' historic visit to northern Iraq to hold prayers at an ancient church destroyed _________ ISIL "sends a clear message to the world that harmony and cohesion _________ the followers of all religions is the only way for the advancement and progress of humanity," the top UN culture official has said.

A. against − for　B. about − with
C. by − between　D. from − on

35. In an emotional address Monday night, South African President Cyril Ramaphosa reintroduced bans on public gatherings and alcohol sales, made mask-wearing required in public and lengthened a _________ as a second wave of coronavirus cases _________ Africa's worst-hit country at "an alarming and unprecedented rate."

A. dislocation − ravages　B. curfew − sweeps
C. mandate − encroaches　D. promulgation − disparages

36. **________ the transformative power of women's equal participation, top United Nations officials called on all ________ to take special measures to advance their equal participation and achieve rapid change.**

A. Underscoring − stakeholders　B. Crystallizing − beneficiaries
C. Courting − contributors　D. Redressing − parties

37. **Security forces in Myanmar again used force Saturday to ________ anti-coup protesters, a day after a UN special envoy urged the Security Council to take action to ________ junta violence that this past week left more than 50 peaceful demonstrators dead and scores injured.**

A. spurn − stifle　B. compromise − quash
C. disperse − quell　D. fault − thwart

38. **As Portugal ________ the presidency of the European Union (EU), to be followed by Slovenia later this year, the UN refugee Agency (UNHCR) on Tuesday called on them to lead the effort to ________ a better protection system for those seeking refuge across the continent and beyond.**

A. surmises − shape　B. assumes − forge
C. relegates − espouse　D. bears − tweak

39. **The director general of the World Health Organization on Friday renewed calls to ________ some intellectual property rights for coronavirus vaccines, a move he said is needed to boost global supply and ensure greater access for poorer countries — ________ for ending the coronavirus pandemic.**

A. waive − requisites　B. relinquish − insolences
C. cede − discretion　D. imperil − reckoning

40. **While the release of more than 200 girls abducted from their school on Friday in northwest Nigeria is a welcome ________ said senior UN officials there on Tuesday, civilians and aid facilities have come under attack in the country's northeast, highlighting the plight of civilians who have suffered years of conflict and ________.**

A. injunction − precariousness　B. dichotomy − schism
C. inkling − upheaval　D. development − insecurity

V. Choose from among the underlined phrases the one that is grammatically or idiomatically incorrect.

41. Tokyo **(A)** on Sunday opened its first major community **(B)** hub for LGBTQ people, part of a pre-Olympics project **(C)** that campaigners hopes will **(D)** tackle stigmas and raise awareness of discrimination.

42. Prime Minister Yoshihide Suga's administration **(A)** is readying legislation to punish **(B)** refuse to comply with **(C)** government-mandated COVID-19 measures, amid **(D)** concerns it may infringe too much on personal freedoms.

43. Countries fighting the coronavirus should not **(A)** impose nationwide or large-scale school closures, **(B)** which is the wrong response and compounds the societal **(C)** cost of the disease, with 320 million children **(D)** locking out of school at the start of December, the UN children's agency UNICEF said on Tuesday.

44. **(A)** Outstanding issues related to Syria's **(B)** initial declaration of his chemical weapons stockpile **(C)** and programme cannot be considered "accurate and complete", the head **(D)** of the world body monitoring States' implementation of the Chemical Weapons Convention told the Security Council on Friday.

45. **(A)** The number of bankruptcies in Japan's restaurant industry **(B)** will likely to hit an all-time high in 2020 **(C)** as many establishments struggle to restore **(D)** their cash flow amid the ongoing coronavirus pandemic, the results of a recent survey showed.

46. Amid continuing uncertainty, fear and anxiety around the world over the COVID-19 pandemic, senior UN officials **(A)** are keen to stress the legitimacy of **(B)** concerns, listening carefully to citizens around the world, and help **(C)** them distinguish between misinformation **(D)** and accurate information, based on science.

47. Relations between Japan and South Korea in 2021 are expected to **(A)** remain at a historical low over **(B)** a wartime labor issue, even though the U.S. administration under President-elect Joe Biden **(C)** is set to increase pressure on **(D)** the two American allies to mend ties.

48. COVID-19 **(A)** has had a "catastrophic" impact on workers, the head of the International Labour Organization (ILO) **(B)** said on Wednesday, with lost working hours **(C)** lower than originally forecast, **(D)** and equivalent to 495 million full-time jobs globally in the second quarter of the year.

49. The coronavirus **(A)** remains actively on human skin for nine hours, Japanese researchers **(B)** have found, in a discovery **(C)** they said showed the need for frequent hand washing **(D)** to combat the COVID-19 pandemic.

50. Ambassadors, senior UN officials, representatives of global sports organizations, **(A)** and managers of some of the world's top athletes **(B)** met virtually on Friday to **(C)** underline the role of sport can play **(D)** in combating violent extremism and radicalization.

Ⅵ. Choose from among the four alternatives the one that most closely corresponds to the meaning of words in bold type and blanks in the following passage.

As international relations (IR) has grown in complexity, the family of theories that IR offers has grown in number, which presents a challenge for newcomers. Theories are constantly emerging and competing with one another. This can be disorientating. As soon as you think you have **(51) found your feet with** one theoretical approach, others appear.

Traditionally there have been two central theories of IR: liberalism and realism. Although they have come under great challenge from other theories, they remain central to the discipline. At its height, liberalism was referred to as a 'utopian' theory and to some degree is still recognised as such today. Its proponents view human beings as **(52)** _________ good and believe peace and harmony between nations is not only achievable, but desirable. In the late eighteenth century, Immanuel Kant developed the idea that states that shared liberal values should have no reason for going to war against one another. In Kant's eyes, the more liberal states there were in the world, the more peaceful it would become, since liberal states are ruled by their citizens and citizens are rarely **(53) disposed** to go to war. This is in contrast to the rule of kings and other non-elected rulers who frequently have selfish desires **(54) out of step** with citizens. His ideas have resonated and continue to be developed by modern liberals, most notably in the democratic peace theory, which posits that democracies do not go to war with each other.

Further, liberals have faith in the idea that the permanent **(55) ending** of war is an attainable goal. Putting liberal ideas into practice, US President Woodrow Wilson addressed his 'Fourteen Points' to the US Congress in January 1918 during the final year of the First World War. The last of his 'points' – ideas for a rebuilt world beyond the war – was the setting up of a general association of nations: this became the League of Nations. Dating back to 1920, the League of Nations was created largely for the purpose of overseeing affairs between states and implementing, as well as maintaining, international peace. **(56)** _________, when the League collapsed due to the outbreak of the Second World War in 1939, its failure was difficult for liberals to comprehend, as events seemed to contradict their theories. Therefore, despite the efforts of figures such as Kant and Wilson, liberalism failed to retain a strong hold and a new theory emerged to explain the continuing presence of war. That theory became known as realism.

Realism gained momentum during the Second World War, when it appeared to offer a convincing account for how and why the most widespread and deadly war in known history followed a period of supposed peace and optimism. **(57)** _________ its name suggests, advocates of realism purport that it reflects the 'reality' of the world and more effectively accounts for change in international politics. Thomas Hobbes is often mentioned in discussions of realism due to his description of the brutality of life during the English Civil War of 1642–1651. Hobbes described human beings as living in an orderless 'state of nature' that he perceived as a war of all against all. To remedy this, he proposed a 'social contract' between the ruler and the people of a state to maintain relative order. Today, such ideas are **(58)** __________ as it is usually clear who rules our states. Each leader, or 'sovereign' (a monarch or a parliament, for example), sets the rules and establishes a system of punishments for those who break them. We accept this in our respective states so that our lives can function with a sense of security and order. It may not be ideal, but it is better than a state of nature. As no such contract exists internationally and there is no sovereign in charge of the world, disorder and fear rules international relations. For realists, we live in a system of 'international anarchy'. That is why war seems more common than peace to realists; indeed, they see it as **(59) inevitable**.

It is important to understand that there is no single variant of each theory. Scholars rarely fully agree with each other, even those who share the same theoretical approach. Each scholar has a particular interpretation of the world, which includes ideas of peace, war and the role of the state in relation to individuals. **(60)** __________, these perspectives can still be grouped into theory families or traditions.

51. **In this context, "found your feet with" is closest in meaning to**

A. adapted easily to　　B. become accustomed to

C. made the most of　　D. reconciled yourself with

52. **From the context, the underlined blank could best be filled with**

A. immovably　　B. indifferently

C. inanely　　D. innately

53. **From the context, "disposed" is best replaced by**

A. averse　　B. inclined

C. loathed　　D. obliged

54. **In this context, "out of step" is closest in meaning to**

A. above and beyond　　B. at odds

C. over the top　　D. wide of the point

55. **From the context, "ending" is best replaced by**

A. arrestment　　B. abeyance

C. cessation　　D. expiration

56. **From the context, the underlined blank could best be filled with**

A. As such　　B. However

C. Notwithstanding　　D. Thereby

57. **From the context, the underlined blank could best be filled with**

A. As
B. Because
C. Regardless
D. Though

58. **From the context, the underlined blank could best be filled with**

A. followed up
B. held back
C. picked up on
D. taken for granted

59. **From the context, "inevitable" is best replaced by**

A. amenable
B. evadable
C. fated
D. unescapable

60. **From the context, the underlined blank could best be filled with**

A. As a result
B. Besides
C. Moreover
D. Nevertheless

Ⅶ. Choose from among the four alternatives the one that best explains each of the underlined words or phrases in the context of the article below.

The COVID-19 pandemic has led to rising antisemitism which shows the world must remain **(61) vigilant** against this persistent form of racism and religious persecution, the UN Secretary-General told an online event on Monday to commemorate the 76th anniversary of the liberation of the Auschwitz-Birkenau concentration camp.

António Guterres said although antisemitism found its most horrific expression in the Holocaust, it did not end there and continues to blight the world today.

"I was honoured to join Holocaust survivors to mark the 76th anniversary of the liberation of the Auschwitz-Birkenau death camp. Holocaust denial, distortion & minimization are **(62) resurgent**. We must continue to stand against lies, bigotry & hatred. It is sad, but not surprising, that the COVID-19 pandemic has **(63) triggered** yet another eruption of this poisonous ideology. We can never let down our guard", he stated.

The ceremony organized by the Park East Synagogue in New York and the UN served to honour the memory of the six million Jews and millions of others who were systematically murdered by the Nazis and their collaborators during the Second World War.

"Our best tribute to those who died in the Holocaust is the creation of a world of equality, justice and dignity for all", the Secretary-General said.

Mr. Guterres warned of the resurgence of Holocaust denial and distortion, and that after decades in the shadows, neo-Nazis and their ideas are **(64) gaining currency**.

"In Europe, the United States and elsewhere, white supremacists are organizing and recruiting across borders, **(65) flaunting** the symbols and **(66) tropes** of the Nazis and their murderous ambitions", he said.

"We have seen shocking examples in this nation's capital in recent days. The Anti-Defamation League found that the American Jewish community experienced the highest level of antisemitic incidents in 2019 since tracking began in 1979."

The pandemic has also opened new fronts for neo-Nazis and white supremacists, who are using social media to disseminate propaganda and **(67) sow** fear and hatred.

However, the Secretary-General said their continued rise "must be seen in the context of a global attack on truth that has reduced the role of science and fact-based analysis in public life."

He warned that when truth dies, it becomes easier to exploit differences between groups, or to invent **(68) scapegoats**. Fragmentation of traditional media and the growth of social media have also contributed to the situation.

"When the truth is just one version among many, lying becomes normalized and history can be distorted and rewritten", he said, referring to Holocaust denial. "As the number of Holocaust survivors diminishes every year, we must make ever greater efforts to elevate the truth and ensure that it lives on."

Addressing the commemoration's theme of recovery and reconstitution after the Holocaust, the Secretary-General noted that this period only marked the beginning of an unimaginably painful and difficult journey for survivors and for the world, as both had been changed forever.

"Today, as we consider the recovery from the COVID-19 pandemic, we can take important lessons from the Holocaust," Mr. Guterres said.

"The recovery must address the fragilities and **(69) fissures** that have been exposed by the pandemic. It must strengthen our mutual bonds, based on our common humanity."

Calling for 2021 to be a year of healing, Mr. Guterres urged political, religious and community leaders to work to build consensus "if we are to emerge safely from these dangerous times."

He underlined the need for coordinated global action to counter the growth and spread of neo-Nazism and white supremacy, and to fight propaganda and disinformation. "History shows that those who undermine truth ultimately undermine themselves," he said.

"The only way out of the COVID-19 pandemic is through science and fact-based analysis. The production of vaccines in record time is **(70) testimony to** the effectiveness of this approach. There is no vaccine for antisemitism and xenophobia. But our best weapon remains the truth."

61. **vigilant**

A. heedful B. oblivious
C. jovial D. gratified

62. **resurgent**

A. dwindling B. waning
C. proliferating D. abating

63. **triggered**

A. arrested B. initiated
C. foregone D. renounced

64. **gaining currency**

A. increasingly rare B. squandering money deliberately
C. a good investment D. amplifying in prevalence

65. **flaunting**

A. concealing B. obscuring
C. displaying D. withholding

66. **tropes**

A. satisfactions | B. embarrassments
C. modesties | D. expressions

67. **sow**

A. disavow | B. disallow
C. disseminate | D. disapprove

68. **scapegoats**

A. stooges | B. heroes
C. mentors | D. champions

69. **fissures**

A. exultations | B. disparities
C. gratifications | D. blisses

70. **testimony to**

A. censure towards | B. disagreement with
C. reproach for | D. endorsement of

Ⅷ. Fill in each of the following blanks with the most appropriate of the four alternatives as required by the context.

The shells started landing inside Hussein Ali Wuhaish's refugee camp days after the Biden administration ended US support for a Saudi-led coalition fighting in Yemen and took steps to lift sanctions on northern rebels.

The rebels, known as Houthis, seemingly **(71)** __________ by the American pivot, had intensified their offensive in strategic Marib province, one of the few safe harbors in the war. Now Wuhaish and his family, who fled to Marib in 2017, were once again **(72)** __________.

"I could hear the screams and the crying of my neighbors' children, as my wife and I tried to calm our own children," said Wuhaish, 38, a doctor and father of five. "We realized that we were again not safe."

"So as the sounds of the fighting got closer, we fled for our lives."

The military escalation in Marib, the last northern stronghold of the internationally recognized Yemeni government, threatens to displace hundreds of thousands of Yemenis, many of whom have already fled violence multiple times. That would significantly worsen a humanitarian crisis already described by the United Nations as the world's most severe, say US and UN officials and aid workers.

The tensions could implode efforts by the United Nations and others to broker an end to the six-year-long war that has killed or injured tens of thousands in the Arab world's poorest nation.

The conflict **(73)** __________ the Iran-aligned Shiite Muslim Houthis against the US-backed coalition of Sunni Muslim nations, led by Saudi Arabia and the United Arab Emirates, seeking to restore the government to power. Today, the conflict is as much a **(74)** __________ war between Saudi Arabia and Iran as it is a civil conflict.

For the past year, the rebels have steadily advanced in Marib province, roughly 100 miles northeast of Sanaa. Capturing it would remove the government's last northern footprint and give the Houthis control over lucrative oil and natural gas reserves — a key ambition.

The province's capture would strengthen the rebels' position in negotiations to end the war and create a new government, analysts say.

"Marib was the success story of the war," said Elisabeth Kendall, a Yemen scholar at Oxford University. "It was a haven in the middle of a war. It's a place that provided hope. Symbolically, having that completely turn around is really tragic."

For the Biden administration, the Marib offensive **(75)** __________ the obstacles it faces in tackling a key foreign policy objective. Two weeks ago, President Biden ended US backing for the coalition's offensive operations, appointed a new Yemen envoy and pledged to accelerate diplomatic efforts to end the fighting.

The administration notified Congress that it would remove the Houthis from a US list of foreign terrorist organizations, reversing a Trump administration decision after aid groups warned it would worsen Yemen's humanitarian situation.

The State Department warned last week that the Houthis should not interpret its pivot on Yemen as a sign of US weakness and seize more territory. It urged the rebels to stop their offensive on Marib.

Martin Griffiths, the UN special envoy to Yemen, declared "the attack on Marib must stop.

The quest for territorial gain by force threatens all of the prospects of the peace process," he said last week.

Mohammed Ali al-Houthi, a senior Houthi official, denounced Griffiths' characterization of the offensive **(76)** _________ an "attack." He blamed the United States for the conflict.

"Six years have passed since Obama and Biden decided to launch the aggression and test the patience of the Yemeni people," al-Houthi tweeted. "We can never accept a peace that makes us subdued, and **(77)** _________ we were to accept that, we would have accepted it in the early days."

In the conflict's first years, Marib province was spared heavy fighting, allowing local authorities to channel oil and gas revenue into developing the economy.

But that stability also attracted at least 850,000 people displaced from areas gripped by fighting, **(78)** _________ the International Organization of Migration, most crowding camps outside Marib city. The conflict's escalation would be catastrophic for the displaced, say the United Nations and aid agencies.

"Many are in urgent need of food, water, health care and other humanitarian assistance," said Muhsin Siddiquey, Yemen country director for Oxfam. "Many families are especially vulnerable as they have already been forced to flee multiple times and may not have the resources to flee again."

The Houthis are **(79)** _________ heavy weaponry and equipment as they push toward the city, according to local reports and aid agencies. Scores of fighters on both sides have been killed in recent days and several displaced people's camps have been shelled, according to aid agencies and local reports.

Wuhaish's family fled their village in Dhamar province after Houthi fighters abducted, jailed and tortured him for speaking out against them, he said. They settled down in the provincial capital, Dhamar city, but in 2017, the Houthis came looking for him again. That's when they fled to Al Zour camp, on the outskirts of Marib city.

This month, their lives were **(80)** _________ again.

As the bombs fell, they fled their camp with only the clothes on their back, Wuhaish said. He said many families are now sleeping in tents or out in the open.

Wuhaish's family was fortunate to stay temporarily in a friend's house. But finding their next refuge could prove difficult. They have little money. The Houthis control the areas west of Marib. To the east is a vast desert with little water. Returning to Dhamar could mean death.

"We have nowhere to go now," said Wuhaish. "I just don't know what tomorrow will bring."

71.	A.	subverted	B.	constrained
	C.	emboldened	D.	purported
72.	A.	on the run	B.	off the ground
	C.	down-to-earth	D.	up in arms
73.	A.	pits	B.	corrals
	C.	compounds	D.	tempers
74.	A.	righteous	B.	proxy
	C.	unvarnished	D.	pugnacious
75.	A.	circumvents	B.	expels
	C.	helms	D.	underscores
76.	A.	with	B.	despite
	C.	as	D.	against
77.	A.	while	B.	if
	C.	though	D.	once
78.	A.	in deference to	B.	according to
	C.	on the basis of	D.	in the interest of
79.	A.	amassing	B.	transfixing
	C.	brandishing	D.	forgoing
80.	A.	flustered	B.	cluttered
	C.	castigated	D.	upended

IX. Write a short essay in English of 150-200 words as your answer to the following question:

How would you explain the overall idea of the United Nations SDGs to someone?

マークシート記入例

東京の本会場でA級を受験する、国連 太郎さん、受験番号が「東京01-20001」、生年月日が「1980年10月24日」の場合の記入例です。

【受験番号/氏名】
それぞれ受験票の記載通りに記入してください。

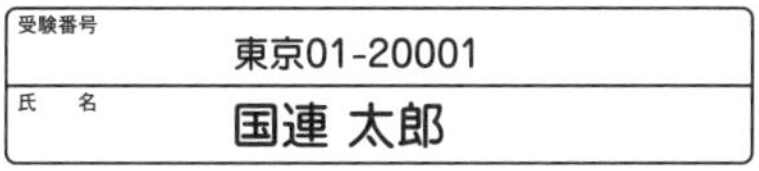

【受験地区】
下段の都道府県部分を塗りつぶしてください。

【会場番号】
都道府県部分に続く２桁の数字を塗りつぶしてください。

【受験番号】
ハイフン（−）以降の５桁の数字を塗りつぶしてください。

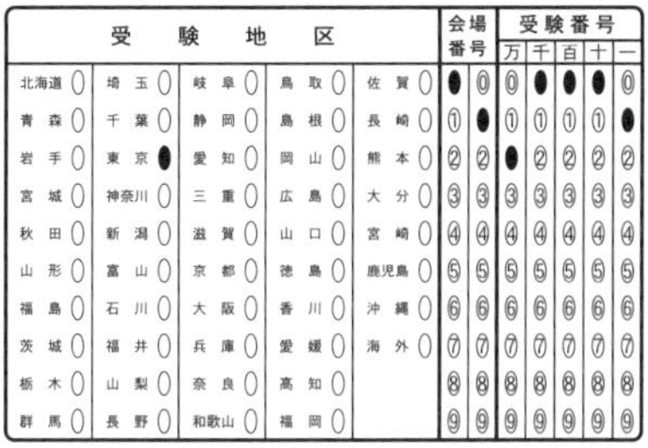

【受験級】
「A」と記入し、下段のA級部分を塗りつぶしてください。

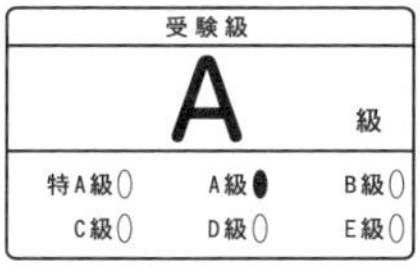

【生年月日】
４桁の西暦・月・日を塗りつぶしてください。
10未満の月・日の十の位は、「０」を塗りつぶしてください。

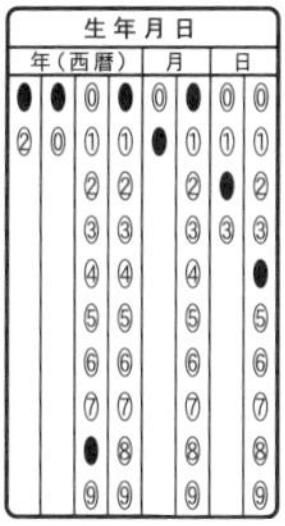

※HB以上の鉛筆を用いてマークをしてください。

※他の地区から会場を変更して受験する場合でも、受験票に記載されている受験地区・会場番号をマークしてください。

2021年
第1回試験

解答・解説

2021年　国連英検A級第1回試験
解答・解説

＊〔　〕内は訳出上の補足や説明

I　『新 わかりやすい国連の活動と世界』に基づき，
空所を埋めるのに最も適切なものを4つの選択肢の中から1つ選びなさい。

1.　解答：D

訳例　21世紀の国連の役割に関するこのようなビジョンから，未来に向けての最も重要な課題が3つ生まれます。貧困の根絶，紛争の防止，そして民主主義の促進です（『新 わかりやすい国連の活動と世界』p.12。以下，書名略）。

2.　解答：C

訳例　私は，今日のアウン・サン・スー・チー国家顧問の演説と，コフィー・アナン氏を議長とするラカイン州に関する諮問委員会の提言をできる限り早期に実施する旨の意思表示に留意します（同 p.25）。

3.　解答：A

訳例　発足時の加盟国51カ国は，サンフランシスコ会議に出席したか，それ以前に連合国宣言に署名し，のち国連憲章に調印，これを批准した国々である（同 p.45）。

4.　解答：C

訳例　安全保障理事会は，国際の平和および安全を危うくするおそれのある紛争に対して調査を行い，その調整方法，あるいは解決の条件を勧告する（同 p.55）。

5.　解答：B

訳例　平和構築委員会は，総会，安全保障理事会，経済社会理事会から選出された31の加盟国によって構成される政府間諮問機関である（同 p.58）。

6.　解答：C

訳例　国連の通常予算は2年ごとに総会によって承認される（同 p.62）。

7. 解答：D

訳例　2005 年，双方の分野における活動の功績が認められ，IAEA 及びモハメド・エルバラダイ事務局長（当時）はノーベル平和賞を受賞した（同 p.76）。

8. 解答：A

訳例　〔WHO の〕主要機関としては，最高意思決定機関である世界保健総会，34 カ国の理事によって構成される執行理事会，そして事務局が設けられている（同 p.79）。

9. 解答：B

訳例　世界貿易機関（WTO）は，多角的な貿易自由化の促進や貿易に関するルール策定を行う国際機関である（同 p.85）。

10. 解答：D

訳例　とりわけ，2004 年以降，日本はドイツ，ブラジル，インドとともに安全保障理事会常任理事国の議席の拡大を要請し，国連におけるより強い発言権の獲得に努めている（同 p.168）。

II

下線を引いた動詞の最も適切な変化形を 4 つの選択肢の中から 1 つ選びなさい。

11. 解答：B

解説　President Donald Trump told ... よりも前のことなので，過去完了の B が正解。

12. 解答：D

解説　下線部は a mob of self-styled revolutionaries の形容詞句の一部になっている。よって，現在分詞の D が正解。

13. 解答：A

解説　過去の出来事について述べているので，A が正解。政権移譲が平和的に行われないのは，暴動よりもあとのことなので，would が使われている。

14. 解答：A

解説　下線部より前で，英文としては完結しているので，付帯状況を表す現在分詞がその後に続いていると考える。よって，A が正解。

15. 解答：B

解説 下線部以降は colleagues の形容詞句になっている。よって，関係代名詞が入った B が正解。

16. 解答：D

解説 下線部は，that 節内の述語動詞に相当する。よって，D が正解。

17. 解答：D

解説 付帯状況の forcing のあとに，目的語の partisans があることから，force O to do の語法であることを見抜く。よって，D が正解。

18. 解答：B

解説 help のあとに動詞が続く場合，help (to) do となる。よって，B が正解。

19. 解答：B

解説 下線部以降は GOP officials の形容詞句になっている。よって，関係代名詞を使うが，時制の観点から B を正解にする。

20. 解答：C

解説 下線部は a video の形容詞句の一部になっている。よって，現在分詞の C が正解。D は時制が適切ではない。

訳例　「我々は決してあきらめない！　決して敗北を認めない！」──ドナルド・トランプ大統領は 1 月 6 日，自身がワシントンに呼び寄せた支持者の群衆にそう告げた。群衆は大統領の言葉を聞き，従った。〔そして〕数時間のうちに，連邦議事堂にはトランプ氏の旗を振る自称革命家の一群が乱入していた。足場をよじ登り，窓を割って〔侵入し〕，大理石のホールを埋め尽くした。議員や職員が慌てて避難する中，建物内で発砲があり，催涙ガスが円形大広間に充満した。米国で平和的な政権移譲が行われなくなるのは，南北戦争以来，初めてのことだ。

この暴動で中断する以前，自らの負けが明らかな大統領選挙の結果を不正にひっくり返そうとするトランプ氏の最後の試みはうまく運んでいなかった。

マイク・ペンス副大統領は，各州の選挙人票の集計〔結果を発表するという〕儀式的役割を果たすと発言，集計結果を認定しないようにとのトランプ氏の要求を拒絶した。共和党のミッチ・マコネル上院院内総務は熱弁を振るい，トランプ氏に味方して〔大統領就任〕手続きを阻止しようとする同党議員を非難した。

トランプ氏率いる〔共和〕党は４年にわたり身を屈してファウスト的な取引に応じたのだった。トランプ氏が有権者から集めている忠誠心を目にして，党関係者は――ある者は嬉々《きき》として，またある者は不承不承ながらも――米国をほとんど限界まで追い込んだ〔この〕大統領の後に「前へならえ」と整列した。共和党は，選挙に勝ち，権力を行使することで，トランプ氏の権威主義的傾向や政治制度に対する激しい攻撃，あるいは共和党党員や共和党が掲げる理想に対する攻撃を無視することが正当化されると判断したのだ。しかし，大統領任期終了まで２週間の時点に至って，トランプ氏に権限を与えることの代償が，共和党にとっても，そして米国にとっても明らかとなった。

トランプ氏は選挙〔結果〕を覆す最後の手段として，数十人の共和党議員を威嚇することで，１月６日に行われたジョー・バイデンの勝利認定に異議を唱えさせた。民主主義と憲法に対する自らの最後の挑戦に党員が味方するよう強いたのだ。その過程でトランプ氏は，ジョージア州の２〔議席をめぐる連邦上院議員選挙の〕決選投票で共和党候補が僅差で敗れ，民主党の上院支配を許す結果を招いた。権力を得るべく自らの原則を放棄した党が，その両方を失ったのだ。

任期満了に先立つ数週間，トランプ氏は暴れ回った。選挙についての自らの根拠のない主張に従おうとしない共和党幹部のキャリアを潰してやると明言したほか，年間国防予算には拒否権を発動，また，共和党が支持しようとしない2,000ドルの景気刺激対策個人給付金については，民主党側に与《くみ》して〔議会の承認を〕要求。ジョージア州で行われた連邦上院選挙では，不正〔が行われた〕と決めつけ，支持者に投票ボイコットを呼びかけた。そして，「愛国者」に呼びかけてワシントンD.C.に集結させ，連邦議事堂で最後の対決を試みた。混乱が拡大する中，トランプ氏は非暴力を求める弱々しい要請をツイートし，数時間後には動画を公開。支持者に退去を命じる一方，支持者を称賛し，なおも選挙の不正を主張した。

III 空所を埋めるのに文法的・論理的に最もふさわしいものを４つの選択肢の中から１つ選びなさい。

21. 解答：D

解説 in computing and data science までが形容詞句で，it が make it possible to do を構成する形式目的語であることに着目する。

22. 解答：B

解説 with に続く名詞句と述語動詞が成立するものを選ぶ。detailed, timely, and relevant の並列構造に着目し，まず A と B に絞り込むことも可能。

23. 解答：A

解説 直前までで英文は成立しているので，ここでは不定詞（副詞的用法）が続く A が正解。不定詞の並列構造にも着目したい。

24. 解答：D

解説 主語を探りつつ，must のあとに動詞の原形，realize のあとに名詞句が続くものを選ぶ。

25. 解答：C

解説 直前の be 動詞に着目し，空所は補語として適切なものを選ぶ。よって，C が正解。

26. 解答：A

解説 One of the key roles ... を受ける補語として適切なものを選ぶ。setting principles and standards のコロケーションに気づけるかもポイント。

27. 解答：D

解説 avoid の目的語が A and B の並列構造になっていることに着目し，D を選ぶ。

28. 解答：C

解説 has を述語動詞と捉えると，構造的にまとまらなくなる。また空所のあとにコンマがあるので，選択肢の後半は C 以外，文法的にありえない。

29. 解答：B

解説 every のあとは単数形の名詞が続くことから，B が正解。

30. 解答：A

解説 connects の目的語としては，文法的にも文脈的にも A の researchers

around the worlds しか候補に残らない。

訳例　世界に存在するデータの量は指数関数的に増加の一途をたどっている。ある推定によると，世界に存在するデータは，過去2年の間に作られたものが90%を占めており，また毎年40%ずつ増加するという。その多くは，携帯電話やクレジットカード，ソーシャルメディアなどのデジタル製品やデジタルサービスとの間で日常的に行われるやりとりから受動的に収集されたデータ，すなわち「廃棄（排気）データ」である。このデジタルデータの洪水はビッグデータと呼ばれている。

数多くの安価な情報感知モバイル機器によるデータ収集がますます進むとともに，世界の情報蓄積能力は1980年代以降，40カ月ごとにほぼ倍増しているため，データは増加する一方だ。

オープンデータ運動，クラウドソーシングの台頭，データ収集のための新しいICT，ビッグデータの爆発的な普及，そして人工知能やモノのインターネットの出現などによるデータ革命は，すでに社会を大きく変えつつある。コンピューターおよびデータ科学の進歩により，いまではビッグデータをリアルタイムで処理・分析することが可能になった。こうしたデータ・マイニングから得られる新たな知見は，公式統計や調査データを補完し，人間の行動や経験に関する情報に深みやニュアンスを加える力を持つ。こうした新しいデータと従来のデータを統合することで，より詳細で適時・適切な，質の高い情報が得られるはずだ。

データは意思決定に不可欠な「血液」であり，説明責任の原料〔のようなもの〕である。現在，民間企業ではビッグデータの分析は当たり前になっており，消費者プロファイリングや個人化サービス，予測分析〔という手法〕がマーケティングや広告，経営管理に利用されている。同様の技術は，人々の幸福度をリアルタイムで把握し，弱い集団に的を絞った援助介入を行う目的でも採用できるだろう。衛星データなどの新しいデータ源や新しい技術，新しい分析手法を責任あるやり方で適用すれば，より迅速で効率的，そして根拠に基づく意思決定が可能となり，持続可能な開発目標（SDGs）の進捗を包括的かつ公平な方法を使って，より適切に測定することができる。

ビッグデータがもたらす機会を現実のものとするには，人権の基本的な要素を保護しなければならない──プライバシー，倫理，データ主権の尊重を図るためには，集団の利益とともに個人の権利について見極める必要がある。多くの新しいデータは，さまざまな人間が残した「デジタルフットプリント」やセンサー機能を有する物体から受動的に収集されるか，アルゴリズムを介して推論される。ビッグデータは個人固有の行動パターンから生まれるのだから，明示的個人情報を削除してもプライバシーを十分に保護できないおそれがある。多数のデータセットを組み合わせることで個人や集団が割り出され，場合によっては被害を受ける可能性があるからだ。データの誤用や処理上のミスを防ぐためには，適切なデータ保護措置を講じる必要がある。

また，不平等や偏見が拡大するリスクも存在する。データを持つ者と持たざる者の間には，すでに大きな格差が生まれつつあり，ここで手を打たなければ，まったく新しい不平等フロンティアが〔生じて〕，世界は知る者と知らざる者とに二分されてしまうだろう。多くの人々が，言語や貧困，不十分な教育，技術インフラの欠如，地理的な遠さ，あるいは偏見や差別によって，データと情報という新しい世界から排除されている。すべての国，特に後発開発途上国（LDC），内陸開発途上国（LLDC），小島嶼《しょうとうしょ》開発途上国（SIDS）の能力を高めるなど，幅広い行動が求められる。

国連やその他の国際・地域機関の重要な役割の１つとして，(26) グローバルコミュニティー内で共通の規範に従って，開発や人道行動の目的でビッグデータを安全に利用する際の集団行動に対して指針となる原則と基準を設定することが挙げられる。そうした基準が目標とするのは，はるかに高いレベルの公開性と透明性によってデータの有用性を高めること，個人や集団に関するデータの悪用によるプライバシーや人権の侵害を回避すること，データの生産，閲覧，それに使用における不平等を最小限に抑えることである。デジタル世界においてSDGsを達成するには，データの悪用を防ぐ必要を認識するだけでなく，データを公共の利益のために責任を持って利用することが可能な場合には，それを確実に実現する必要〔があること〕をも認識しなければならない。

事務総長〔直属〕の「持続可能な開発のためのデータ革命に関する独立専門家諮問グループ（IEAG）」は，こうした課題にどう取り組むかについてすでに具体的な勧告を行い，持続可能な開発のためのデータ革命を遂行する国連主導の取り組みを〔行うよう〕呼びかけている。

たとえば，世界中の人々が毎日［ツイッターアプリを使って］数十言語で送信するツイートの数は何億件にものぼる。こうした社交的なやりとりには，食費や求人の状況，医療の受けやすさ，教育の良し悪し，自然災害についての知らせなど，多くの問題に関するリアルタイムの情報が含まれている。［ツイッターと国連の間で］結ばれた提携により，国連の開発および人道支援を担当する機関は，公開済みデータをすぐに使える情報に作り替えることで，世界中のコミュニティーを支援できる。

その他の提携例としては，GSM［Global System for Mobile Communications］アソシエーションの「社会的善のためのビッグデータ」イニシアチブ（携帯電話事業者のビッグデータ能力を活用して，伝染病や自然災害などの人道的危機に対応）や，「気候〔変動防止〕行動のためのデータ」（世界中の研究者と先進企業のデータやツールを結び付けることで，データ主導の気候変動対策を実行するコンテスト），「データ・コラボレーション」（官民連携モデルの枠を超えた新しい形の協働。異なるセクター〈特に企業〉の参加者がデータをやりとりすることで公共的価値を創出する）などがある。

IV 以下の文章に最も適切に当てはまる語句のペアを4つの選択肢の中から1つ選びなさい。

31. 解答：B

解説 第1空所は文脈からB. sworn in, C. inaugurated, D. inductedが候補に残る。第2空所は直後のfromに着目してB. reelingを選ぶ。

訳例 ジョー・バイデン氏が水曜日，米国大統領に就任し，疲弊した経済と国内の死者が40万以上に達したコロナ禍に揺らぐ，深い分裂の中にある〔米〕国に対して，結束と復興のメッセージを発信した。

32. 解答：D

解説 第1空所はrelease from ... からD. detentionを選ぶ。第2空所はアレクセイ・ナワリヌイ氏がthe court processに対して示した反応なのでD. slammedが正解。

訳例 モスクワの判事は木曜日，ロシア政府批判〔で服役中〕の野党指導者，アレクセイ・ナワリヌイ氏が拘留停止を求めた申し立てを棄却した。これに先立ち同氏は裁判手続きを非難し，同氏の支持者が「おじけづくことなどあり得ない」ことをデモ参加者が示してくれことに感謝していた。

33. 解答：B

解説 第1空所は「〔韓国最高裁〕判決に ______」という文脈からB. in accordance withとD. in light ofが候補に残る。第2空所は徴用工のことを指しているのでB. requisitioned以外は不可。

訳例 韓国の文在寅大統領は月曜日，日本企業に徴用工への賠償を命じた〔韓国最高裁〕判決に従って，日本企業から差し押さえた資産を換金〔売却〕することは，日韓関係の観点から望ましくないと述べた。

34. 解答：C

解説 第1空所はdestroyed ... ISILが直前の名詞を修飾する形容詞句であることからC. byを選ぶ。第2空所はharmony and cohesion ... the followers of all religionsに注目しC. betweenが正解。

訳例 ローマ教皇フランシスコがイラク北部へ歴史的な訪問を行い，ISILによって破壊された古い教会で祈りを捧げたが，このことは「すべての宗教の信者間の調和と結束こそ，人類の進歩のために〔残された〕唯一の道だとの明確なメッセージを世界に送るものだ」。国連ユネスコのオドレ・アズレ事務局長が述べた。

35. 解答：B

解説 第 1 空所はコロナ禍の中，南アフリカの大統領が行ってきた政策という観点から B. curfew しか適さない。第 2 空所は国を荒廃させると捉えれば A. ravage も候補になる。

訳例 〔コロナ禍で〕アフリカ最大の被害を受けた南アフリカ。感染〔拡大〕の第 2 波が「驚くべき前例のないペース」で猛威を振るう中，シリル・ラマポーザ大統領は月曜夜，感情もあらわに演説し，集会やアルコール販売の禁止措置を再び実施するとともに，公共の場でのマスク着用義務化と外出禁止令の延長〔を発表した〕。

36. 解答：A

解説 第 1 空所は女性の機会均等について述べているので A. Underscoring と B. Crystallizing が候補に残る。第 2 空所は国連高官の呼びかけを受ける団体という文脈から A. stakeholders が正解。

訳例 国連高官らが女性の平等な参加によってもたらされる変革の力を強調〔するメッセージを発信し〕，女性の平等な参加を進めるとともに，迅速な変革を実現する特別な措置をとるようすべての関係者に呼びかけた。

37. 解答：C

解説 第 1 空所は治安維持の文脈で ... anti-coup protesters とあるので C. disperse を選ぶ。第 2 空所はどの選択肢でも候補になりうる。

訳例 ミャンマーの治安部隊が土曜日，クーデターに反対して抗議の声を上げる人々に再び武力を行使して解散させた。国連特使が〔前日〕安保理に対し，先週の平和的なデモの参加者から死者 50 人以上と多数の負傷者を出した軍事政権の暴力をやめさせるため行動をとるよう求めた〔矢先のこと〕。

38. 解答：B

解説 第 1 空所は Portugal ... the presidency から，B. assumes と D. bears が候補に残る。第 2 空所は「よりよい保護システムを______」とあるので B. forge が正解。D. tweak は improve の意味なので文意に合わない。

訳例 ポルトガルが欧州連合（EU）の議長国に就任し，今年後半にはスロベニアが交代することになったが，国連難民高等弁務官事務所（UNHCR）は両国に対し火曜日，欧州内外に避難を求める人々のためによりよい保護システムを構築する取り組みを主導するよう求めた。

39. 解答：A

解説 第1空所はワクチンの普及という文脈で ... some intellectual property rights とあるので A. waive, B. relinquish, C. cede が候補になる。第2空所はa moveの補足説明に相当する。... for ending the coronavirus pandemic から A. requisites が正解。

訳例 世界保健機関（WHO）の〔テドロス〕事務局長は金曜日，コロナウイルス・ワクチンの知的財産権の一部放棄を改めて呼びかけた。〔これについて〕同氏は，コロナ禍を終息させる要件である世界的供給の拡大と貧しい国々における接種増進のために必要な措置だと述べた。

40. 解答：D

解説 第1空所は誘拐されていた少女たちの解放を a welcome ... と述べているので D. development が正解。第2空所はどの選択肢でも候補になりうる。

訳例 ナイジェリア北西部で金曜日に学校から誘拐された200人以上の少女が解放されたことは喜ばしいことだが，同国北東部では市民や援助施設が攻撃を受け，長年の紛争と不安定に苦しんできた市民の苦境が浮き彫りになっている。ナイジェリア駐在の国連高官らが火曜日，述べた。

V

文法的，語法的にふさわしくないものを下線の中から1つ選びなさい。

41. 解答：C

解説 hopes → hope。campaigners hope は関係代名詞に続く挿入箇所。主語が複数形なので三人称単数の s は外す。

訳例 東京では日曜日，オリンピックに先立つプロジェクトの一環として，日本で初めてとなる LGBTQ の人々のための大型総合センターがオープンした。運動を推進する人々は，同施設が〔LGBTQ に対する〕烙印《らくいん》づけと闘い，差別についての意識を高めることを期待している。

42. 解答：B

解説 refuse → refusal。punish は他動詞なので名詞が続く。

訳例 菅義偉首相率いる政府は，政府が行うコロナウィルス感染対策に従わなかった場合〔に適用する〕罰則を定める法案の準備を進めているが，個人の自由をあまりに大きく侵害するとの懸念の声が上がっている。

43. 解答：D

解説 locking → locked。付帯状況の目的語が 320 million children なので，「学校から～された」とするには過去分詞にしなければならない。

訳例 コロナウィルスとの闘いを続ける国々は，全国的あるいは大規模な学校閉鎖を実施すべきではない。それは間違った対応であり，学校が休校となっている子供の数が 12 月初めの時点で世界 3 億 2,000 万人に達する中，コロナ感染症に伴う社会的コストを悪化させる――国連児童基金（ユニセフ）が火曜日，発表した。

44. 解答：B

解説 his → its。この代名詞は Syria を指すので its になる。

訳例 化学兵器禁止条約の実施状況を監視する世界機関の長〔アリアス化学兵器禁止機関事務局長〕は金曜日，安全保障理事会〔のオンライン会議に出席し〕，「シリアが化学兵器備蓄と開発計画について行った初期の宣言をめぐる未解決の問題は，『正確かつ完全』と考えることはできない」と述べた。

45. 解答：B

解説 to hit → hit。助動詞 will を受けるには動詞の原形にしなければならない。

訳例 日本の外食産業の倒産件数は 2020 年，過去最高となる見通しとなった。コロナ禍が続く中，多くの店で資金繰りの立て直しが難航しているため。このほど発表された調査結果で分かった。

46. 解答：B

解説 listening → listen。A, B, and C の並列構造なので，stress ..., listen ..., and help とすべて動詞の原形にそろえる。

訳例 コロナウィルスの感染拡大に対して，世界中で引き続き不透明感や怖れ，不安が広がる中，国連の高官らは，懸念を抱くことが正当だとしっかり伝え，世界中の市民の声に注意深く耳を傾けたい，そして市民が誤った情報と科学に基づく正確な情報を区別する助けとなりたいと，強い意欲を示している。

47. 解答：A

解説 historical → historic。ここでは concerning history ではなく famous or important in history の意味で使われている。

訳例 2021 年の日韓関係は，ジョー・バイデン次期大統領率いる米政権が両国に対して関係修復への圧力を強めることは確実であるものの，戦時中の徴用工問題をめぐって歴史的な低水準にとどまることが予想される。

48. 解答：C

解説 lower → higher。失われた労働時間が予想と比べてどうだったか，という文脈なので lower では文意に合わない。

訳例 国際労働機関（ILO）の〔ガイ・ライダー〕事務局長は水曜日，コロナ禍は働く人々に「壊滅的な」影響を及ぼしたと述べた。失われた労働時間は当初の予想より多く，今年〔2020 年〕第 2 四半期には全世界で常勤労働者 4 億 9,500 万人分に相当する量に達した。

49. 解答：A

解説 actively → active。remain のあとは副詞ではなく形容詞。

訳例 コロナウィルスがヒトの皮膚の上で 9 時間活性を保つことを日本の研究者らが突き止めた。研究者らは，この発見によりコロナ禍と闘う上で頻繁な手洗いの必要性が示されたとしている。

50. 解答：C

解説 of →トル。the role を修飾する関係代名詞節が続いている。

訳例 各国の大使や国連高官をはじめ，世界的なスポーツ団体の代表者，世界のトップアスリートの指導者らが金曜日，オンラインで集まって会議を開き，暴力的急進主義や過激化と闘う上でスポーツが果たせる役割についてアピールした。

VI

以下の文章の中に含まれる太字の語句および空所の意味として文脈上最も近いものを 4 つの選択肢の中から 1 つ選びなさい。

51. 解答：B

解説 find one’s feet は「物事に慣れる」という意味の熟語なので，B. become accustomed to が正解。

52.　解答：D

解説　view human beings as ... good という文脈から D. innately が正解。

53.　解答：B

解説　この dispose は incline someone toward a particular activity の意味なので，B. inclined が正解。

54.　解答：B

解説　out of step は not conforming to what others are doing or thinking の意味なので，B. at odds が正解。

55.　解答：C

解説　C. cessation は ending の同義語。

56.　解答：B

解説　1920 年に国際連盟が設立，1939 年に崩壊と空所前後で対比が見られる。よって，B. However が正解。C. Notwithstanding は in spite of this と同義で without being affected by the particular factor mentioned を意味する。

57.　解答：A

解説　it reflects the 'reality' of the world に着目して，A. As を選ぶ。

58.　解答：D

解説　as it is usually clear who rules our states に着目して，assume that something is true without questioning it を意味する D. taken for granted を選ぶ。C の pick up on（= become aware of）では，such ideas が定着しているニュアンスは出せない。

59.　解答：D

解説　inevitable は unavoidable と同義なので，unable to be avoided を意味する D. unescapable が正解。C. fated は be destined to happen の意。現実主義者が国際関係事象の説明に「運命」を持ち出すとは考えにくい。

60.　解答：D

解説　Each scholar has a particular interpretation of the world ... をD. Neverthelessでつなげば，「学者それぞれ世界解釈があるけれども，互いに共通性を持つものもあるのでグループ分けが可能」としっくりくる。

訳例　国際関係論（IR）が複雑化するにつれて，IRが提供する理論群も拡大し，新たに学ぶ者にとってやっかいな問題となっている。さまざまな理論が絶えず現れ，互いに競合している状況は，人をまごつかせるばかりである。ある理論的アプローチに慣れたかと思うと，すぐに別の理論が出てくる〔のだから〕。

伝統的に，IRの中心理論には自由主義と現実主義の2つがあった。この2つの理論は，他の理論から激しい挑戦を受けながらも，この学問の中心であり続けている。自由主義は，その絶頂期には「ユートピア」理論とも呼ばれたが，現在でもある程度はそのようなものと見なされている。〔自由主義を〕支持する者は，人間を生来善なるものと見なし，国家間の平和と調和については，達成可能であるばかりか，これを望ましいと考えている。18世紀末，イマヌエル・カントは，自由主義の価値観を共有する国家の間では戦争する理由が存在しえないとの思想を展開した。カントの目には，世界に存在する自由主義国家が多いほど，それだけ世界は平和になるように思われた。なぜなら，自由主義国家は市民によって統治されており，市民が好んで戦争をすることはまれであるから。これは，市民とは懸け離れた利己的な欲望をしばしば抱く王や，その他選挙によらずに〔地位に就いた〕支配者による統治とは対照的である。カントの思想は現代の自由主義者の共鳴を呼び，その後も常に展開されてきた。特に，民主政国家は互いに戦争をしないとする民主的平和理論において顕著である。

さらに自由主義者は，戦争の永久廃止が達成可能な目標であるとの考え方を信奉している。自由主義の思想を実践した米国大統領，ウッドロウ・ウィルソンは，第1次世界大戦末期の1918年1月，米国議会で演説し，「14カ条〔の平和原則〕」を示した。戦争終結後の復興された世界のあり方を示したこれら「原則」の最後の条には，諸国家の連合体の設立が謳《うた》われており，これが〔のちに〕国際連盟となった。国際連盟は1920年に設立され，国家間の問題を監視し，国際平和の実現・維持を図ることを主な目的としていた。しかし，この国際連盟が1939年の第2次世界大戦の勃発によって崩壊した際，その破綻は自由主義者にとっては不可解なものであった。自由主義の理論に矛盾すると思われる出来事が生じたためである。したがって，カントやウィルソンなどの努力にもかかわらず，自由主義は強固な支持を保つことができなかった。そこで，戦争が続いてやまない〔理由〕を説明する新しい理論が現れ，現実主義と呼ばれるようになった。

現実主義は第２次世界大戦中に勢いを増した。当時それは，主観的な平和と楽観主義の時代に続いて，歴史上最も広範，かつ最も凄惨《せいさん》な戦争が起きた経緯と原因について，説得力ある説明を提示するように思われた。現実主義という名が示すとおり，現実主義の支持者は次のように唱える。すなわち，現実主義は世界の「現実」を反映するもので，国際政治における変化をより効果的に説明できると。トマス・ホッブズは，1642 ～ 1651 年のイングランド内戦期における生の過酷さを描いたことから，現実主義に関する議論ではしばしば引き合いに出される〔思想家である〕。ホッブズは人間の生を秩序なき「自然状態」と見なし，それを「万人の万人に対する戦い」であると考えた。〔そして〕これを是正するため，相対的な秩序を維持する目的で支配者と国家に属する人民との間の「社会契約」〔という概念〕を提起した。今日では，国家を誰が支配しているかは通常明らかであるため，このような考え方は当然とされている。各指導者，すなわち「主権者」（君主や議会など）がルールを定め，違反者に対する刑罰の体系を確立している。これを我々は，生活が安心感と秩序感の中で営まれるように，それぞれの国家において受け入れているのである。理想的とは言えないまでも，自然状態よりはましであろう。〔一方〕国際的には，そのような契約は存在せず，世界を支配する主権者もいないため，国際関係は無秩序と恐怖によって支配されている。現実主義者によれば，人間は「国際的無政府」システムの下で生きている。そのため現実主義者にとっては，平和よりも戦争が普通の状態であり，実際，現実主義者は戦争は不可避であると考えている。

〔しかし〕それぞれの理論に唯一の型が存在するわけではないことを理解することが重要である。学者というものは，理論上同じアプローチを共有する場合でも，見解が完全に一致することはきわめて稀《まれ》であり，おのおの世界に対する固有の解釈を持っている。そうした解釈の中には，平和や戦争，それに個人との関係における国家の役割に関する考え方が含まれる。とはいっても，そうした〔さまざまに異なる〕切り口もやはり，理論群や流派に分類することは可能なのである。

Ⅶ 下線部の単語や句の意味を最もよくあらわしているものを４つの選択肢の中から１つ選びなさい。

61. 解答：A

解説 vigilant は keeping careful watch for possible danger の意。よって最も近いのは A. heedful。語根の heed は careful attention の意。

62. 解答：C

解説 resurgent は increasing or reviving after a period の意。よって最も近

いのはC. proliferating。proliferateはincrease rapidly in numberの意。

63. 解答：B

解説 原形のtriggerはこの場合cause a situation to happenの意。よって最も近いのはB. initiate。

64. 解答：D

解説 currencyはこの場合prevalenceの意。よってD. amplifying in prevalenceが正解。

65. 解答：C

解説 原形のflauntはdisplay something ostentatiouslyの意。よってC. displayingが正解。

66. 解答：D

解説 tropeはa figurative use of a word or expressionの意。よってD. expressionsが正解。

67. 解答：C

解説 sowはこの場合disseminateの意。よってCが正解。

68. 解答：A

解説 scapegoatはa person who is blamed for the wrongdoings for reasons of expediencyの意。よって最も近いのはa subordinate used by another to do unpleasant routineの意をもつA. stooges。

69. 解答：B

解説 fissureはa state of incompatibility or disagreementの意。よって最も近いのはB. disparities。

70. 解答：D

解説 testimonyはこの場合evidence or proofの意。よって最も近いのはD.

endorsement of。

訳例　コロナ禍によって反ユダヤ主義が台頭してきたが，このことは，世界がこの根強い人種差別と宗教的迫害に対して警戒を怠ってはならないことを示している――国連の〔アントニオ・グテーレス〕事務総長は月曜日，アウシュビッツ＝ビルケナウ強制収容所の解放 76 周年を記念して行われたオンラインの式典でこう述べた。

事務総長は，反ユダヤ主義はホロコーストにおいてその最も恐るべき形態を示したが，そこで終わらずに今日も世界を苦しめ続けている，と述べた。

「アウシュヴィッツ・ビルケナウ絶滅収容所の解放 76 周年を記念する〔式典に〕ホロコーストの生存者の皆様とともに参加できることを光栄に思う。ホロコーストに対する否定や歪曲《わいきょく》，矮小《わいしょう》化《か》がいまや息を吹き返してきた。我々はうそや偏狭，憎悪に対して引き続き反対していかなければならない。コロナ禍によってこの有害なイデオロギーの新たな噴出がもたらされたことは，悲しいことではあるが，驚くには当たらない。我々は決して油断してはならない」(同)。

ニューヨークのパーク・イースト・シナゴーグと国連が共同で主催したこの式典は，第 2 次世界大戦中にナチとその協力者によって組織的に殺害されたユダヤ人 600 万人とそのほかの数百万人を追悼するもの。

「ホロコーストで命を落とされた方々を偲《しの》ぶに当たり，我々〔にできる〕最高の贈り物は，すべての人にとって平等と正義と尊厳ある世界を作り出すことだ」(同)。

グテーレス氏は，ホロコーストに対する否定と歪曲が息を吹き返してきたことに警鐘を鳴らし，何十年も影を潜めていたネオナチとその思想が広まりつつあることに注意を促した。

「欧州や米国などで，白人至上主義者が国境を越えて組織化と仲間集めを進めており，ナチを象徴する図柄や比喩を堂々と用いたり，その残忍な野望を誇示したりしている。

この数日，この国〔米国〕の首都で衝撃的な出来事が起きた。名誉棄損防止組合は，米国のユダヤ人コミュニティーが 2019 年に確認した反ユダヤ主義的事件の件数が，追跡調査を開始した 1979 年以来，最高の水準に達したことを明らかにした」(同)。

コロナ禍はまた，ネオナチや白人至上主義者にとって新たな戦線を開いた。〔すなわち〕ソーシャルメディアを使ってプロパガンダを拡散し，恐怖と憎しみを植え付ける〔ことが行われている〕。

しかし事務総長は，これら勢力の台頭が続いていることについて，「公共の場において科学や事実に基づく分析が果たす役割を弱める働きをしてきた，地球規模での真実に対する攻撃という文脈で見る必要がある」と述べた。

また,「真実が失われると，集団間の違いを利用したり，スケープゴートをでっち上げたりすることが容易になる。伝統的なメディアの分断とソーシャルメディアの発展も，この状況を助長してきた」として，警鐘を鳴らした。

ホロコーストに対する否定に触れつつ，同氏は次のように述べた。「真実が多くの〔命題〕の中の1つのバージョンでしかないとなれば，虚言が常態化し，歴史がゆがめられ，書き換えられる。ホロコーストの生存者が年々減少する中，我々は真実が持つ力を強め，真実が存続するように，これまで以上に努力しなければならない」。

事務総長は，記念式典のテーマであるホロコースト後の復興・再建〔期の問題〕を取り上げ，次のように指摘した――生存者にとっても世界にとっても，この時期は想像を絶するほど辛く困難な旅の始まりにすぎない，なぜなら両者とも永遠に変わってしまったのだから。

「今日，コロナ禍からの復興を考えるに当たっては，ホロコーストから重要な教訓を引き出すことができる。

この復興は，感染拡大によって露呈した脆弱性《ぜいじゃくせい》と分断を手当てするとともに，我々共通の人間性を基に，相互の結びつきを強化するものでなければならない」(同)。

グテーレス氏は2021年が癒《いや》しの年となるように呼びかけるとともに，政治，宗教，コミュニティーの指導者らに対し，「この危難の時代を無事に脱出するため」合意形成に取り組むよう促した。

〔そして〕ネオナチズムと白人至上主義の発展と拡散に対抗し，プロパガンダと虚偽情報と闘うために，グローバルな協調行動の必要性を強調した。「真実を掘り崩す者が結局は自らを掘り崩すことを歴史は示している。

コロナ禍を抜け出す唯一の道は，科学と事実に基づく分析であり，記録的な速さでワクチンが製造されたことが，このアプローチの有効性を証明している。反ユダヤ主義や外国人嫌いを防ぐワクチンは存在しないが，真実というものこそが，いつも変わらず我々の最大の武器となるのである」(同)。

VIII 文脈上，空所を埋めるのに最もふさわしいものを4つの選択肢の中から1つ選びなさい。

71. 解答：C

解説 前の段落でアメリカの方針転換が反政府勢力の攻撃を誘発したとある。よってC. emboldenedが正解。emboldenはgive courageの意。

72.　解答：A

解説　2017年にマリブに逃げてきたが，The rebels ... intensified their offensive in strategic Maribとあるので，trying to avoid being capturedを意味するA. on the runを選ぶ。... we fled for our livesもヒントになる。

73.　解答：A

解説　The conflict ... the Iran-aligned Shiite Muslim Houthis against ...に着目し，set someone in conflictを意味するA. pitsを選ぶ。

74.　解答：B

解説　空所前に，この紛争はシーア派とスンニ派の間で行われているとある。よってB. proxyが正解。proxy warでa war instigated by a major powerの意。

75.　解答：D

解説　2週間前のバイデン政権はaccelerate diplomatic efforts to end the fightingとあるので，the Marib offensive ... the obstacles it facesにはD. underscoresが入る。underscoreはemphasizeの意。

76.　解答：C

解説　denounced Griffiths' characterization of the offensive ... an "attack"に着目しC. asを選ぶ。

77.　解答：B

解説　「和平は絶対に受け入れられない」に続いてwe were to accept that, we would have accepted it in the early daysとあるので，仮定法と解釈しB. ifを選ぶ。

78.　解答：B

解説　that stability also attracted at least 850,000 peopleと具体的な事実を述べたあとthe International Organization of Migrationと組織名が続くのでB. according toを選ぶ。

79. 解答：A

解説 as they push toward the city からフーシ派が攻撃に向けた準備を着々と進めていることが読み取れる。よって A. amassing が正解。amass は accumulate a large amount of material の意。

80. 解答：D

解説 数々の苦難のあと「今月になって，一家の生活は再び ______」とある。よって D. upended を選ぶ。upend は turn something upside down の意。

訳例　フセイン・アリ・ウハイシュが暮らす難民キャンプ内に砲弾が着弾しはじめた。バイデン政権がイエメンで戦うサウジアラビア主導の連合軍に対する米国の支援を打ち切り，北部の反政府勢力に対する制裁を解除する措置をとって数日後のことだ。

フーシと呼ばれる反政府勢力は，米国の方針転換によって勢いづいたかのように，この戦争における数少ない安全な避難場所として戦略的に重要なマリブ県で攻勢を強めていた。2017年にマリブに逃れたウハイシュ一家は，いま再び逃亡の身となった。

ウハイシュさんは医師で5児の父親。「妻といっしょに子供たちをなだめていると，ご近所の子供たちの叫び声と泣き声が聞こえてきました。また，安全ではいられなくなったのだとはっきり分かりました」と話す。

「ですから戦闘の物音が近づく中，命からがら逃げ出したのです」。

国際的に承認されているイエメン政府の北部最後の拠点であるマリブにおける戦闘激化によって，何十万人ものイエメン人が避難を余儀なくさせられる恐れが出てきた。その多くはすでに何度も暴力を逃れてきた人たちだ。そうなれば，〔この〕人道危機は国連がすでに世界で最も深刻だと指摘しているものだが，それが大幅に悪化してしまう。米国および国連の高官や援助関係者はそう話している。

この緊張は，このアラブ圏の最貧国で何万人もの死傷者を出しているこの6年間続く戦争を終結させるべく国連などが行っている取り組みを崩壊させる可能性がある。

この紛争の当事者は，イランと連携するイスラム教シーア派のフーシと，米国の支援を受けた，サウジアラビアやアラブ首長国連邦を中心とするイスラム教スンニ派諸国の連合〔の二者〕で，後者はイエメン政府の政権復帰を目指している。現在では，内戦であると同時に，サウジアラビアとイランの代理戦争〔という性格を帯びるにいたった〕。

この1年間，反政府勢力はサヌアの北東約100マイルにあるマリブ県で着実に力を伸ばしてきた。ここを奪取すれば，政府が擁する北部最後の拠点がなくなり，フーシは主要な獲得目標である，利益を生む油田や天然ガス田を支配下に置くこととなる。

同県を占領すれば，戦争の終結と新政府の樹立を目指す交渉において反政府勢力の立場が強まるとアナリストらは指摘している。

オックスフォード大学のイエメン研究者，エリザベス・ケンドール氏は言う。「マリブはこの戦争の成功物語でした。戦争のただ中にあっても安全地帯でした。希望を与えてくれる場所でした。それをまったく別物に変えさせてしまうことは，象徴的な意味できわめて悲劇的です」。

バイデン政権からすれば，〔フーシによる〕マリブへの攻勢は，重要な外交政策目標に取り組む上で抱えているさまざまな障害を浮き彫りにするものだ。バイデン大統領は2週間前，連合軍の攻撃作戦に対する米国の支援を打ち切るとともに，新しいイエメン特使を任命し，戦闘終結に向けた外交努力を加速させることを約束した。

同政権は，米国の外国テロ組織リストからフーシ派を削除することを議会に通知した。それを行えばイエメンの人道状況が悪化するとの各援助団体からの警告を受けてトランプ政権が下した判断を覆した形だ。

国務省は先週，フーシ派に対し，イエメンに対するこの方針転換を米国の弱さの表れと受け取り，さらに領土を奪取することがあってはならないと警告するとともに，マリブへの攻撃を停止するよう求めた。

マーティン・グリフィス国連イエメン特使は先週，「マリブへの攻撃は止めなければならない。武力による領土獲得を目指すことは，和平プロセスのあらゆる見通しを損なう脅威となる」と述べた。

フーシ派高官のモハメド・アリ・アル・フーシ氏は，グリフィス氏が攻勢を「攻撃」と呼んだことを非難するとともに，この紛争の責任は米国にあると述べた。

同氏はツイッターで次のように述べた。「オバマとバイデンが侵略を開始することでイエメン人の忍耐力を試すと決めてから，6年が経過した。我々は我々を制圧させるような和平は絶対に受け入れられない。もし受け入れるのであれば，早い段階で受け入れていただろう」。

紛争の最初の数年間，マリブ県は激しい戦闘を免れたため，現地当局は石油やガスで得た収益を経済発展に回すことができた。

しかし国際移住機関によれば，その安定は戦闘に見舞われた地域から少なくとも85万人の避難民を引き寄せ，そのほとんどがマリブ市郊外のキャンプに押し寄せた。紛争が激化すれば，避難民は壊滅的な打撃を受けるだろうと，国連や支援機関は発言している。

オックスファムのイエメン担当ディレクターを務めるムーシン・シディキー

は次のように述べた。「多くの人が食糧，水，医療，その他の人道支援を緊急に必要としている。多くの家族が特に弱い立場に置かれている。すでに何度も避難を余儀なくされ，再び避難するための資源を持っていない可能性があるためだ」。

現地報道や援助機関によると，フーシ派は市内に向けて進みながら，重火器や装備を蓄えつつある。また，ここ数日，双方の戦闘員数名が死亡し，避難民キャンプ数カ所が砲撃されたとの援助機関や現地報道からの〔情報もある〕。

ウハイシュさんの話によると，自分がフーシ派を声高に批判したため拉《ら》致《ち》されて監禁・拷問を受けたことから，一家はザマル県の村から逃げ出したという。その後，県都のザマル市に落ち着いたが，2017年，フーシ派が再びウハイシュさんを探してやってきた。そこで一家はマリブ市郊外にあるアル・ズール・キャンプに逃げ込んだ。

今月になって，一家の生活は再び一変してしまった。

爆弾が降る中，衣服だけを背負ってキャンプから逃げ出したという。ウハイシュさんの話によると，多くの家族がテントの中か，さもなければ野外で寝泊りしているという。

ウハイシュ一家は，幸いにも友人の家に一時的に身を寄せることができたが，次の避難先を見つけるのは難しいかもしれない。一家には所持金はほとんどない。フーシ派はマリブの西側を支配している。その東は広大な砂漠で，水はほとんどない。ダマールに戻ることは死を意味する。

ウハイシュさんは言った。「今はもう行くところがありません。明日どうなるか分からない状態です」。

IX

以下の質問に対し，150～200語の短いエッセイを英語で書きなさい。

質問文：国連SDGsの全体的な考え方を誰かに説明するとしたら，どうするか？

解答例 My explanation imagines SDGs as a three-layer wedding cake. Each level—environment, society, economy—supports the layer above. In 2015, the UN adopted 17 sustainable goals—measured using 169 targets and 232 achievement indicators—for 193 countries to attain by 2030. Goals are connected.

First, environment supports everything. SDGs for clean water, climate action, life on land, and life below water must be reached to sustain our planetary existence. I think SDG#13 is most important because it coordinates other goals on this level.

Second, societal goals—no poverty; zero hunger; good health and well-being; quality education; gender equality; affordable clean energy; sustainable cities and communities; and peace, justice, and strong institutions—are essential for human civilization. SDG#5, gender equality, is imperative because it doubles humanity's power, as an effectively skilled and mutually supportive team, to tackle all other problems.

Third, economic aims—decent work and business-related growth; industry, innovation, and infrastructure; reduced inequalities; and responsible consumption—result from social action. SDG#10, reducing inequalities, must accelerate the freeing and mobilizing of our global population toward achieving sustainable goals more quickly.

Try asking, "what's your most important part of the cake?" and start your own interesting conversation with someone about the SDGs.

解説　国連 SDGs に関する正確な知識を織り交ぜながら，テーマに沿って意見をまとめるとよい。

第 1 パラグラフでは，SDGs の「採択年」「目標数」「目標年」等を明記しつつ，導入として「環境」「社会」「経済」の 3 つの分野を 3 層のケーキに例えている。

第 2 パラグラフでは，環境について複数の具体的目標を示しつつ，とりわけ気候変動に関する目標 13 がもっとも影響力が大きいとしている。

第 3 パラグラフでは，社会について目標をいくつか列挙したのち，ジェンダー平等に関する目標 5 が，他の問題に取り組む上で人類のチーム力アップにつながると主張している。

第 4 パラグラフでは，経済について同様に複数の目標を提示したのち，人や国の不平等をなくしていく目標 10 には，人類の解放と結集が必要と訴えている。

第 5 パラグラフでは，説明を聞いてくれている相手に 3 層のケーキの中でどの部分が一番大切かを聞いてみることを提案し，結びとしている。

訳例　私の説明は，SDGs を 3 段のウェディングケーキに見立てるもので，環境，社会，経済の層がそれぞれ上の層を支える形となっている。国連は 2015 年，2030 年までに 193 カ国が達成すべき 17 の持続可能な〔開発〕目標（169 のターゲットと 232 の指標により測定）を採択した。〔これらの〕目標は〔相互に〕関連している。

まず，環境はあらゆるものを支える〔基盤である〕。安全な水，気候変動対策，陸の豊かさ，海の豊かさに関するSDGsの達成が必要なのは，地球上における我々の生存を持続させるためである。〔特に〕SDG目標13はこのレベルにおいて他の目標を調整するものであるから，私はこれを最も重要と考える。

第二に，社会に関する目標の「貧困をなくそう」，「飢餓をゼロに」，「すべての人に健康と福祉を」，「質の高い教育をみんなに」，「ジェンダー平等を実現しよう」，「エネルギーをみんなに，そしてクリーンに」，「住み続けられるまちづくりを」，「平和と公正をすべての人に」は，人類の文明にとって不可欠なものだ。SDG目標5「ジェンダー平等を実現しよう」が必須である理由は，それによって人類が役立つ技能を備えた，互いに支え合うチームとして，他のすべての問題に取り組む力が倍増するからである。

第三に，経済目標の「働きがいも経済成長も」，「産業と技術革新の基盤をつくろう」，「人や国の不平等をなくそう」，「つくる責任，〔つかう責任〕」は，社会的行動の結果として実現するものである。SDG目標10「人や国の不平等をなくそう」〔の実現に〕は，持続可能な〔開発〕目標の達成に向けて，世界人類の解放と結集を加速させる必要がある。

〔説明する〕相手に「このケーキで一番大事と思う部分はどこ？」と尋ねてみよう。そしてそれをきっかけに，SDGsについて興味の赴くまま話し合ってみてはどうだろうか。

2021年A級第1回試験　正解一覧

Ⅰ
1. D　2. C　3. A　4. C　5. B　6. C　7. D　8. A　9. B　10. D

Ⅱ
11. B　12. D　13. A　14. A　15. B　16. D　17. D　18. B　19. B　20. C

Ⅲ
21. D　22. B　23. A　24. D　25. C　26. A　27. D　28. C　29. B　30. A

Ⅳ
31. B　32. D　33. B　34. C　35. B　36. A　37. C　38. B　39. A　40. D

Ⅴ
41. C　42. B　43. D　44. B　45. B　46. B　47. A　48. C　49. A　50. C

Ⅵ
51. B　52. D　53. B　54. B　55. C　56. B　57. A　58. D　59. D　60. D

Ⅶ
61. A　62. C　63. B　64. D　65. C　66. D　67. C　68. A　69. B　70. D

Ⅷ
71. C　72. A　73. A　74. B　75. D　76. C　77. B　78. B　79. A　80. D

2021年
第2回試験

問題

Ａ級第１次試験問題用紙

Ａ級

外務省後援

２０２１年度第２回国際連合公用語

英語検定試験（120分）

受験上の注意

1．問題用紙は試験開始の合図があるまで開いてはいけません。その間に、この**受験上の注意を熟読しておいてください。**

2．**受験番号と氏名を解答用紙（マークシートと作文用紙）**に記入してください。

3．解答用紙の配布は１人１部のみです。複数の配布は致しません。

4．試験開始前は、答案への解答記入は禁止です。

5．マークシートの記入は、１～100までの記入箇所がありますが、この級では１～80までを使います。

6．マークシートの記入は、必ずＨＢ以上の濃い鉛筆を使って該当箇所を黒く塗りつぶしてください。書き間違いの場合は「アト」が残らないように消してください。マークシートは絶対に折ったり曲げたりしないでください。

7．受験級、受験地区、会場番号、受験番号のマークシートへの記入は監督者の指示に従い、間違いなく記入してください。**（裏表紙の「マークシート記入例」参照）**

8．作文は、⑴読みやすい文字をペン、ボールペンまたはＨＢ以上の濃い鉛筆で書いてください。⑵使用語数の150～200語を目安にしてください。

9．試験問題についての質問は、印刷が不鮮明な場合を除き、一切受けつけません。

10．中途退室の際は、マークシートと作文用紙を持って監督者に渡し、他の受験者の迷惑にならないように静かに退室してください。中途退室後の再入室はできません。

11．試験中は他の受験者の妨げとなる行動は慎んでください。また携帯電話等の電源はお切りください。

12．マークシートと作文用紙は監督者に提出し、問題用紙はご自由にお持ち帰りください。

＊試験問題の複製や転載、インターネットへのアップロード等、いかなる媒体への転用を禁止します。

試験結果について

1．第１次試験の結果は2021年11月24日㈬頃に受験申込書に記載された住所に郵送で通知します。

2．その間に住所変更をされた方は、郵便局へ住所変更の届け出を忘れずに行ってください。

3．発表前の試験結果のお問合せには応じられません。

第２次試験について

1．第１次試験合格者には、試験結果発表と同時に試験日時、会場を指定して通知します。（第１次試験を特別会場で受験した合格者には最寄りの２次試験会場が指定されます。）

2．第２次試験は2021年12月12日㈰です。Ａ級の試験地は札幌・仙台・東京・名古屋・大阪・福岡・鹿児島・沖縄のいずれかになります。（特Ａ級との併願で特Ａ級の第１次試験に合格された方の試験地は東京と大阪になります。）あらかじめご了承願います。

公益財団法人 日本国際連合協会
http://www.unaj.or.jp/

I.	Fill in each of the following blanks with the most appropriate of the four alternatives according to the knowledge and information gained from *New Today's Guide to the United Nations*.

1. **Foreword**

The United Nations, whose membership comprises almost all the States in the world, is founded on the principle of the equal worth of every ________.

A. human being　　B. nation
C. religion　　D. people

2. **Address to the General Assembly**

I am grateful to the General Assembly for approving one of my first reform initiatives: the establishment of the UN Office on ________.

A. Mediation　　B. Counter-Terrorism
C. Climate Change　　D. International Humanitarian Law

3. **Membership**

Japan joined the United Nations on 18 December 1956. Membership of the Organization has more than tripled to ________ nations, as of November 2017.

A. 179　　B. 189
C. 193　　D. 202

4. **Security Counsel**

Each member of the Security Council has one vote. Decisions on matters of procedure require the approval of at least nine of the ________ members.

A. 7　　B. 10
C. 12　　D. 15

5. **Peacebuilding Commission**

The establishment of the Peacebuilding Commission (PBC) was proposed during the ________ of the United Nations in 2005.

A. General Assembly　　B. World Summit
C. Security Council　　D. International Court of Justice

6. **Secretariat**

The present Secretary-General is António Guterres of ________, who assumed office in January 2017.

A. Portugal　　B. Austria
C. Italy　　D. Peru

7. **Food and Agriculture Organization of the United Nations (FAO)**

The Food and Agriculture Organization of the United Nations (FAO) was founded at a conference in Quebec on 16 October ________.

A. 1945 B. 1946

C. 1948 D. 1956

8. **United Nations Educational, Scientific and Cultural Organization (UNESCO)**

Owing to the increase of member countries from newly independent countries beginning the 1960s, UNESCO developed more ________ policies, aggravating conflict with the United States.

A. detailed B. coherent

C. independent D. integrated

9. **World Health Organization (WHO)**

The World Health Organization (WHO) came into being on 7 April 1948, when 26 United Nations member States had its ________ ratified.

A. Convention B. Constitution

C. Treaty D. Declaration

10. **Relationship with UN Specialized Agencies**

In the mid-1980s, although major member States such as the U.S. and ________ withdrew from UNESCO, Japan chose to stay in while devoting itself to UNESCO's internal reform efforts as the de facto number-one donor to the organization's regular budget.

A. Soviet Union B. China

C. France D. the U.K.

Ⅱ. Choose from among the four alternatives the one that is the most appropriate form of each of the underlined verbs.

Isolation and the absence of family and friends have taken a toll on athletes' mental health at the Tokyo Olympics, with some **(11)** **struggle** to cope with the challenges posed by the pandemic while carrying their country's hopes on the global sports stage.

After her stunning exit from the women's gymnastics team event on Tuesday, Simone Biles said she felt she **(12)** **carry** the weight of the world on her shoulders. That burden seems to **(13)** **exacerbate** a year of a grief, loss and restrictions tied to the COVID-19 pandemic.

"Usually you hang out in the village, all that stuff," Biles said. "It does suck when you feel the weight of the world. There are no outlets with the amount of training that we do."

Athletes have seen their pre-Olympic training **(14)** **disrupt** lockdowns and restricted access to athletic facilities, and the postponement of the Games fueled concern about qualification schedules and the ability to travel internationally without contracting the virus.

Their families and friends can't cheer for them in the stands in Tokyo and their movements are heavily restricted.

The pandemic prompted the U.S. women's gymnastics team **(15)** **steer** clear of the bustle of the athletes village and stay at a nearby hotel for security reasons, something that takes the shine off an Olympic experience.

"Not saying that we don't have a great set up," Biles said. "We chose that **(16)** **be** COVID safe."

Biles said she had been able to keep in touch with family by FaceTime and text messages, **(17)** **give** her "all the support that I absolutely needed."

"We have tons of resources available to us," Biles added. "But I wanted to tough it out to the last minute, but obviously it **(18)** **not work** that way."

U.S. swimmer Katie Ledecky, **(19)** **also come** into the Games with high expectations, said she understood the pressure Biles felt as an Olympian of her stature. She said their compatriots should be more concerned about what is happening in the world than whether she wins an Olympic title.

"Being Olympians it's something that we all have to watch out for each other and help each other through and in times of need," Ledecky said after winning gold in the first 1,500 meters swimming event for women ever **(20)** **stage** at the Olympics.

11. A. struggled B. struggling
C. are struggling D. struggle

12. A. is carrying B. would be carrying
C. had been carrying D. has been carrying

13. A. have been exacerbating B. be exacerbating
C. exacerbate D. have been exacerbated by

14. A. disrupting B. is disrupting
C. is disrupted by D. disrupted by

15. A. to steer B. steering
C. which steers D. should steer

16. A. for being B. being
C. was D. to be

17. A. gave B. to give
C. which give D. giving

18. A. hadn't worked B. didn't work
C. won't work D. isn't working

19. A. also had come B. also came
C. who also came D. was also coming

20. A. staged B. have staged
C. staging D. had staged

Ⅲ. Fill in each of the following blanks with the most grammatically and logically appropriate of the four alternatives.

A case of Ebola virus has been confirmed in Côte d'Ivoire for the first time since 1994, the country's Ministry of Health has confirmed. The World Health Organization (WHO) is coordinating the delivery of vaccines to the country.

In a statement released on Saturday, the Côte d'Ivoire country office of the WHO said that the **(21)** ______________________________ who was hospitalized in the commercial capital of Abidjan, after arriving from Guinea. Initial investigations found that the patient had travelled to Côte d'Ivoire by road and arrived in Abidjan on 12 August. The patient was admitted to hospital **(22)** ______________________________.

Earlier this year, Guinea experienced a four-month long Ebola outbreak, which was declared over on the 19 June 2021. The WHO said **(23)** ______________________________ case in Côte d'Ivoire is linked to the Guinea outbreak, but added that further investigation will identify the strain, and determine if there is a connection between the two outbreaks.

This year Ebola outbreaks have been declared in the Democratic Republic of the Congo and Guinea, but it is the first time an outbreak has occurred in a large capital city such as Abidjan since the 2014–2016 West African Ebola outbreak.

"It is of immense concern that this outbreak has been declared in Abidjan, a metropolis of more than 4 million people," said Dr Matshidiso Moeti, World Health Organization (WHO) Regional Director for Africa. "However, much of the **(24)** ______________________________ continent and Côte d'Ivoire can tap into this experience and bring the response to full speed. The country is one of **(25)** ______________________________ up their Ebola readiness and this quick diagnosis shows preparedness is paying off."

WHO is helping to coordinate cross-border Ebola response activities, and 5,000 Ebola vaccines doses which the organization helped secure to fight the outbreak in Guinea are now being transferred to Côte d'Ivoire, following an agreement between the ministries of health of Côte d'Ivoire and Guinea. People at high risk, including health workers, first responders and contacts of confirmed cases, will be prioritised for vaccination.

Ebola is a severe, often fatal illness affecting humans and other primates. Fatality rates have varied from 25% to 90% in past outbreaks; there is now effective treatment available and if patients receive treatment early, as well as supportive care, their chances of survival improve significantly.

The vaccination against Ebola of high-risk populations began on Monday in Côte d'Ivoire **(26)** ______________________________ three days earlier. The swift response came after vaccines manufactured by Merck, which the World Health Organization (WHO) helped to secure to fight a four-month long outbreak in neighboring

Guinea, were quickly sent to the country.

The deployment from Guinea included 2,000 doses that are being used under the "ring strategy," where people **(27)** ____ ____ patient are given the vaccine, as well as first responders and health workers. Guinea also sent around 3,000 vaccine doses manufactured by Johnson & Johnson. These are being used as booster jabs in areas not experiencing active transmission.

"The Ebola vaccine is a critical tool in the fight against the virus and so it's a top priority to move rapidly and start protecting people at high risk of the disease," said WHO Regional Director for Africa, Dr. Matshidiso Moeti, who described the quick response as "remarkable and shows that with effective sub-regional solidarity we **(28)** __________ ________________________________ can potentially flare up into large outbreaks."

The outbreak was declared in Côte d'Ivoire after the Ebola virus was confirmed in a patient who travelled to Abidjan by road from Guinea. One suspected case and nine contacts have also been identified and are being monitored, although no deaths have been reported.

There is no indication yet that the current outbreak in Côte d'Ivoire is linked with the one that was in Guinea and further analysis and genomic sequencing is being carried out to help determine any connection.

The outbreak is Côte d'Ivoire's first since 1994 and to support the country's efforts to control its spread, the WHO is **(29)** ________________________________ __________ ramp up infection prevention and control, diagnostics, contact tracing, treatment, community mobilization and cross-border surveillance. The UN agency is also assessing whether additional vaccines will be needed to curb the disease.

In Guinea, the health authorities are stepping up surveillance, carrying out further investigations, identifying contacts in readiness for vaccination and readying an Ebola treatment center.

Since **(30)** ____ year, the WHO has been supporting six countries, including Côte d'Ivoire, to prepare for a potential outbreak. This included support in disease surveillance, screenings at border crossing points and in high-risk communities as well as setting up rapid response teams, improving testing and treatment capacity and reinforcing community outreach and collaboration.

21. A. samples was found in a patient from collected virus
B. patient found was in samples collected a virus from
C. collected patient was found a virus from in samples
D. virus was found in samples collected from a patient

22. A. after experiencing a fever and is currently receiving treatment
B. experiencing receiving treatment currently and is a fever after
C. receiving currently treatment experiencing and is after a fever
D. treatment a fever and is currently receiving after experiencing

23. A. that current is there no indication that the currently
B. currently that the indication that current there no is
C. there is that no currently indication current that the
D. that there is currently no indication that the current

24. A. Ebola is here tackling in on the expertise world's
B. expertise in world's Ebola is here on the tackling
C. world's expertise in tackling Ebola is here on the
D. tackling the Ebola world's in expertise is here on

25. A. recently six that WHO has the beef supported to
B. the six that WHO has supported recently to beef
C. six supported that WHO has recently to beef the
D. WHO that six has recently supported to the beef

26. A. following the discovery of an outbreak in the country
B. in an outbreak following the discovery of the country
C. the country in outbreak of an discovery the following
D. of following the country discovery an outbreak in the

27. A. come into contact with a confirmed Ebola who have
B. into contact with Ebola who have come confirmed a
C. who have come into contact with a confirmed Ebola
D. with a confirmed Ebola have come into contact who

28. A. can quickly take measures to extinguish lethal infections that
B. extinguish lethal measures that can quickly take to infections
C. quickly can take lethal infections to extinguish measures that
D. to take infections measures that can quickly extinguish lethal

29. A. country-based deploying experts to join to help their counterparts
B. deploying experts to join their country-based counterparts to help
C. help to country-based experts to join their counterparts deploying
D. join country-based counterparts deploying experts to their help to

30. A. declared earlier this Ebola was in the Guinea outbreak
B. earlier outbreak in Ebola declared this was the Guinea
C. Guinea was declared this in Ebola outbreak the earlier
D. the Ebola outbreak was declared in Guinea earlier this

Ⅳ. Choose from among the four alternatives the one that best completes the following sentence.

31. **President Joe Biden on Monday said the United States is _________ new sanctions against Belarus, marking the one-year anniversary of Alexander Lukashenko's election as president in an election that the US and international community have said was _________ with irregularities.**

A. revoking – marred
B. imposing – distraught
C. levying – fraught
D. enforcing – eluded

32. **The continued recruitment and presence of mercenaries in Libya is _________ "progress in the peace process" and an obstacle to upcoming elections, independent UN human rights experts said on Friday, calling for their "long _________" departure.**

A. crippling – imminent
B. corroborating – abrupt
C. expediting – laborious
D. impeding – overdue

33. **At least 227 people were killed and hundreds were injured and missing after a 7.2 magnitude earthquake struck Haiti on Saturday, and Prime Minister Ariel Henry said he was _________ aid to areas where towns were destroyed and hospitals _________ with incoming patients.**

A. rushing – overwhelmed
B. withholding – inundated
C. securing – frequented
D. granting – admitted

34. **The top UN rights official once more _________ the alarm on Thursday over the plight of civilians in Syria, as intense fighting and indiscriminate shelling by Government forces and armed opposition groups _________ neighborhoods in and around the southern city of Daraa.**

A. articulated – disregard
B. sounded – paralyze
C. heeded – tout
D. disdained – deprive

35. **A Chinese court sentenced Canadian entrepreneur Michael Spavor to 11 years in prison Wednesday in a spying case that has been linked _________ Beijing's pressure campaign against the Canadian government _________ the arrest of an executive at tech giant Huawei.**

A. for – under
B. with – toward
C. from – without
D. to – over

36. **Belarus has ________ an unprecedented human rights crisis over the past year, the independent expert appointed to monitor the country said on Monday, calling on authorities to immediately end their policy of repression and fully respect the legitimate ________ of their people.**

A. witnessed – aspirations B. weathered – formalities
C. defused – credentials D. precipitated – conjunctures

37. **At least three people were killed in anti-Taliban protests in the Afghan city of Jalalabad on Wednesday, witnesses said, as the Islamist group moved to ________ power and Western countries ________ evacuations from a chaotic Kabul airport.**

A. confer – fortified B. relinquish – hampered
C. consolidate – ramped up D. wield – codified

38. **Last year was the deadliest on record for Rohingya refugees journeying through the Bay of Bengal and Andaman Sea, the UN refugee agency (UNHCR) said in a new report on Thursday, ________ that some two-thirds of those attempting the ________ voyages were women and children - risking even further abuse by smugglers.**

A. rekindling – arduous B. highlighting – perilous
C. underscoring – epic D. rebuking – maiden

39. **With coronavirus deaths rising in Myanmar, ________ are growing from residents and human rights activists that the military government, which ________ control in February, is using the pandemic to consolidate power and crush opposition.**

A. grievances – perpetuated B. enmities – renounced
C. predicaments – delegated D. allegations – seized

40. **________ the Taliban's lightning takeover of Afghanistan, Russian officials moved quickly into a ________ approach: cautiously reaching out to the Taliban even as Russia expanded military exercises with Tajikistan along the Afghan border.**

A. In defiance of – practical B. For fear of – intrepid
C. In the wake of – two-pronged D. In line with – pliant

V. Choose from among the underlined phrases the one that is grammatically or idiomatically incorrect.

41. Three **(A)** Chinese naval vessels, including a large **(B)** guided-missile destroyer, has been **(C)** spotted in the Strait of Tsushima, north of Japan's Kyushu main island, **(D)** sailing into the Sea of Japan, the Defense Ministry said.

42. The UN Secretary-General **(A)** on Friday called on Taliban militants to **(B)** "immediate halt" their offensive against Government forces **(C)** and return to the negotiating table in good faith, **(D)** "in the interest of Afghanistan, and its people."

43. Japan decided Tuesday **(A)** to extend its unilateral sanctions on North Korea, including **(B)** a ban on all trade, by two years to maintain pressure **(C)** on the country to give up its nuclear and missile programs, **(D)** and making progress on the issue of its past abductions of Japanese nationals.

44. The Japanese government plans **(A)** to extend the COVID-19 state of emergency set to **(B)** expire at the end of May in Tokyo and eight prefectures **(C)** to June 20, a senior official said Thursday, as **(D)** the increase in infections has slowed and hospitals remain under strain.

45. **(A)** A new study released on Friday by the UN cultural agency **(B)** reveals that more than 100 million more children **(C)** as expected are falling behind the minimum proficiency level **(D)** in reading, due to COVID-related school closures.

46. **(A)** A growing number of people who have recently **(B)** arrived in Japan are raising concerns over malfunctioning monitoring tools **(C)** and confusing guidelines may have put them **(D)** on the government's blacklist for violating quarantine.

47. The looming **(A)** threat to a fifth wave of COVID-19 infections **(B)** has put plans for allowing spectators at the Tokyo Olympics **(C)** in doubt, as the ultimate choice on how many — **(D)** if any — will be able to watch the events has moved into the political arena.

48. Over 140,000 species, **(A)** including 55 per cent of all fish, **(B)** rely on freshwater inhabitants for their survival. Freshwater species are important to local ecosystems, provide sources of food and income to humans, and are **(C)** key to flood and erosion control. Yet wetland species are **(D)** going extinct more rapidly than terrestrial or marine species.

49. **(A)** Achieving equal rights for women is "the **(B)** unfinished human rights struggle of this century", UN Secretary-General **(C)** António Guterres said in remarks to **(D)** the Generation Equality Forum began online from Mexico City on Monday.

50. **(A)** Leading athletes, influencers and innovators **(B)** have been sharing their thoughts on the role that sport **(C)** can play in building a better world for all, in UN-led **(D)** online discussions held to coincide the Tokyo Olympics.

VI. Choose from among the four alternatives the one that most closely corresponds to the meaning of words in bold type and blanks in the following passage.

Defining Micro-States: It has been noted by many that there is no consensus as to what constitutes a small state, including micro-states. This is because there are many ways to define small states, there are many variables that can be used to define small states and because different academics are studying small states for different purposes. Archer and Nugent write, 'ultimately a judgmental element must **(51) creep** into the exercise of categorising states by size' (2002, 5). Variables like territorial size, population and economic outputs are commonly cited as ways to define small states. Moreover, size is a relative concept in political science as all states are different sizes. David Vital (1967) proposed a two-fold means of defining small states involving a combination of industrial/economic capability and population size. Vital argued that small states were either advanced industrial states with populations of 10–15 million or under-developed states with populations of 20–30 million. While this template was formulated during the Cold War, it still has some **(52) resonance** today.

Within small state studies, the sub-field of micro-states also has a range of competing definitions. A range of scholars have produced different definitions of micro-states including Blair (1967) who uses a population threshold of 300,000 and Plischke (1977) who **(53)** __________ a format in which micro-states have populations of under 100,000 or between 100,000–300,000 and are UN members. Ali Naseer Mohamed (2002) suggests a **(54) threshold** of 1.5 million, while Armstrong and Read (1995) use a population threshold of 3 million to define micro-states. **(55)** __________, many scholars indicate that a population threshold of 1 million is sufficient to constitute a micro-state. Scholars such as Simpson (2008) use the one million residents or less as a means of identifying micro-states. Though Wivel and Oest (2010, 434) add that micro-states, '[are] permanently stuck as the weak party in asymmetric relationships.' The central point is that micro-states are very small states, usually in both population and territorial terms. **(56)** __________, there are important consequences of this smallness such as having smaller governments, fewer economic resources, weaker bureaucracies, smaller militaries, and they are vulnerable to external pressures. Ogashiwa (1991, x) summarises, 'micro-states which have very small populations and land areas also in most cases are economically, militarily and politically vulnerable.'

Statehood, Self-Determination and UN Membership: Initiated by President Woodrow Wilson in 1918, the concept of self-determination was established and it became a guiding principle of his 'Fourteen Points' at the Versailles Peace Conference following the First World War. However, it became a principle of international law in 1945 at the **(57) insistence** of the Soviet Union and was incorporated into the UN Charter through Articles 1 and 55. Self-determination is, 'the search for full independence and sovereignty by a community with the result to redraw international boundaries at the expense of the existing state' (Danspeckgruber 2002, 3). This means that a 'people' or a 'nation' have the right to possess their own sovereign state. International law, according to Article 1 of the 1933 Montevideo Convention on the Rights and Duties of States, presents four **(58) criteria** of statehood: a) a permanent population, b) a defined territory, c) government, and d) capacity to enter into relations with other states. Importantly, international law does not specify a minimum threshold for territory or population; this allows for micro-states.

An unwritten fifth criterion is constitutional independence, which is essential to self-determination. In 1948 the International Court of Justice presented five criteria for UN membership, **(59)** ________ applicants a) must be a state, b) be peace-loving, c) accept UN obligations as set in the UN Charter, d) be able to carry out these obligations, e) be willing to do so. With UN membership being by application, this placed conditions on membership. For example, the term 'peace-loving' was—in reality—political **(60) code** for being part of the Grand Alliance that defeated Nazism, thus excluding many states including neutral states.

51. **In this context, "creep" is closest in meaning to**

A. clamber B. enter
C. skulk D. slink

52. **In this context, "resonance" is closest in meaning to**

A. quality B. reverberation
C. significance D. timbre

53. **From the context, the underlined blank could best be filled with**

A. follows up B. gets down
C. sets out D. takes on

54. **From the context, "threshold" is best replaced by**

A. base B. factor
C. maximum D. perimeter

55. **From the context, the underlined blank could best be filled with**

A. As such B. In this sense
C. Besides D. However

56. **From the context, the underlined blank could best be filled with**

A. Conversely B. Moreover
C. Notwithstanding D. To say the least

57. **In this context, "insistence" is closest in meaning to**

A. assurance
B. demand
C. edict
D. proclamation

58. **In this context, "criteria" is closest in meaning to**

A. conditions
B. notions
C. principles
D. yardsticks

59. **From the context, the underlined blank could best be filled with**

A. for instance
B. namely that
C. therein
D. vis-à-vis

60. **In this context, "code" is closest in meaning to**

A. behaviour
B. expectations
C. guidelines
D. phrasing

Ⅶ. Choose from among the four alternatives the one that best explains each of the underlined words or phrases in the context of the article below.

Thousands of boys and girls have been killed or injured over the past two years in Afghanistan, according to the latest UN report on Children and Armed Conflict, which was issued on Monday, a day after the Taliban **(61)** **consolidated** their control over the country.

The study found that 5,770 Afghan youngsters were killed or maimed between January 2019 and December 2020, the reporting period. Meanwhile, child casualties hit their highest levels ever during the first half of this year, with hundreds killed in recent weeks amid the **(62)** **deteriorating** political and security situation.

Virginia Gamba, the UN Secretary-General's Special Representative for Children and Armed Conflict, said Afghanistan continues to be one of the most dangerous places to be a child.

"I am **(63)** **appalled** by the continuing and rising high levels of violence endured by children in Afghanistan, including those caught up in combat," she said.

"As the already dramatic situation continues to evolve rapidly and **(64)** **concerning** reports of human rights violations keep **(65)** **arising**, I call for all abuses to stop, and I urge the Taliban and all other parties to abide by their obligations under international humanitarian law and international human rights law, as well as by national commitments and protect the lives and rights of all people, including those of women and girls."

The research revealed that during the reporting period, one in three **(66)** **casualties** was a child. Armed groups, particularly the Taliban, were responsible for most incidents, or 46 per cent, with Government and pro-Government forces accounting for 35 per cent, followed by landmines and explosive remnants of war.

"It is urgent that all parties take the necessary actions to minimize harm to children and prioritize their protection in the conduct of hostilities as well as protect schools and hospitals," said Ms. Gamba.

"Such harm is otherwise bound to affect generations to come, when Afghan children have already had their childhood taken away from them. With **(67)** **figures** already alarmingly high and the Taliban identified in the report as a major perpetrator of violence against children, the future of children, especially girls in Afghanistan is grim."

The UN also verified more than 6,470 **(68)** **grave** violations against children during the reporting period, with nearly half attributed to the Taliban. Some 297 attacks on schools and hospitals also were verified. Despite a decrease in assaults on schools, the report's authors noted that attacks on hospitals and protected personnel rose, which they found particularly **(69)** **egregious**, given the fragile state of the Afghan healthcare system and the challenges of the COVID-19 pandemic.

Meanwhile, deliberate Taliban attacks on girls' schools remain "a worrisome trend". Ms. Gamba appealed for the group, and all other parties to the conflict, to respect human rights, including the right to education for girls.

Warring sides, mainly the Taliban, also recruited 260 boys into the hostilities, mostly in combat roles. Ms. Gamba explained that the pandemic exacerbated boys' vulnerability: a situation she said will deepen given the current levels of violence.

"Today, I call on all parties, especially the Taliban, to prevent recruitment and use, abduction, and the killing and maiming of children and to cease all violations and urgently take concrete measures to protect children, schools, and hospitals, and mitigate child casualties," she said.

The UN Special Representative further called for Afghanistan to uphold the criminalization of the practice of bacha bazi, a form of sexual abuse against boys, in line with revisions to the penal code in 2018.

She **(70)** **stressed** that true protection for Afghanistan's children will only come through peaceful resolution of the conflict. "I call on all parties, especially the Taliban today, to ensure that child protection issues are prioritized by all actors involved in peace negotiations to sustainably prevent grave violations against children from occurring again and to contribute to enhancing the viability of peace," said Ms. Gamba.

61. **consolidated**

A. ceded　　B. established
C. relinquished　　D. waived

62. **deteriorating**

A. gratifying　　B. heartwarming
C. humanizing　　D. worsening

63. **appalled**

A. aghast　　B. elated
C. reassured　　D. uplifted

64. **concerning**

A. alarming　　B. enriching
C. inspiring　　D. soothing

65. **arising**

A. amounting to nothing　　B. coming to light
C. failing to materialize　　D. proving themselves false

66. **casualties**

A. boys freed from becoming soldiers

B. children able to escape harm

C. individuals who are injured

D. people who cause problems

67. **figures**

A. numbers of occurrences

B. protection for children

C. shapes of future plans

D. the availability of food

68. **grave**

A. adolescent

B. burial place

C. negligible

D. serious

69. **egregious**

A. disgraceful

B. hallowed

C. revered

D. venerable

70. **stressed**

A. did not feel

B. misconstrued

C. pretended

D. emphasized

Ⅷ. Fill in each of the following blanks with the most appropriate of the four alternatives as required by the context.

RIO DE JANEIRO — Rodrigo Lucas thinks of himself as a Bolsonaro man. He has supported Jair Bolsonaro's demands that the coronavirus be treated with unproven and ineffective medications. He has condemned the Brazilian president's critics on social media. His background image on Twitter is of Bolsonaro. And he describes himself as "right wing to the root."

But there's one place where Lucas, 37, has refused to follow Bolsonaro: vaccine skepticism. "In a war, we have to use weapons that we have," Lucas said. "**(71)** _________ it came about in six months or a year, if the laboratories are recognized, we have to believe in it. I'm not going to find a conspiracy theory in everything."

All of the pieces were in place for Brazil to follow the United States down the path toward vaccine resistance. The country is politically polarized and **(72)** _________ with disinformation. Brazilians, who have watched politician after politician get sent off to prison, are primed to mistrust. And they're led by a man who has repeatedly worked to undermine faith in scientific research, the country's institutions — and the vaccine itself.

Bolsonaro, who was infected with the coronavirus last year, has declined to get his shots. He once predicted fewer than half of Brazilians would seek to be inoculated.

"I don't consider myself vaccinated; I am vaccinated," he said. "Everyone who has contracted this virus are [has been] vaccinated, even in a way that's more effective than the vaccine itself. So don't argue it: Anyone who has contracted the virus is immunized."

But Brazilians, even those who support Bolsonaro, have been largely tuning him out. As the delta variant bears down **(73)** _________ Brazil, a country at odds over nearly everything has found common ground on the vaccine, **(74)** _________ fears that vaccine skepticism would undermine the country's response to its devastating outbreak, and showing the limits of Bolsonaro's powers of persuasion.

Polls show the number of Brazilians who say they intend to get vaccinated has risen dramatically in recent months, from around 3 in 4 — and even lower in São Paulo — to around 9 in 10.

However, getting the vaccine has been another matter. The country has reported more than 20.3 million cases of covid-19 and more than 569,000 deaths — second only to the United States — but it has continued to suffer vaccine delays and shortages. Where there's a vaccine, however, the Brazilian answer has largely been: Yes, please.

More than 72 percent of all Brazilian adults have gotten one shot of the vaccine — a rate that puts it even with the United States. In São Paulo state, the figure is 86 percent. In the south, where many have supported Bolsonaro, 77 percent of adults have received at least one dose in Rio Grande do Sul, and 76 percent have done the same in Paraná.

"I didn't have any doubt that as soon as they were available, people would put the politics **(75)** _________," said Carla Domingues, an epidemiologist who once directed

Brazil's immunization program. "Brazil believes in the vaccine and Brazil wants the vaccine."

Some have broken the law to get jabbed. Prosecutors across the country have prosecuted people for cutting vaccine lines. Clandestine vaccination clinics have opened.

For some Brazilians, one or two doses has not been enough. One retired teacher in the state in Minas Gerais got two shots of the Chinese Coronavac vaccine. Then another of the AstraZeneca. Then one more of the Pfizer.

In Brazil's **(76)** _________ of vaccines, epidemiologists see the strength of the country's long-standing inoculation culture. Its mass vaccination campaigns have historically reached just about everyone, and quickly. Nearly ninety million Brazilians were vaccinated against H1N1 in three months. It conducted in 2018 the world's largest yellow-fever mass vaccination campaign. The country's vaccine mascot, Zé Gotinha — he looks like the Pillsbury doughboy on a diet — is an ever-present figure.

"We need to take into account Brazilian culture," said Margareth Dalcolmo, a pneumologist and researcher at the research institution Fiocruz. "Brazil, since the creation of the national vaccination plan in 1973, has always had great trust in vaccines."

The **(77)** _________ to get vaccinated suggests the political weakness of Bolsonaro, now the target of a damaging congressional investigation into his government's hands-off approach to the pandemic. Bolsonaro, who once suggested a vaccine might turn recipients into alligators, has himself refused to get the vaccine — but not his son Flávio Bolsonaro, a federal senator. His vice president, Hamilton Mourão, has also been immunized. One of his ministers, Luiz Eduardo Ramos, went out and got it, secretly, while at the shopping mall.

"I, like any other human being, want to live," he said.

Mauro Paulino, the director of the prominent Brazilian polling service Datafolha, said vaccine hesitancy is strong among about a third of Bolsonaro's most **(78)** _________ supporters. "Bolsonaro is the leader and he is influencing his supporters, without a doubt," he said.

But he said the share of the electorate that say they will **(79)** _________ vote for Bolsonaro — he called them the "convinced Bolsonaristas" — is a shrinking sliver of the electorate.

"The data shows very clearly that the federal government has an influence over the opinion of Bolsonaro followers," he said. "But what's happening is he has fewer and fewer supporters."

One die-hard is Carlos de Lima Belucio, 44. A resident of the northern state of Pará, he has advocated for Bolsonaro to **(80)** _________ a military takeover of the country. He says there's no way he'll get the vaccine.

Belucio said he's already gotten the coronavirus twice — maybe even three times — and doesn't find it very threatening. The only way he would consider getting vaccinated, he said, is if it came with a guarantee he would never catch the virus again.

"I don't trust the vaccine," he said. "I'm not a guinea pig."

71. A. While B. Whether
C. Even though D. Once

72. A. discrete B. non-aligned
C. tantalized D. rife

73. A. to B. with
C. on D. from

74. A. instilling B. divulging
C. assuaging D. striking

75. A. in the way B. to the side
C. on its feet D. under control

76. A. inauguration B. unrest
C. proliferation D. embrace

77. A. drive B. instability
C. apprehension D. affliction

78. A. reluctant B. ardent
C. vitriolic D. oblivious

79. A. certainly B. narrowly
C. promptly D. formally

80. A. foil B. partake
C. stage D. obliterate

IX. Write a short essay in English of 150-200 words as your answer to the following question:

What actions is the UN taking to support the younger generation and how is that support mutually beneficial?

マークシート記入例

東京の本会場でA級を受験する、国連 太郎さん、受験番号が「東京01-20001」、生年月日が「1980年10月24日」の場合の記入例です。

【受験番号/氏名】
それぞれ受験票の記載通りに記入してください。

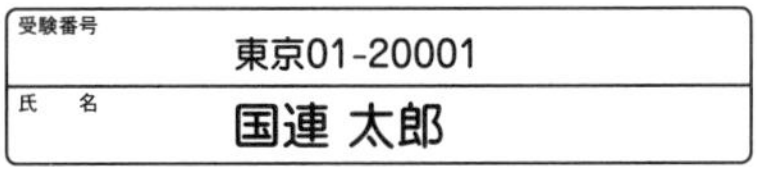

【受験地区】
下段の都道府県部分を塗りつぶしてください。

【会場番号】
都道府県部分に続く2桁の数字を塗りつぶしてください。

【受験番号】
ハイフン（−）以降の5桁の数字を塗りつぶしてください。

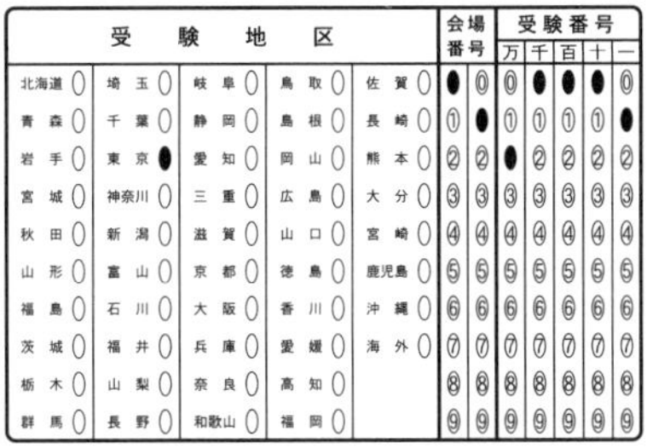

【受験級】
「A」と記入し、下段のA級部分を塗りつぶしてください。

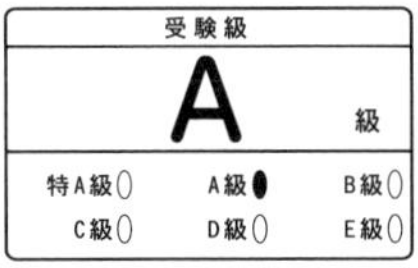

【生年月日】
4桁の西暦・月・日を塗りつぶしてください。
10未満の月・日の十の位は、「0」を塗りつぶしてください。

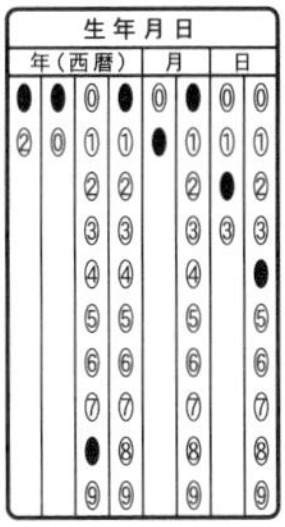

※HB以上の鉛筆を用いてマークをしてください。

※他の地区から会場を変更して受験する場合でも、受験票に記載されている受験地区・会場番号をマークしてください。

2021年

第2回試験

解答・解説

2021年　国連英検A級第2回試験
解答・解説

＊〔　〕内は訳出上の補足や説明

I　『新 わかりやすい国連の活動と世界』に基づき，
空所を埋めるのに最も適切なものを4つの選択肢の中から1つ選びなさい。

1. 解答：A

訳例　国連は世界のほとんどすべての国が加盟しており，すべての人間に等しく価値があるとの信念の上に成り立っています（『新 わかりやすい国連の活動と世界』p.15。以下，書名略）。

2. 解答：B

訳例　私の初の改革イニシアチブのひとつである，国連テロ対策局の設置を承認した総会に感謝いたします（p.25）。

3. 解答：C

訳例　日本が国連に加盟したのは，1956年12月18日である。加盟国は2017年11月現在，当初の3倍以上の193カ国に達している（p.45）。

4. 解答：D

訳例　安全保障理事国は，それぞれ1票の投票権を持つ。手続き事項の決定には，15理事国のうち少なくとも9理事国の賛成を必要とする（p.55）。

5. 解答：B

訳例　平和構築委員会（PBC）は，2005年の世界サミット開催時にその設置が提案された（p.57）。

6. 解答：A

訳例　現在の事務総長は，2017年1月に就任したポルトガル出身のアントニオ・グテーレスである（p.61）。

7. 解答：A

訳例　国連食糧農業機関（FAO）は 1945 年 10 月 16 日，ケベック会議において創設された（p.77）。

8. 解答：C

訳例　1960 年代以降，ユネスコの加盟国が増えると，新興独立国の支持を背景に，ユネスコが自立的な政策を展開するようになり，アメリカと対立を深めていった（p.78）。

9. 解答：B

訳例　世界保健機関（WHO）は，国連加盟国 26 カ国が同機関の憲章を批准した 1948 年 4 月 7 日に発足した（p.79）。

10. 解答：D

訳例　1980 年代半ば，米英などの主要加盟国がユネスコとたもとを分かった後も，日本は同組織内に踏み止まり，事実上最大の予算拠出国としてその改革に助力し続けていた（p.169）。

II

下線を引いた動詞の最も適切な変化形を 4 つの選択肢の中から 1 つ選びなさい。

11. 解答：B

解説　with some (athletes) ... で付帯状況。前置詞の目的語と分詞に能動の関係が成立していることから，現在分詞の B が正解。

12. 解答：C

解説　said 以下に来る（that）節は，Biles said 以前の彼女の苦しみについて述べている。よって，過去完了形の C が正解。

13. 解答：D

解説　that burden と exacerbate との関係は受け身。よって，過去分詞の D が正解。

14. 解答：D

解説　see O＋C の知覚構文なので，目的語である their pre-Olympic training

との関係性に着目する。disrupted ... and restricted と並列構造になっていることもヒントになる。過去分詞の D が正解。

15. 解答：A

解説 steer clear of は keep away from と同義の熟語。また the U.S. women's gymnastics team は prompt の目的語である。よって，prompt O to do の A が正解。

16. 解答：D

解説 COVID safe は形容詞。よって，choose O to do の語法を活かせる D が正解。

17. 解答：D

解説 give の主語は前文（she had been able to ...）を指し，下線部は and it gives と置き換え可能。よって，分詞構文の D が正解。

18. 解答：B

解説 S+V（過去形），but S+V という構造になっている。よって，過去形の B が正解。

19. 解答：C

解説 コンマで囲まれた部分は Katie Ledecky の補足説明になっている。よって，関係代名詞（非制限用法）の C が正解。

20. 解答：A

解説 下線部は swimming event を修飾している。よって，過去分詞（形容詞的用法）の A が正解。

訳例　東京オリンピックでは，〔選手らが周囲から〕隔離され，家族や友人も〔近くに〕いないために，その精神状態に多大な影響が出ている。一部には，この世界的なスポーツの大舞台で国の期待を背負いながら，コロナ禍がもたらす課題への対応に悪戦苦闘している選手もいる。

　火曜日に行われた体操女子の団体戦を〔途中で〕棄権して話題となったシモ

ーネ・バイルズ選手。その後，世界の〔すべての〕重さを背負ってきたように感じると語った。重圧は，コロナ禍に伴い1年〔続いた〕苦悩や損失，行動制限によって悪化していたようだ。

バイルズ選手は次のように述べた。「ふつうは選手村の中をぶらついたりするけど，世界の重さを感じたら最悪。こなしている練習量〔が多い〕から〔ストレスの〕はけ口がない」。

選手たちは，ロックダウンや競技施設の使用制限によって事前のトレーニングが中断されるという目に遭った。また，大会の延期によって，予選の予定についての懸念や，ウィルスに感染せずに国境を越えて移動できるかどうかという心配も高まった。

今回の東京〔オリンピック〕では，家族や友人にもスタンドでの応援は許されない上，移動も厳しく制限されている。

コロナ禍のため，米国の体操女子チームは安全を考慮し，選手村の喧騒《けんそう》を離れて近くのホテルに滞在することに。オリンピック出場というきらめく体験も台無しだ。

「施設がよくないというのではなく，コロナに感染しない安全策を取ったということだ」(バイルズ)。

バイルズの話では，家族とは〔ビデオ通話アプリ〕フェースタイムやテキストメッセージで連絡を取ることができ，「自分にとって絶対に必要なすべてのサポート」をもらっているという。

「使える設備などはたくさんそろっているが，最後の一瞬までやり抜きたいと思った。ご覧のとおり，うまく行かなかったが……」(同)。

競泳〔女子〕米国代表のケイティー・レデッキー選手も大きな期待を胸に大会に臨んだ。〔すでに〕オリンピック〔で〕輝かしい名声を築いた同選手だが，バイルズ選手が感じたプレッシャーは分かるという。レデッキー選手は，米国人はメダルの獲得よりも世界の状況に関心をもつべきだという。

また，オリンピック史上初めて行われた競泳女子1,500メートルで金メダルを獲得した後も，「*オリンピック選手の場合，〔プレッシャー〕はお互いの状態に気を配って，克服できるようにするもの。また困ってる人がいたらお互い助け合うもの」と話した。

＊訳注：このセンテンスは，関係代名詞 that 以下の関係節が文法的でないため，母語話者インフォーマントの意見を参考に意訳した。

III 空所を埋めるのに文法的・論理的に最もふさわしいものを4つの選択肢の中から1つ選びなさい。

21.　解答：D

解説 直前の that は接続詞なので，空所は S+V の完全文。加えて，直後の

who が関係代名詞であることに着目する。

22. 解答：A

解説 直前までで文は成立している。よって，after ... ing で副詞句となる A が正解。

23. 解答：D

解説 said に続く that 節が文法的に成立しているものを選ぶ。

24. 解答：C

解説 expertise は in とセットになることが多い名詞。加えて，直後の continent の前置詞としては on が適切である。

25. 解答：B

解説 one of に続く名詞句において名詞を裸で置くことはできない。beef up のコロケーションもヒントになる。

26. 解答：A

解説 構造的に空所には副詞句が入るが，B の in an outbreak と following the discovery of the country では文意に合わない。

27. 解答：C

解説 関係副詞 where に続く S+V は，people ... are given。よって，関係代名詞 who を直後に配置すれば文法的に成立する。

28. 解答：A

解説 take measures と lethal infections のコロケーションに注目して，文法的に成立するものを選ぶ。

29. 解答：B

解説 the WHO is に続くものとして適切なのは，現在進行形の B しかない。

30. 解答：D

解説 空所はsince（接続詞）に続くS＋Vだが，Ebora outbreak was declaredのつながりは外せない。

訳例　コートジボワールで1994年以来初めてとなるエボラ出血熱の感染者が確認された。同国保健省が発表した。世界保健機関（WHO）では，同国へワクチンを移送する手配を進めている。

WHOのコートジボワール事務所は土曜日に発表した声明の中で，ウィルスが検出された検体は，ギニアから商業都市アビジャンに到着後に同市内に入院していた患者から採取されたことを明らかにした。これまでの調査で，患者は陸路でコートジボワールに入り，8月12日にアビジャンに到着したことが判明した。患者は発熱後に入院し，現在治療を受けている。

今年初め，ギニアで4カ月に及ぶエボラ出血熱の流行が発生し，2021年6月19日に終息が宣言された。WHOは，今回のコートジボワールの患者はこのギニアでの流行と関連しているとした上で，さらなる調査によってウィルス株を特定し，2件の流行の間のつながりについて判断すると述べた。

エボラ出血熱の流行は今年これまでに，コンゴ民主共和国とギニアで宣言されているが，アビジャンのような大きな〔実質上の〕首都で発生したのは，2014～2016年の西アフリカ・エボラ出血熱流行以来，初めての例となる。

世界保健機関（WHO）のアフリカ地域事務局長を務めるマシディソ・モエティ医師は次のように話している。「今回の流行が，人口400万人超のアビジャンのような大都市で宣言されたことは，計り知れないほど大きな懸念材料だ。しかし，エボラ出血熱対策に関する世界の専門的知見はアフリカ大陸に集中していることから，コートジボワールはこの知見を活用して対応をフル回転までスピードアップできる。コートジボワールは，WHOが最近支援してエボラ出血熱への備えを強化された6カ国の中に含まれる国で，今回の速やかな診断〔が行われたこと〕も，備えが功を奏していることを示している」。

WHOは，国境を越えたエボラ出血熱対策活動の調整を支援しており，ギニアでの流行に対処すべく同機関が支援して確保したエボラワクチン5,000回分が，コートジボワールとギニアの両保健省間の合意を受けて現在，コートジボワールへ移送中である。〔今後〕医療や警察・消防・救急，それに確認済み患者の窓口業務の従事者など，〔感染〕リスクが高い人が優先的にワクチン接種を受けることになる。

エボラは，ヒトや他の霊長類に感染し，しばしば死を招く重症疾患。過去の流行では致死率は25%から90%とバラツキがあるが，現在では有効な治療法が確立されているため，早期に治療を行い，支持療法を施せば，生存率は大きく高まる。

コートジボワールでは3日前の流行確認を受けて，月曜日から，リスクの高い人に対するエボラ出血熱の予防接種が始まった。この速やかな対応〔が可能になったの〕は，隣国ギニアで4カ月続いた流行に対処すべく世界保健機関（WHO）が協力して確保したメルク社製ワクチンがただちに同国へ送られたことによる。

ギニアから配備される〔ワクチン〕には，「リング戦略」で使用されている2,000回分が含まれる。同戦略は，エボラ出血熱の確認済み感染者と接触した人のほか，警察・消防・救急などの要員や医療従事者にワクチンを投与するもの。ギニアからはこのほか，ジョンソン・エンド・ジョンソン社製のワクチン約3,000回分も届いており，感染があまり広がっていない地域でブースター接種用として使用されている。

WHOアフリカ地域事務局長のマシディソ・モエティ博士は，「エボラワクチンはウィルスとの闘いにおける重要なツールなので，速やかに動いて感染リスクが高い人を守る取り組みを始めることが最優先課題だ」と述べた。また，この迅速な対応については「注目に値するものであり，大流行に発展しかねないような死に至る感染症〔であっても〕，有効な準地域的連帯によって，撲滅へ向けた対策を速やかに実施できることを示すもの」としている。

コートジボワールで流行の発生が宣言されたのは，ギニアから陸路でアビジャンに移動した患者からのエボラウィルス検出を受けてのことで，〔これまでに〕疑い例1名と接触者9名も確認され，経過観察中である。なお，死亡者は報告されていない。

コートジボワールの現在の流行とギニアの事例との関連はまだはっきりしておらず，何らかのつながりがあるかを判断するため，現在，さらなる分析とゲノム解読が進められている。

今回の流行はコートジボワールでは1994年以来初となるもので，WHOでは感染拡大を抑えるため専門家を派遣し，国内の専門家と協力して，感染予防と管理，診断，接触者追跡，治療，それにコミュニティの結束や国境を越えた監視を強化する支援を行っている。WHOではまた，エボラ抑制のために追加のワクチンが必要かどうかについての評価も進めている。

ギニアでは，保健当局が監視の強化やさらなる調査のほか，ワクチン接種の準備作業として接触者の特定，それにエボラ治療センターの準備を進めている。

今年前半〔2021年3月〕にギニアでエボラ出血熱の流行が宣言されて以来，WHOはコートジボワールを含む6カ国に対し，発生した場合に備える支援を行ってきた。この対象となる支援分野としては，疾病監視，国境通過地点やリスクの高いコミュニティでのスクリーニングのほか，迅速対応チームの設置，検査・治療能力の向上，コミュニティへの働きかけや協力態勢の強化などがある。

IV 以下の文章に最も適切に当てはまる語句のペアを4つの選択肢の中から1つ選びなさい。

31. 解答：C

解説 第1空所は制裁を課すという文脈から，B. imposing，C. levying，D. enforcing が候補に残る。第2空所は with irregularities に着目して，filled と同義の C. fraught が正解。

訳例 〔ベラルーシの〕大統領選挙でアレクサンドル・ルカシェンコ氏が当選を果たしてから1周年となる月曜日，ジョー・バイデン米大統領はベラルーシに対して新たな制裁を科すと発表した。同選挙をめぐっては，不正が横行したことが米国をはじめとする国際社会から指摘されている。

32. 解答：D

解説 第1空所は progress in the peace process を修飾するので文脈から A. crippling と D. impeding が候補に残る。第2空所は their “long ... departure に着目して，D. overdue が正解。long overdue で needed for a long time の意。

訳例 リビアでは傭兵の募集と使用が続いており，それによって「和平プロセスの進展」が妨げられているほか，来るべき選挙の障害になっている――国連の独立人権専門家ら〔傭兵の使用に関する国連作業部会〕は金曜日，このように述べるとともに，「長年の懸案」である傭兵の退去を求めた。

33. 解答：A

解説 第1空所は援助をどうするか，という文脈から A. rushing，C. securing，D. granting が候補に残る。第2空所は hospitals (were) ... with incoming patients に着目して，B. inundated と同義の A. overwhelmed が正解。

訳例 ハイチで土曜日，マグニチュード 7.2 の地震が発生し，少なくとも 227 人が死亡，数百人が負傷または行方不明となっている。アリエル・アンリ首相は，街区が破壊された地域や病院が患者であふれている地域に対して，早急に支援を届けるよう作業を進めている，と述べた。

34. 解答：B

解説 第1空所は C. heeded でも良さそうだが，the alarm とのコロケーションから B. sounded を選ぶ。第2空所は intense fighting and indiscriminate shelling ... neighborhoods に着目すれば，B. paralyze しか残らない。

訳例　シリアでは，政府軍と反政府武装勢力による激しい戦闘と無差別砲撃により，南部の都市ダルアーと周辺地域が麻痺《まひ》状態に陥っている。これを受けて国連人権高等弁務官は木曜日，シリア市民の窮状について重ねて警鐘を鳴らした。

35.　解答：D

解説　第 1 空所は linked に続く前置詞として D. to を選ぶ。第 2 空所も，Beijing's pressure campaign ... the arrest of an executive に着目すれば，about と同義の D. over しか残らない。

訳例　ハイテク大手，華為技術（ファーウェイ）社の幹部逮捕をめぐり中国政府がカナダ政府に対して行った圧力作戦に関わるスパイ事件で，中国の裁判所が水曜日，カナダ人実業家のマイケル・スパヴァー被告に懲役 11 年〔の有罪判決〕を言い渡した。

36.　解答：A

解説　第 1 空所は国際情勢および their policy of repression から A. witnessed と D. precipitated が候補になる。第 2 空所は respect the legitimate ... of their people から ambition と同義の A. aspirations が正解。

訳例　ベラルーシを監視する任に当たる独立専門家〔アナイス・マラン特別報告者〕は月曜日，同国で過去 1 年間に前例のない人権危機が発生したことを明らかにするとともに，当局に対し，弾圧政策を直ちに終了し，国民の正当な希望を十分に尊重するよう求めた。

37.　解答：C

解説　第 1 空所はタリバンが政権を奪ったあとの状況について述べているので，C. consolidate と D. wield が候補になる。第 2 空所は Western countries ... evacuations from a chaotic Kabul airport から increase と同義の C. ramp up が正解。

訳例　〔アフガニスタンで〕タリバンが権力基盤を固めようと動き，混乱を極めるカブール空港から〔自国民などを〕出国させる活動を欧米諸国が強化する中，〔東部の〕都市ジャラーラーバードで水曜日，イスラム主義組織タリバンに反対する抗議行動が行われ，目撃者の情報によると少なくとも 3 人が死亡した。

38. 解答：B

解説 第1空所はUN refugee agencyがthat以降の悲惨な状況を～する，という文脈からB. highlightingとC. underscoringが候補になる。第2空所はattempting the ... voyagesからdangerousと同義のB. perilousが正解。

訳例 国連難民高等弁務官事務所（UNHCR）は木曜日，新たな報告書〔Left Adrift at Seaを発表し〕昨年〔2020年〕はベンガル湾やアンダマン海を渡るロヒンギャ難民にとって，記録が残る中で最も悲惨な年となったと述べた。危険な渡航を試みる人は女性と子どもが約3分の2を占め，人身売買業者によりさらに虐待される恐れがある，と強調している。

39. 解答：D

解説 第1空所はWith coronavirus deaths rising in Myanmarから，どれも正解になりうる。第2空所は軍事政権を説明している個所なので，直後のpowerに着目してD. seizedが正解。

訳例 ミャンマーではコロナウィルスによる死者が増えており，住民や人権活動家からは，2月に支配権を握った軍事政権が権力基盤の強化と反対派の鎮圧のためにコロナ禍を利用しているとの声が高まりつつある。

40. 解答：C

解説 第1空所はthe Taliban's lightening takeoverに対するロシアの出方に関わるので，C. In the wake ofとD. In line withが候補になる。第2空所はcautiously reaching outとexpanded military exercisesという一見矛盾するapproachからC. two-prongedが正解。

訳例 タリバンがアフガニスタンを電撃的に占領した後，ロシア当局は，タジキスタンの対アフガニスタン国境付近で〔実施した〕タジキスタンとの〔共同〕軍事演習を拡大しながらも，タリバンとの接触を慎重に行うという二股政策にいち早く踏み切った。

V 文法的，語法的にふさわしくないものを下線の中から1つ選びなさい。

41. 解答：B

解説 has → have。主語がThree Chinese naval vesselsと複数形になっている。

訳例　防衛省によると，大型の誘導ミサイル駆逐艦を含む中国海軍の艦艇３隻が，日本の九州本土の北にある対馬海峡から日本海へ航行するのが確認された。

42.　解答：B

解説　immediate → immediately。halt を修飾するには副詞にしなくてはならない。

訳例　国連事務総長は金曜日，タリバン過激派に対し，政府軍に対する攻撃を「直ちに停止」し，「アフガニスタンとアフガニスタン国民の利益のために」誠意をもって交渉に復帰するよう呼びかけた。

43.　解答：D

解説　making → to make。extend its unilateral sanctions の目的を表すのが to maintain と to make いう構造になっている。

訳例　日本は火曜日，北朝鮮に対する独自の制裁を２年延長することを決定した。貿易の全面禁止などを柱とするもので，過去の日本人拉致問題で進展を得るため，核とミサイルの開発計画を放棄させる圧力を維持することが狙い。

44.　解答：D

解説　increase → decline。extend the COVID-19 state of emergency の背景として，the increase in infections has slowed では意味をなさない。

訳例　日本政府は，５月末に１都８県で期限を迎える新型コロナウィルス緊急事態宣言を６月 20 日まで延長する。政府高官が木曜日，発表した。感染者数の減少が鈍化傾向となり，病院〔医療〕の逼迫《ひっぱく》が続いているため。

45.　解答：C

解説　as → than。100 million more children から比較級であることがわかる。

訳例　〔国連教育科学文化機関（ユネスコ）〕が金曜日に発表した新しい調査で，コロナ禍に伴い〔世界各地で〕学校の閉鎖〔が相次いだ〕結果，最低限の読解力に達していない子どもが予測を１億人以上も上回っていることが明らかになった。

46.　解答：B

解説　over → that。malfunctioning monitoring tools and confusing guidelines が S，have put が V という構造で concerns を説明している

ので同格のthatにしなくてはならない。

訳例 最近日本に入国した人の間で，ある懸念が広がっている。〔コロナウィルス感染〕監視ツールの誤作動と分かりにくいガイドラインが原因で検疫違反となり，政府のブラックリストに載ってしまったのではないか〔と心配する声が上がっている〕。

47. 解答：A

解説 to → of。ここは「新型コロナウィルス第5波の脅威」という意味なので，a threat of violenceのように同格のofを使用する。

訳例 新型コロナウィルス第5波の脅威が迫っていることから，東京オリンピックについて観客の入場を認める計画が疑問視され，（入場を認めるとした場合）観客数〔をどう設定するかという〕究極の選択が政治問題となってきた。

48. 解答：B

解説 inhabitants → habitats。Over 140,000 species ... rely on freshwater ...に着目すると，a person or animal that lives in or occupies a placeという意味のinhabitantsでは文意に合わない。

訳例 淡水を生息域とする〔生物〕種は全魚類の55%を含む14万種以上。淡水生物は地域の生態系にとって重要であるうえ，人間に食料と収入の源を提供し，洪水や浸食防止のカギとなる。にもかかわらず，〔淡水種の中でも〕湿地に生息する種は，陸上生物や海洋生物よりも急速に絶滅に向かっている。

49. 解答：D

解説 began → which began。in remarks to the Generation Equality Forumまでで文としては成立しているので，そのあとにbeganがくることはない。

訳例 国連のアントニオ・グテーレス事務総長は，月曜日にメキシコシティからのオンライン中継で開幕した「ジェンダー平等を目指す全ての世代のためのフォーラム」で発言し，女性の平等な権利の実現は「人権を求める今世紀未完の闘い」である，と述べた。

50. 解答：D

解説 coincide → coincide with。coincideはwithと共起することが多い自動詞。

訳例　東京オリンピックに合わせて開催中の国連主導のオンライン会議。一流のアスリートやインフルエンサー，イノベーターらが〔参加し〕すべての人にとってよりよい世界を築くためにスポーツが果たしうる役割について意見交換を行ってきた。

VI　以下の文章の中に含まれる太字の語句および空所の意味として文脈上最も近いものを４つの選択肢の中から１つ選びなさい。

51.　解答：B

解説　この creep は into と共起して occur or develop gradually and almost imperceptibly を意味するので go into を意味する B. enter がもっとも近い。C. skulk と D. slink には逃げるニュアンスがあるので，ここでは適さない。

52.　解答：C

解説　resonance は richness or significance in evoking ensuring images を意味するので，C. significance が正解。B. reverberation は主に悪い意味で使われる。

53.　解答：C

解説　前後でも，学者たちが micro-states の定義に関して見解を述べている。よって，present ideas を意味する C. set out が正解。

54.　解答：C

解説　threshold は the level at which something starts to have an effect を意味する。ここでは micro-states を定義しているので，upper limit と同義の C. maximum が正解。

55.　解答：D

解説　threshold については 30 万人から 300 万人までさまざまな学説が存在するが，a population threshold of 1 million is sufficient とあるので，D. However が正解。

56. 解答：B

解説 micro-states は人口や領土的に小さいが，それが原因で smaller governments, fewer economic resources, weaker bureaucracies ... とあるので，B. Moreover が正解。

57. 解答：B

解説 insistence と同義なのは，B. demand。

58. 解答：A

解説 criteria は standard と同義なので，a situation that must exist を意味する A. conditions が正解。

59. 解答：B

解説 five criteria の具体的な記述が続いているので，to be specific を意味する B. namely that が正解。A. for instance は as an example の意。

60. 解答：D

解説 code は a phrase or concept used to represent another in an indirect way を意味するので，D. phrasing が正解。

訳例　極小国家の定義：小国家（極小国家を含む）が何をもって構成されるかについて意見の一致がないことについては，すでに多くの人が指摘している。その理由としては，小国家を定義する方法が数多くあること，小国家を定義する上で使える変数が多いことに加え，学者によって小国家を研究する目的が異なることが挙げられる。アーチャーとニュージェントは，「結局のところ，国家を規模によって分類する作業には，判断の要素が入り込まざるを得ない」(2002) と述べている。小国家を定義する基準としては，領土面積，人口，経済生産高などの変数が引き合いに出されることが多い。さらに，領土面積は，国によってすべて異なるという理由から政治学においては相対的な概念となっている。デイヴィッド・ヴァイタル（1967）は，小国家を定義する方法として，産業力 / 経済力と人口規模を組み合わせた二重方式を提唱した。ヴァイタルは，小国家とは人口 1,000 万から 1,500 万の先進工業国か，2,000 万から 3,000 万の低開発国のいずれかであると主張した。この定式は冷戦時代に作られたものであるが，今日でもある程度，重要性を持っている。

小国家研究の中では，極小国家という下位分野に対しても，さまざまな定義が競合している。さまざまな学者が極小国家について異なる定義づけをしている。たとえばブレア（1967）は，人口30万というしきい値を用いているし，プリシュケ（1977）は，人口が10万以下あるいは10万から30万の間で，かつ国連加盟国であるという条件を設けている。また，アリ・ナセル・モハメド（2002）が〔人口〕150万という上限を提案しているほか，アームストロング，リード（1995）は300万を上限として極小国家を定義している。しかし，多くの学者は，極小国家の構成要件としては人口100万という区切りで十分であるとしている。また，シンプソン（2008）などは，人口100万以下を極小国家の判定基準として用いている。ただし，ヴィーヴェル，ウスト（2010）は，極小国家は「非対称な関係における弱者〔の地位〕に永久にはまり込んだ状態」と付言している。その中心的なポイントは，極小国家は通常，人口と領土面積のいずれの面から言ってもきわめて小さな国家であるということである。さらに，この小ささから重要な帰結が生じる。すなわち，〔他に比べて〕政府が小さい，経済資源が少ない，官僚機構が弱小，軍隊が小さい，そして，外圧に対して弱いという点である。小柏（1991）は〔以上を〕要約する形で「人口と国土面積がきわめて小さい極小国家はほとんどの場合，経済的，軍事的，政治的に脆弱《ぜいじゃく》である」と述べている。

国家性，自決，国連加盟：1918年，ウッドロウ・ウィルソン大統領の提唱により自決の概念が確立され，第1次世界大戦後のヴェルサイユ講和会議においては同氏〔が先に発表していた〕「14カ条」の指導原理となった。しかし，1945年にはソ連の主張により国際法の1原則となり，国連憲章の第1条および第55条に盛り込まれた。自決とは，「ある共同体が完全な独立と主権を追求し，その結果として既存の国家を犠牲にして国境線を引き直すという結果を招くこと」（ダンスペックグルーバー2002）である。これは，「国民」または「民族」が自らの主権国家を保有する権利を持つことを意味する。国際法は，1933年のモンテビデオ条約（国家の権利及び義務に関する条約）の第1条によれば，国家の資格要件として，a）永住人口，b）明確な領土，c）政府，d）他国と関係を結ぶ能力の4点を明記している。重要なのは，国際法が領土面積や人口の最低基準を定めていないことで，これによって極小国家というものが認められることとなる。

明記されていないがもう1つ，第5の要件として，憲法を持つ独立〔国家であること〕が挙げられる。これは自決にとって不可欠〔の条件〕である。1948年，国際司法裁判所は国連加盟のための5つの基準を示した。すなわち，申請者は以下の要件を満たさなければならない：a）国家であること，b）平和を愛好すること，c）国連憲章に掲げる国連の義務を受諾し，d）義務履行の能力と，e）その意思があること。国連への加盟は申請制であったため，これが加盟の条件となった。たとえば，「平和を愛好する」という文言は，実際には，ナチズムを打ち破った「大同盟」の一員であることを示す政治的符号であり，中立国を含む多くの国を排除するものであった。

VII 下線部の単語や句の意味を最もよく表しているものを4つの選択肢の中から1つ選びなさい。

61.　解答：B

解説 consolidate は strengthen の意。よって，最も近いのは set up on a firm or permanent basis を意味する B. established。

62.　解答：D

解説 deteriorating と同義なのは D. worsening。

63.　解答：A

解説 appalled も A. aghast も horrified を意味する。

64.　解答：A

解説 concerning の意味は making someone anxious or worried なので，最も近いのは making someone feel worried or frightened を意味する A. alarming。

65.　解答：B

解説 arise は emerge と同義なので，これに近いのは B. coming to light。

66.　解答：C

解説 casualty は a person killed or injured in a war or accident の意。よって，C が正解。

67.　解答：A

解説 これまで子どもたちの死傷者数や被害の状況について述べられており，With figures already alarming high とあるので，A. numbers of occurrences が正解。

68.　解答：D

解説 grave は serious と同義なので，D が正解。

69. 解答：A

解説 egregious は shocking と同義なので，最も近いのは shockingly unaccceptable を意味する A. disgraceful。

70. 解答：D

解説 stress は emphasize と同義なので，D が正解。

訳例　アフガニスタンでは過去2年間に数千人の子どもが殺傷されたことが，国連の最新報告書「子どもと武力紛争」で明らかになった。同報告書は，タリバンが支配を固めた〔2021年8月15日の〕翌日の月曜日に発表された。

調査によると，報告期間の2019年1月から2020年12月の間にアフガニスタンの子ども5,770人が殺害または傷を負わされたという。また，今年上半期の数字は過去最高を記録。〔特に〕ここ数週間は政治や治安の状況の悪化に伴い，数百人が殺害されている。

ヴァージニア・ガンバ国連特別代表（子どもと武力紛争担当）は，アフガニスタンは依然として子どもにとって世界で最も危険な国の部類に入ると述べた。

同氏は次のように述べた。「アフガニスタンの子どもたち，戦闘に巻き込まれた子どもたちは無論だが，その周囲で起きている重度の暴力が継続し，さらに悪化しつつあることに愕然《がくぜん》としている」。

「それでなくとも悲惨な状況が急速に進行し続けている上，人権侵害に関する憂慮すべき報告が次々となされる中，私はすべての虐待を止めるよう求めるとともに，タリバンと他のすべての当事者に対し，国際人道法と国際人権法の下での義務に加え，国内公約を遵守し，女性と少女を含むすべての人の生命と権利を守るよう強く求める」。

調査の結果，報告期間中の死傷者は3人に1人が子どもであることが分かった。武装集団，特にタリバンによるケースが46%と最も多く，政府軍と親政府勢力によるものが35%，次に地雷と爆発性戦争残存物（ERW）によるものとなっている。

ガンバ氏は次のように述べた。「戦闘行為において子どもの被害を最小限に抑え，子どもの保護を優先し，学校や病院を保護するため，すべての当事者が必要な行動をとることが急務である」。

「アフガニスタンの子どもたちはすでに子ども時代を奪われているだけに，上の措置が実現しないならば，そうした〔戦闘行為から受けた〕被害は必ずや将来の世代にも影響を及ぼすことになろう。〔死傷者の〕数はすでに驚くほど多いほか，報告書では子どもに対する暴力の主な加害者をタリバンと特定していることから，アフガニスタンの子どもの将来，特に女子の将来はきわめて厳しい〔というべきだ〕」。

国連はまた，報告期間中に子どもに対する重大な侵害を6,470件以上確認したが，その約半分はタリバンによるものだった。学校や病院に対する攻撃も297件確認された。学校への攻撃は減少したものの，報告書の著者らは病院と被保護人員への攻撃が増加したことを指摘。この問題について，アフガニスタンの医療システムの脆弱《ぜいじゃく》な状態とコロナ禍で発生している難題から考えて，きわめて悪質〔な行為〕だとしている。

一方，女子校に対するタリバンの意図的な攻撃は，依然として「気がかりな動向」だ。ガンバ氏は，タリバンと他のすべての紛争当事者に対し，女子の教育を受ける権利を含め，人権を尊重するよう訴えた。

さらに，紛争当事者（主にタリバン）は少年260人を敵対行為に引き入れ，大半の少年を戦闘任務に就かせた。ガンバ氏の説明によると，コロナ禍によって少年の弱い立場がさらに弱くなっており，現在の暴力の程度を考えると，この状況は今後も悪化が予測されるという。

同氏は「本日，私はすべての当事者，とりわけタリバンに対し，子どもの兵員採用や使用，拉致《らち》，殺傷を防止すること，あらゆる侵害を停止すること，そして子どもや学校，病院を保護し，子どもの犠牲を軽減する具体的な措置を早急に取ることを要請する」と述べた。

また，アフガニスタンに対しては，少年に対する性的虐待の一形態であるバチャ・バジという慣習について，2018年の刑法改正に沿って犯罪化する方針を堅持するよう求めた。

同氏は，アフガニスタンの子どもたちを本当の意味で守るということは，紛争の平和的解決によってしか実現しない，と強調した。「私が本日，すべての当事者，特にタリバンに対して呼びかけたいのは，子どもの保護問題が和平交渉に関わるすべての関係者によって確実に優先されるようにして欲しい，そしてそれによって子どもに対する重大な侵害の再発を持続的に防止し，平和の実現可能性を高める上で一役買って欲しい，ということだ」。

VIII 文脈上，空所を埋めるのに最もふさわしいものを4つの選択肢の中から1つ選びなさい。

71. 解答：B

解説 ... it came about in six months or a year は we have to believe in it の副詞節で，it は vaccine を指す。A or B に着目し，in either of two cases を意味する B. Whether を選ぶ。

72. 解答：D

解説 ブラジルはアメリカと同様，politically polarized and ... with

disinformation とあるので，widespread を意味する D. rife が正解。

73. 解答：C

解説 the delta variant bears down ... Brazil に着目し，C. on を選ぶ。bear down on で move quickly towards a place in an intimidating way の意。

74. 解答：C

解説 何でも意見が分かれることが多いブラジルでも，ワクチンに関してはそうではない，そのことが ... fears that vaccine skepticism would undermine the country's response とあるので，C が正解。assuage は ease と同義。

75. 解答：B

解説 as soon as they were available, people would put the politics ... という文脈から，B が正解。put ... to the side で save something to be dealth with later の意。

76. 解答：D

解説 In Brazil's ... of vaccines で，ブラジルのワクチンに対する姿勢を表しているので，an act of accepting something willingly を意味する D. embrace が正解。

77. 解答：A

解説 Brazil ... has always had great trust in vaccinesの直後にThe ... to get vaccinated とあるので，urge と同義の A. drive が正解。

78. 解答：B

解説 he is influencing his supporters, without a doubtから，このsupportersがどれほど大統領を支持しているかが読み取れる。よって，passionate を意味する B. ardent が正解。

79. 解答：A

解説 he called them the “convicted Bolsonaristas” から，支持者は確実に Bolsonaro に投票することが読み取れる。よって，A. certainly が正解。

80. 解答：C

解説 Bolsonaroの熱烈な支持者がfor Bolsonaro to ... a military takeover of the country と主張しているので，organize を意味する C. stage が正解。

訳例　リオデジャネイロ――ボルソナーロ派を自任するロドリゴ・ルーカスさん(37)。コロナウィルス〔感染症〕の治療に未確認で薬効がない薬を使用せよというジャイール・ボルソナーロ〔ブラジル大統領〕の主張を支持し，ソーシャルメディアでは，大統領を批判する人たちを叩いてきた。ツイッターのヘッダー画像にもボルソナーロ氏〔の顔が付いているし〕，自分のことは「根っからの右翼」だと言っている。

しかし，ルーカスさんがボルソナーロ氏に従わないところが1つある。ワクチン懐疑論だ。

「いざ戦争となったときは，手持ちの武器を使わなければいけない」と言うルーカスさん。「半年後か1年後か，どっちにしても製薬メーカーが承認されれば信じるしかない。何でもかんでも陰謀論だと言うつもりはない」。

ブラジルが米国に続いてワクチン抵抗勢力となる道を進むための「駒」はすべてそろっていた。この国は政治的に偏向しており，偽情報が蔓延《まんえん》している。政治家が次々と刑務所に送られるのを見てきたブラジル人は，〔政治家を〕容易に信用しないよう鍛えられている。しかも〔今〕ブラジル人の指導者となっているのが，科学的研究や国の制度，それにワクチンそのものに対する信頼を損ねる言動を繰り返してきた人物なのだ。

ボルソナーロ氏は昨年コロナウィルスに感染したが，これまでワクチン接種を受けることを拒否している。同氏はかつて，ブラジル人で接種を受けるのは半分以下だろうという見通しを述べた。

同氏は次のように述べた。「私がワクチン接種を受けたというのは勝手な思い込みではなく，実際にワクチン接種を済ませたわけだ。このウィルスに感染した人は皆，ワクチン接種済みになる。ワクチンを打つより効果のあるやり方で接種済みになるのだから，議論はおしまいだ。コロナに感染した人は皆，免疫を獲得している」。

しかしブラジル人は，ボルソナーロ氏を支持する人たちでさえ，大半がこれを無視する態度を取っている。デルタ株が猛威を振るう中，ほぼすべての問題について対立が〔絶えない〕ブラジルも，ワクチンに関しては共通の基盤を見いだした。そして，ワクチン懐疑論が壊滅的な感染拡大への対応を鈍らせるという懸念を鎮めるとともに，ボルソナーロ氏の説得力の限界を示した。

世論調査によると，予防接種を受けるつもりだと答えたブラジル人はここ数カ月で大きく増えており，4人に3人だった（サンパウロではさらに少なかった）ものが，10人に9人ほどにまで〔増加した〕。

しかし，ワクチンの確保はまた別の問題だ。ブラジルではこれまでコロナウィルス感染者2,030万人以上，死者56万9,000人以上（米国に次いで世界で2番目）が報告されているが，ワクチンの遅れと不足に悩まされ続けている。しかしワクチンがある場合は，ブラジル人の答えはほぼ決まっている。「はい，打ちます」だ。

ブラジル成人のワクチン接種率は72%以上と，米国と同レベル。サンパウロ州では86%に達している。ボルソナーロ氏の支持者が多い南部では，リオグランデ・ド・スル州で成人の1回以上の接種率が77%，パラナ州でも76%となっている。

「ワクチンが打てるようになれば，国民は政治のことは考えなくなるだろうと確信していた」と話すのは，ブラジルの予防接種プログラムをかつて指揮した疫学者のカルラ・ドミンゲス氏。「ブラジルはワクチン〔の効果〕を信じているし，ブラジルはワクチン〔接種〕を希望している」。

中には法律を破ってまで接種を受けようとする人もいる。全国各地の検察は，ワクチン〔接種の順番待ちの〕列へ割り込みをした者を起訴処分としてきた。隠れて営業する〔違法な〕ワクチン接種クリニックも現れた。

一部のブラジル人は，1回や2回の接種では不十分〔だと思った〕。ミナスジェライス州のある退職教師は，中国製のコロナバック・ワクチンを2回接種したが，その後アストラゼネカ製を1回，さらにもう1回，ファイザー製を打った。

ブラジルのワクチン受容度の高さは，疫学者の間では，長年にわたる予防接種文化の長所と受け止められている。ブラジルの大規模なワクチン接種キャンペーンはこれまでも，ほぼすべての人に，しかも速やかに行き渡った。H1N1ワクチンの場合は，3カ月で9,000万人近くのブラジル人が接種を受けた。また，2018年には世界最大規模となる黄熱病の集団予防接種キャンペーンを実施した。〔これらのキャンペーンには〕ブラジルのワクチンマスコット，ゼ・ゴティーニャ（〔米国の食品大手〕ピルズベリー社のマスコット，ドウボーイがダイエットをしている感じ）が常に登場する。

「ブラジルの文化を考慮する必要がある」と話すのは，研究機関オズヴァルド・クルスの研究者で呼吸器学が専門のマルガレート・ダルコルモ氏だ。「ブラジルは，1973年に国家予防接種計画を策定して以来，常にワクチンに対して大きな信頼を寄せてきた」という。

ワクチン接種の動きはボルソナーロ氏の政治的弱点を示すもので，〔実際〕その問題は現在，コロナ禍を放置したボルソナーロ政権の政策に対する議会の調査の対象となっており，〔政権に〕打撃を与えている。ボルソナーロ氏はかつて，ワクチンを打つとワニになるかもしれないぞと発言しており，自らはワクチン接種を拒否しているが，息子で連邦上院議員でのフラヴィオ・ボルソナーロ氏は違う。副大統領のハミルトン・モウラン氏もワクチン接種を受けている。閣僚の１人，ルイス・エドゥアルド・ラモス氏に至っては，ショッピングモールに出かけた際にこっそりと接種を受けた。

「私も他の人と同じで命が惜しいからね」と同氏は述べた。

ブラジルの有名世論調査会社，ダータフォーリャのマウロ・パウリーノディレクターは，ワクチン接種を最もためらっているのはボルソナーロ氏の最も熱心な支持者の３分の１ほどだ，としている。「ボルソナーロは指導者であり，間違いなく支持者に影響を与えている」（同）。

しかし，同氏によれば，ボルソナーロ氏に必ず投票するという有権者（同氏がいう「信念あるボルソナーロ派」）は有権者のほんの一握りで，しかも減少している，という。

「連邦政府がボルソナーロ支持者の意見に影響を及ぼしていることが，このデータから非常にはっきり分かる。しかし，今起きているのはボルソナーロ氏の支持者急減という事態だ」（同）。

〔その〕熱烈な支持者の１人がカルロス・デ・リマ・ベルシオさん（44）。北部パラ州在住。ボルソナーロ氏はブラジルを軍事的に乗っ取るべきだと主張してきた。ワクチンを接種することはあり得ないという。

ベルシオさんはすでにコロナウィルスに２回（おそらくは３回）感染しているが，あまり怖いとは思っていない。ワクチン接種を考えるとすれば，もう二度とウィルスに感染しない保証がある場合だけだ，という。

「私はワクチン〔の効果〕を信用していない。モルモットにはなりたくないから」。

IX

以下の質問に対し，150～200語の短いエッセイを英語で書きなさい。

質問文：国連は若い世代を支援するためにどのような行動をとっているか？　また，その支援はどのようにお互いに利益をもたらしているか？

解答例 I will discuss ways the UN supports the younger generation and make specific reference to youth environmentalists.

First, the UN youth strategy, “Youth 2030”, outlines plans supporting 1.8 billion young people—90% of whom are from developing countries—within the “SDG 2030” goals. The five “Youth

2030" priorities include incorporating all UN work to partner with young people and their organizations; education and health services for youth; economic empowerment through greater access to decent work; protecting young people's political action rights; and supporting young people as catalysts for peace, security and humanitarian action.

Second, using SDG13, climate action, as a specific example, highlights connections between humanitarian action and youth activism. Filipino climate justice advocate Mitzi Jonelle asserts that the climate crisis is also a humanitarian crisis involving ordinary people, not just scientists; climate activist Greta Thunberg says, on Twitter, that inequality and climate injustice is at the heart of the climate crisis. Grassroots youth environmental organizations and associations have enormous impact by publicizing and popularizing urgent issues; they excite public demand for immediate measures to reverse climate change and protect the environment.

This is one example of the mutual benefit that UN action supporting youth confers on all of us.

解説　国連の若い世代への取り組みについて事実を述べつつ，テーマに沿って意見をまとめるとよい。

第1パラグラフでは，国連の若者への支援策と青年環境保護活動家への言及を本論の柱にすると明示している。

第2パラグラフでは，国連の若者戦略として「ユース 2030」を取り上げ，その対象となる人数が 18 億人に及ぶことや，若者の組織と国連活動との統合といった優先事項を5つ列挙している。

第3パラグラフでは，SDGs 目標 13（気候変動に具体的な対策）を活用することが人道的行動とミッチ・ジョネルやグレタ・トゥンベリといった若者の積極的活動との間のつながりを強調していることに触れ，青年環境保護団体が気候変動と環境保護の世論形成にとって大きな影響力をもつ，つまり若者を支援する国連の活動が双方にとって利益があると述べている。

訳例　国連がどのように若い世代を支援しているかを述べるとともに，青年の環境保護活動家についても具体的に言及したい。

まず，国連の若者戦略「ユース 2030」では，「SDGs 2030」の目標の枠内において，若者18億人（うち9割が途上国出身者）を支援する計画の概要を示している。「ユース2030」の5つの優先事項は，若者や若者の組織と提携する国連のあらゆる活動の統合，若者のための教育と医療サービス，まともな仕事に就く機会の拡大を通じた経済地位向上，若者が政治活動をする権利の尊重，それに平和・安全・人道活動の触媒としての若者に対する支援サポートである。

第二に，SDG目標13（気候変動に具体的な対策を）を具体例として用いることで，人道的行動と若者の積極的活動との間のつながりが強調されている。フィリピンの気候正義活動家，ミッチ・ジョネル〔・タン〕は，気候危機は科学者だけでなく一般人を巻き込む人道危機でもあると主張しているし，気候活動家のグレタ・トゥンベリはツイッターで，不平等と気候不正義が気候危機の核心だと述べている。草の根の青年環境保護団体や協会は，緊急の課題について公表し，広く知らせることで大きな影響力を持つ。そして，気候変動を逆転させ，環境を保護するための緊急の対策を求める世論を喚起する。

このことは，若者を支援する国連の活動が我々すべてにもたらす相互利益の一例である。

2021年A級第2回試験　正解一覧

Ⅰ

1. A　2. B　3. C　4. D　5. B　6. A　7. A　8. C　9. B　10. D

Ⅱ

11. B　12. C　13. D　14. D　15. A　16. D　17. D　18. B　19. C　20. A

Ⅲ

21. D　22. A　23. D　24. C　25. B　26. A　27. C　28. A　29. B　30. D

Ⅳ

31. C　32. D　33. A　34. B　35. D　36. A　37. C　38. B　39. D　40. C

Ⅴ

41. B　42. B　43. D　44. D　45. C　46. B　47. A　48. B　49. D　50. D

Ⅵ

51. B　52. C　53. C　54. C　55. D　56. B　57. B　58. A　59. B　60. D

Ⅶ

61. B　62. D　63. A　64. A　65. B　66. C　67. A　68. D　69. A　70. D

Ⅷ

71. B　72. D　73. C　74. C　75. B　76. D　77. A　78. B　79. A　80. C

2022年
第1回試験
問題

A級第１次試験問題用紙

A級

外務省後援

２０２２年度第１回国際連合公用語

英語検定試験（120分）

受験上の注意

1．問題用紙は試験開始の合図があるまで開いてはいけません。その間に、この**受験上の注意を熟読しておいてください。**

2．**受験番号と氏名を解答用紙（マークシートと作文用紙）**に記入してください。

3．解答用紙の配布は１人１部のみです。複数の配布は致しません。

4．試験開始前は、答案への解答記入は禁止です。

5．マークシートの記入は、１～100までの記入箇所がありますが、この級では１～80までを使います。

6．マークシートの記入は、必ずＨＢ以上の濃い鉛筆を使って該当箇所を黒く塗りつぶしてください。書き間違いの場合は「アト」が残らないように消してください。マークシートは絶対に折ったり曲げたりしないでください。

7．受験級、受験地区、会場番号、受験番号のマークシートへの記入は監督者の指示に従い、間違いなく記入してください。**（裏表紙の「マークシート記入例」参照）**

8．作文は、⑴読みやすい文字をペン、ボールペンまたはＨＢ以上の濃い鉛筆で書いてください。⑵使用語数の150～200語を目安にしてください。

9．試験問題についての質問は、印刷が不鮮明な場合を除き、一切受けつけません。

10．中途退室の際は、マークシートと作文用紙を持って監督者に渡し、他の受験者の迷惑にならないように静かに退室してください。中途退室後の再入室はできません。

11．試験中は他の受験者の妨げとなる行動は慎んでください。また携帯電話等の電源はお切りください。

12．マークシートと作文用紙は監督者に提出し、問題用紙はご自由にお持ち帰りください。

＊試験問題の複製や転載、インターネットへのアップロード等、いかなる媒体への転用を禁止します。

試験結果について

1．第１次試験の結果は2022年6月29日㈬頃に受験申込書に記載された住所に郵送で通知します。

2．その間に住所変更をされた方は、郵便局へ住所変更の届け出を忘れずに行ってください。

3．発表前の試験結果のお問合せには応じられません。

第２次試験について

1．第１次試験合格者には、試験結果発表と同時に試験日時、会場を指定して通知します。（第１次試験を特別会場で受験した合格者には最寄りの２次試験会場が指定されます。）

2．第２次試験は2022年7月10日㈰です。Ａ級の試験地は札幌・仙台・東京・名古屋・大阪・福岡・鹿児島・沖縄のいずれかになります。（特Ａ級との併願で特Ａ級の第１次試験に合格された方の試験地は東京と大阪になります。）あらかじめご了承願います。

公益財団法人 日本国際連合協会
http://www.unaj.or.jp/

I. Fill in each of the following blanks with the most appropriate of the four alternatives according to the knowledge and information gained from *New Today's Guide to the United Nations.*

1. Foreword

The rights of the individual are of no less importance to immigrants and minorities in _________ and the Americas than to women in Afghanistan or children in Africa.

A. South-East Asia
B. the Caribbean
C. Middle East
D. Europe

2. Address to the General Assembly

Let me turn to the global threat of terrorism. Nothing justifies terrorism—no cause, no _________.

A. gain
B. atrocity
C. grievance
D. integrity

3. Basic Facts about the United Nations

Other than those principal organs, there are _________ related organizations and specialized agencies which operate in areas as diverse as health, setting standards for radiation protection, international postal regulation and meteorology.

A. 10
B. 23
C. 35
D. 46

4. Charter of the United Nations

The purposes of the United Nations are set forth in _________ of the Charter of the United Nations.

A. Article 1
B. Article 3
C. Article 33
D. Article 55

5. Economic and Social Council

The Economic and Social Council (ECOSOC), which operates under the authority of the _________, coordinates the economic and social work of the United Nations and its specialized agencies.

A. Security Council
B. General Assembly
C. World Trade Organization
D. Department of Economic and Social Affairs

6. <u>International Court of Justice</u>

The jurisdiction of the International Court of Justice covers all questions _________ refer to it, and all the matters provided for in the Charter of the United Nations or in treaties or conventions in force.

A. States B. authorized United Nations organs
C. specialized agencies D. the Members of the United Nations

7. <u>Secretariat</u>

The General Assembly, on the recommendation of the Security Council, appoints the Secretary-General for a term of _________ years.

A. 3 B. 5
C. 7 D. 10

8. <u>United Nations Educational, Scientific and Cultural Organization (UNESCO)</u>

The United Nations Educational, Scientific and Cultural Organization (UNESCO) was formed on 4 November _________.

A. 1946 B. 1948
C. 1956 D. 1995

9. <u>International Monetary Fund (IMF)</u>

In order to prevent the re-introduction of exchange control and discriminatory _________, the 1944 Bretton Woods Conference discussed the international economic order to be formed for the postwar world and drew up the Articles of Agreement of the International Monetary Fund (IMF).

A. treatments B. policies
C. prices D. tariffs

10. <u>Relationship with UN Specialized Agencies</u>

Unlike what was the case in the _________ of Nations founded in the aftermath of the First World War, Japan was not an original member of the UN established in the final days of the Second World War.

A. Confederation B. Alliance
C. League D. Partnership

Ⅱ. Choose from among the four alternatives the one that is the most appropriate form of each of the underlined verbs.

Around eight in the evening of Sunday December 8th 1991, Mikhail Gorbachev, the president of the Soviet Union, picked up a phone call on a top-security line. The caller was Stanislav Shushkevich, a modest physics professor whom Mr Gorbachev's reforms **(11) place** at the helm of the Soviet Republic of Belarus a few months before. Mr Shushkevich was phoning from a hunting lodge in the magnificent Belovezh forest **(12) tell** the great reformer that he was out of a job: the Soviet Union was over.

In retrospect, its last gasp had come in August, when the KGB, hardline communists and the army had placed Mr Gorbachev under house arrest and mounted a coup. After three days of peaceful resistance **(13) lead** Boris Yeltsin, president of the Russian Soviet Republic, they backed down. That ruled out any return to a Soviet past. But Mr Gorbachev still clung to hopes for some sort of post-Soviet liberal successor as a way to hold at least some of the republics together. Mr Shushkevich's call killed any such aspiration.

One of its triggers was Russia's economic collapse. As Yegor Gaidar, Yeltsin's top economic reformer, was later **(14) write**, it was an autumn of "grim food lines ... pristinely empty stores ... women rushing around in search of some food, any food ... an average salary of seven dollars a month." To successfully enact the sweeping reforms Mr Gaidar was designing, Yeltsin needed a Russia which controlled its own currency. That meant **(15) leave** the USSR.

Mr Shuskevich, too, was motivated by the dreadful economy. He had invited Yeltsin to the retreat in the forest in the hope that by wining and dining him he would ensure that Russian gas and electricity would keep flowing to Belarus. It **(16) be** a hard winter without them. The venue he chose was a lodge called Viskuli, where Leonid Brezhnev and Nikita Khrushchev had entertained themselves **(17) shoot** bison and other game (hence its hard-wired connection to Moscow).

Yeltsin suggested that Leonid Kravchuk, the president of the Ukrainian republic, **(18) join** them. The previous Sunday, Ukraine had voted overwhelmingly to ratify the declaration of independence from the Soviet Union **(19) pass** in its parliament, the Rada, immediately after the August coup.

Yeltsin did not just want what Mr Kravchuk had achieved in Ukraine for economic reasons. Independence would, he felt, be crucial to consolidating his power and pursuing liberal democracy. And Ukraine—never, until the 19th century, a well-defined territory, and home to various ethnic enclaves and deep cultural divides—becoming an independent unitary state within its Soviet borders set a precedent for Russia to define itself the same way, **(20) refuse** independence to restive territories such as Chechnya. That was why the Russian republic was one of the first three polities in the world to recognise it as an independent state.

11.	A.	had placed	B.	to place
	C.	was placed	D.	will place
12.	A.	told	B.	to tell
	C.	and tell	D.	who told
13.	A.	to lead	B.	led by
	C.	that led by	D.	leading
14.	A.	written	B.	to write
	C.	and wrote	D.	wrote
15.	A.	and left	B.	by leaving
	C.	to leave	D.	leaving
16.	A.	would have been	B.	will be
	C.	had been	D.	ought to be
17.	A.	to shoot	B.	and shooting
	C.	shooting	D.	shot
18.	A.	joining	B.	and joined
	C.	join	D.	to join
19.	A.	which had been passed	B.	to be passed
	C.	and passed	D.	that would be passed
20.	A.	to refuse	B.	and refuse
	C.	which refused	D.	refused

Ⅲ. Fill in each of the following blanks with the best and most grammatically and logically appropriate of the four alternatives in the context of the article below.

The UN Secretary-General on Saturday said that Africa was "a source of hope" for the world, highlighting the examples of the African Continental Free Trade Area and the Decade of Financial and Economic Inclusion for African Women. António Guterres also argued that, for the last 20 years, the African Union (AU) "has helped to bring this hope to life, in order to enable the continent to realize its enormous potential." The **(21)** ________________________________ of State and Government of the AU, taking place in Addis Ababa this weekend, via a video message. He is being represented in the Ethiopian capital, by Deputy Secretary-General, Amina Mohammed.

According to Mr. Guterres, the collaboration between the UN and AU "is stronger than ever", with the 2030 Agenda for Sustainable Development and Agenda 2063 (Africa's blueprint for a peaceful, integrated and more prosperous continent) as the central pillars.

The Secretary-General argued that "injustice is deeply embedded in global systems", but it is Africans who "are paying the heaviest price." He remembered **(22)** ________________________________ times higher than in Africa and stated that "a morally bankrupt global financial system has abandoned the countries of the South. The unethical inequalities that suffocate Africa fuel armed conflict, political, economic, ethnic and social tensions, human rights abuses, violence against women, terrorism, military coups and a sentiment of impunity", he continued. Because of that, Mr. Guterres said, tens of **(23)** ________________________________ the democratic institutions are in peril.

The Secretary-General then offered the UN's support to ignite "four engines of recovery." First, he said, everyone needs to get their vaccine. In this regard, he highlighted the African Vaccine Acquisition Task Team (AVATT) and the benefits that **(24)** ________________________________ countries will generate.

"I urge you to **(25)** ________________________________ capable of producing tests, vaccines and treatments to multiply, including by addressing intellectual property issues and providing the technical and finance needed", he said.

Second, Mr. Guterres said Member States need to **(26)** ________________________________ global financial system. "But the deck is stacked against Africa. Sub-Saharan Africa is facing cumulative economic growth per capita over the next five years that is 75 per cent less than the rest of the world", he said.

He called for re-directing Special Drawing Rights—an IMF-created reserve currency asset—to countries that need support now, reform of the international debt architecture, and more concessional forms of finance.

Thirdly, the UN chief pointed to a green recovery across the continent. The **(27)** ________________________________ greenhouse gas emissions, but many of the worst impacts of climate change are being felt there. "To address today's tragic reality, we **(28)** ____ mitigation on the continent", Mr. Guterres said. According to him, the Glasgow COP26 commitment to double adaptation finance, from $20 billion, must be implemented, but it is not enough.

He called on wealthier **(29)** ____ finance commitment to developing countries, starting this year, and hold to account private sector partners who have also made commitments. "We are in emergency mode, and we need all hands on deck", he said, pointing to the next UN Climate Conference (COP27), happening later this year in Egypt, as "an essential opportunity for Africa and our world."

Lastly, the UN chief said peace across the continent can also work as an engine for recovery. In multi-ethnic, multi-religious and multi-cultural States across Africa, Mr. Guterres believes an organization like the African Union "is about showing how people can co-exist—even flourish—by working together."

According to him, this requires "inclusive and participatory structures" and so Member States need **(30)** ____. This is especially true for young Africans, Mr. Guterres added, who need more connectivity to access information, benefit from faster communication, better education and jobs.

21. A. addressed Assembly Secretary-General the 35th Heads of the UN
B. Secretary-General UN of the Heads addressed the Assembly 35th
C. 35th of the UN Secretary-General addressed Heads the Assembly
D. UN Secretary-General addressed the 35th Assembly of the Heads

22. A. countries seven that the vaccination rate in high-income is
B. that the vaccination rate in high-income countries is seven
C. the vaccination rate that in high-income seven countries is
D. seven high-income in countries is that the vaccination rate

23. A. continent are displaced millions of the people and across
B. displaced people are of across the continent and millions
C. millions of people are displaced across the continent and
D. people displaced of the continent across and millions are

24. A. South African greater vaccine production in other Africa and
B. other production greater in African South vaccine and Africa
C. greater vaccine production in South Africa and other African
D. Africa and other African South production vaccine greater in

25. A. African conditions for the number of the countries create
B. create the conditions for the number of African countries
C. number the conditions for create the African countries of
D. the countries African for create the number of conditions

26. A. engine ignite by the reforming of the economic recovery
B. ignite the engine of economic recovery by reforming the
C. reforming recovery by the ignite of the economic engine
D. the recovery by reforming economic of the engine ignite

27. A. continent global just three percent contributes of vast
B. global vast contributes just three percent of continent
C. three global continent contributes vast percent of just
D. vast continent contributes just three percent of global

28. A. adaptation for funding need in a radical boost and
B. boost in funding for radical adaptation and need a
C. funding for adaptation need and a boost in radical
D. need a radical boost in funding for adaptation and

29. A. countries to make good on the $100 billion climate
B. good climate countries to make $100 billion on the
C. make good countries on the climate to $100 billion
D. $100 billion countries to make good climate on the

30. A. governance to make good a reality through them
B. good to make them a reality through governance
C. through them a good governance to make reality
D. to make them a reality through good governance

Ⅳ. Choose from among the four alternatives the one that best completes the following sentence.

31. France is ________ a total military withdrawal from Mali, blaming soured relations with the West African nation's military rulers and the arrival of Russian ________, according to the European power's top diplomat and two Western officials with knowledge of the plan.

A. suppressing − sleeper cells B. weighing − mercenaries
C. calling for − delegates D. relinquishing − troops

32. A new report commissioned by the World Wildlife Fund contains ________ findings: Plastic, which constitutes 60% of marine pollution, has ________ even the most remote parts of the ocean; broken down into micro and nano sizes, it has likely been ingested by almost all marine species; and may have found its way back to households through the food that people consume.

A. conflicting − circulated B. stringent − defied
C. grim − infiltrated D. auspicious − strained

33. Russia launched broad attacks on Ukraine early Thursday morning local time, the ________ of weeks of a military buildup that prompted NATO members to ________ troops to Eastern Europe and send weapons and other aid to the government in Kyiv.

A. outcry − annihilate B. commemoration − endow
C. culmination − deploy D. onset − repulse

34. South Sudan's unity government marked its two-year anniversary ________ stalled constitutional progress and ongoing cycles of community violence—often ________ by political groups and armed militias—the senior UN official in the country told the Security Council on Monday.

A. on account of − exasperated B. against a backdrop of − fueled
C. under the auspices of − admonished D. in anticipation of − encroached

35. Bodies are piling up at Hong Kong's hospitals so quickly that they are sitting unattended in the hallways as the ________ fill up. Grocery stores are ________ of food. Rumors of a citywide lockdown have sent residents into a panic and prompted a new wave of departures.

A. mortuaries − stripped B. enclosures − depraved
C. meadows − stashed D. subdivisions − ebbed

36. **Prime Minister Justin Trudeau ________ emergency powers Monday to quell the paralyzing protests by truckers and others angry over Canada's COVID-19 restrictions, ________ plans not only to tow away their rigs but to strike at their bank accounts and their livelihoods.**

A. obliterated − itemizing B. expropriated − dictating
C. invoked − outlining D. wielded − compromising

37. **Russia's invasion of Ukraine has cast a shadow ________ talks to revive the Iran nuclear deal, which extended beyond a presumed deadline Tuesday amid growing doubts that a new agreement is in ________.**

A. of − need B. for − charge
C. from − check D. over − sight

38. **World leaders promised to protect Earth's forests, cut methane emissions and help South Africa ________ itself off coal at the U.N. climate summit Tuesday—part of a flurry of deals intended to ________ catastrophic global warming.**

A. wean − avert B. sever − exonerate
C. disparage − spell D. clamor − weather

39. **China on Saturday cut its annual economic growth target to its lowest level in decades as Beijing struggles to ________ a slump at a time when Russia's war on Ukraine is pushing up oil prices and ________ the global economy.**

A. upend − steering B. reverse − roiling
C. protract − proscribing D. precipitate − curbing

40. **Six months after the ________ of Afghanistan to the Taliban, it is time for concerned countries to deepen their engagement with the country's new authorities and take action to prevent an ________ economic collapse, the top UN official in Kabul told the Security Council on Wednesday.**

A. amalgamation − drawn-out B. onslaught − abrupt
C. capitulation − congenital D. fall − irreversible

V. Choose from among the underlined phrases the one that is grammatically or idiomatically incorrect.

41. A Western intelligence report indicated that Chinese officials **(A)** in early February requested that senior Russian officials **(B)** waited until after the Beijing Olympics had finished before beginning an invasion into Ukraine. US officials **(C)** broadly view the report as credible, but **(D)** its particulars are open to interpretation.

42. Without trains, it's unlikely India **(A)** would have developed into the economic superpower we see today. However, while traditional **(B)** systems might have served India well, they've become increasingly outdated, **(C)** especially when contrasted to the rapid progress **(D)** being made by India's neighbor and rival for regional supremacy—China.

43. Chinese policymakers face **(A)** mounting challenges to keep growing steady, as the country **(B)** contends with a real estate crisis and Beijing's zero-tolerance **(C)** approach to the coronavirus. The fallout from the Ukraine crisis **(D)** could also slow growth by driving commodity prices higher.

44. **(A)** More than a century after it sank off the coast of Antarctica, polar explorer Ernest Shackleton's ship HMS Endurance **(B)** has been located, apparently intact and in good condition. **(C)** The ship, which sank in 1915, is 3,008 meters deep in the Weddell Sea, a pocket in the Southern Ocean **(D)** along northern coast of Antarctica, south of the Falkland Islands.

45. In just over a year, **(A)** Africa has experienced three successful coups, one unsuccessful coup attempt in Niger, **(B)** and an arbitrary military transfer of power in Chad. These **(C)** power grabs threaten a reversal of the democratization process Africa **(D)** has underwent in the past two decades and a return to the era of coups as the norm.

46. An honorary plaque listing the names **(A)** of all police officers who responded to the Jan. 6, 2021, attack on the U.S. Capitol **(B)** will be in placed at the western front of the building, per a massive spending bill advancing in Congress this week. The provision **(C)** marking the heroism of those who faced the deadly insurrection was **(D)** tucked inside the spending bill lawmakers are racing to pass in order to avert a government shutdown by midnight on Friday.

47. **(A)** Two preprint studies posted Saturday offer further evidence that the coronavirus originated in animals and **(B)** spread to humans in late 2019 at the Huanan Seafood Market in Wuhan, China. One of the studies—neither of which has been peer-reviewed or published in a professional journal—**(C)** used spatial analysis to show that the earliest known Covid-19 cases, diagnosed in December 2019, **(D)** was centered on the market.

48. India's Prime Minister Narendra Modi called him a "dear friend." Chinese leader Xi Jinping **(A)** went a step further, calling him his "best and bosom friend." But Russian strongman Vladimir Putin's **(B)** unprovoked assault to Ukraine has thrown Russia's previously **(C)** warm relations with the Asian powers into question. Yet both China and India have **(D)** refused to condemn Russia's brutal invasion outright.

49. **(A)** For patients suffering from pain in the emergency room, just 10 minutes with a dog may help reduce pain, according to a study published Wednesday. **(B)** The results support that dog lovers everywhere have long suspected. **(C)** Canine affection cures many ailments, and it provides a bit of optimism for patients and health care **(D)** providers frequently grappling with limited hospital resources.

50. US House lawmakers probing Amazon for possible antitrust violations **(A)** now accuse the tech giant for lying to Congress and want the Justice Department **(B)** to investigate "potentially criminal conduct" from the company and some of its executives. Lawmakers **(C)** say "Amazon lied through a senior executive's sworn testimony" about (D) how the company had used the data it collects from third-party sellers.

Ⅵ. Choose from among the four alternatives the one that most closely corresponds to the meaning of words in bold type and blanks in the following passage.

The "one country, two systems" principle serves as the solution to prevent a clash between two political units that have significant differences. Hong Kong owes its prosperity to a capitalist system, which it **(51)** _________ during 156 years of British rule, while, since 1949, the PRC has been built upon socialism with Chinese characteristics. In addition to political and ideological differences, both political units do not share the same language, currency, degree of freedom and legal system. As a result, it would be politically irresponsible to forcefully put two political units together—this could bring **(52) catastrophic** political instability to both Hong Kong and the PRC.

The mini-constitution of Hong Kong has various articles that reflect the principle of "one country, two systems." For example, Article 2 grants Hong Kong the right to 'exercise a high degree of **(53) autonomy** and enjoy executive, legislative and independent judicial power.' Further, Article 9 certifies English as one of the official languages. A win-win situation was established; Hong Kong operates on its own terms and Beijing also has Hong Kong back under the umbrella of "one country, two systems" **(54)** _________ causing a direct political and organisational collision—in addition to gaining economic prosperity from the Pearl of the Orient.

However, this political balance is being undermined due to the **(55) ambiguity** of the Basic Law. Article 45 promises the democratisation of Hong Kong stating that 'the ultimate aim is the selection of the Chief Executive (CE) [···] by a broadly representative nominating committee **(56)** _________ democratic procedures.' Nevertheless, on 31 August 2014 the Standing Committee of the National People's Congress (NPCSC) interpreted the meaning of the "broadly representative nominating committee" as a 1,200 member strong committee with a heavily pro-Beijing bias (Flowerdew and Jones 2016, 520–521).

It was such an interpretation from Beijing that led to the massive Occupy Movement in 2014. The NPCSC decision is one of the greatest political threats against Hongkongers' identity, political autonomy and democratisation. The internal and external **(57) legitimacy** of both Hong Kong and the PRC has been eroded, not only because of the NPCSC's decision but also due to numerous incidents of police misconduct in the suppression of peaceful protesters—such as the firing of 87 rounds of teargas and the clandestine beating of a handcuffed protester (Bhatia 2016; Jones and Li 2016).

Undermining the "one country, two systems" disrupts the organisational stability of all involved political units and their citizens' well-being. According to Hongkongers, **(58)** _________ their freedom is being existentially threatened, their way of life that has been guaranteed by the "one country, two systems" principle is also under siege. One of the central notions of the Occupy Movement, "I want true universal suffrage," was aimed at reclaiming the democratisation promised by the Joint Declaration and the Basic Law

(Li 2014). The array of incidents involving police misconduct also **(59) demonstrates** how Hong Kong's law-enforcement system has been corrupted due to political reasons. All these discourses are centred on the rhetoric that Hong Kong's autonomy is politically threatened by influences from another political unit that undermines the principle of "one country, two systems."

During these securitising attempts, the discussion has moved towards autonomy, self-determination and even independence. Pro-establishment politicians and the Hong Kong government have raised various emergency measures such as the legislation of Article 23 to prohibit **(60) treason** against the PRC. This chapter concludes that it does not matter which side successfully securitises the political security of Hong Kong in the future—it will be a lose-lose situation for both political units. This is because the political equilibrium established by the "one country, two systems" will inevitably be undermined.

51. From the context, the underlined blank could best be filled with

A. granted B. inherited
C. overruled D. resisted

52. In this context, "catastrophic" is best replaced by

A. auspicious B. disastrous
C. hapless D. ill-fated

53. From the context, "autonomy" is best replaced by

A. compulsion B. emancipation
C. partiality D. self-governance

54. From the context, the underlined blank could best be filled with

A. by B. despite
C. without D. while

55. From the context, "ambiguity" is best replaced by

A. haziness B. fogginess
C. profoundness D. vagueness

56. From the context, the underlined blank could best be filled with

A. at the expense of B. excluding
C. in accordance with D. notwithstanding

57. **In this context, "legitimacy" is closest in meaning to**

A. faithfulness B. genuineness
C. sincerity D. validity

58. **From the context, the underlined blank could best be filled with**

A. albeit B. despite
C. not only D. nevertheless

59. **In this context, "demonstrates" is closest in meaning to**

A. clashes B. disputes
C. protests D. reveals

60. **In this context, "treason" is closest in meaning to**

A. disloyalty B. infidelity
C. mutiny D. sabotage

Ⅶ. Choose from among the four alternatives the one that best explains each of the underlined words or phrases in the context of the article below.

Deadly wildfires, noise pollution and other **(61) looming** environmental threats could cause widespread ecological damage, and need to be urgently addressed, the UN Environment Programme (UNEP) said in a new report published on Thursday.

"The Frontiers Report identifies and offers solutions to three environmental issues that merit attention and action from governments and the public at large," said UNEP Executive Director Inger Andersen.

Noise, Blazes and Mismatches: Emerging Issues of Environmental Concern, the 2022 edition of the report, draws attention to emerging environmental concerns with the potential to **(62) wreak** regional or global **havoc**, if not addressed early.

The latest report, released days before the UN Environment Assembly (UNEA) resumes, spotlights growing public health threats that are disrupting natural life cycles and having profound ecological consequences worldwide.

"Urban noise pollution, wildfires and phenological shifts—the three topics of this Frontiers Report—are issues that highlight the urgent need to address the triple planetary crisis of climate change, pollution and biodiversity loss," said Ms. Andersen.

Unwanted, prolonged and high-level sounds from road traffic, railways, or leisure activities, impair human health and well-being, according to the report.

(63) Chronic annoyance and sleep disturbance caused by traffic can result in severe heart diseases and metabolic disorders with the very young, and mostly affect the elderly and marginalized communities near busy roads.

Noise pollution also threatens animals by altering the communication and behaviour of various species, including birds, insects, and amphibians.

The report encourages urban planners to prioritize noise reduction by investing in urban infrastructure that creates positive soundscapes such as tree belts, green walls, and more green spaces in cities—also offering diverse health benefits.

London's Ultra-Low Emission Zone, Berlin's new cycle lanes on wide roads, and Egypt's national plan to combat noise, are positive examples that can be **(64) harnessed** as the world builds back better from COVID.

Interactions with the climate and the rhythms of plants and animals must also be considered. Phenology is the timing of recurring life cycle stages, driven by environmental forces, and how species interacting within an ecosystem, respond to changing conditions.

Plants and animals in **(65) terrestrial**, aquatic and marine ecosystems use temperature, day length or rainfall as cues for when to **(66) bear** fruit, migrate or transform in other ways.

However, climate change disrupts these natural rhythms as plants and animals are being pushed **(67) out of synch** with their natural rhythms, leading to mismatches, such as when plants shift life cycle stages faster than herbivores, the report says.

Meanwhile, local climatic cues that trigger migration for birds may no longer accurately predict conditions at their destination and resting sites along the route. And in crops, phenological shifts in seasonal variations challenge food production.

The report flags the crucial importance of conservation goals, such as maintaining suitable habitats and ecological connectivity, strengthening the **(68) integrity** of biological diversity and coordinating international efforts along migratory routes.

Above all, it underscores the importance of reducing CO2 emissions to limit the rate of warming.

The need to stem wildfires is another area of concern. The report outlined that between 2002 and 2016, an average of 423 million hectares of the Earth's land surface—about the size of the European Union—burned, projecting that dangerous wildfires will likely become more frequent, intense and longer lasting, including in areas previously unaffected by fires.

Climate change can prompt extreme wildfires, generating lightning that can ignite other fires, far beyond the fire front and creating a so-called hazardous **(69) feedback loop**.

Long-term effects on human health extend beyond those fighting wildfires, or the evacuated, or those who have lost homes, and **(70) exacerbate** impacts among those with pre-existing illness, women, children, the elderly and the poor.

At the same time, black carbon and other pollutants generated from wildfires can contaminate water sources, speed up glacier melt, trigger landslides and turn rainforests into carbon sinks.

To address this, the report calls for greater investment in reducing wildfire risks; developing prevention and response management approaches; and refinancing remote sensing capabilities, such as satellites and radar.

61. **looming**

A. auspicious　　B. favorable

C. ominous　　D. providential

62. **wreak havoc**

A. provide stability　　B. ensure tranquility

C. furnish constancy　　D. inflict chaos

63. **Chronic**

A. Habitual　　B. Infrequent

C. Scarce　　D. Uncommon

64. **harnessed**

A. disregarded B. excluded
C. ignored D. utilized

65. **terrestrial**

A. earthly B. interstellar
C. terrorist D. transmissible

66. **bear**

A. bring B. move
C. produce D. take

67. **out of synch**

A. away from stress B. in balance
C. in equilibrium D. into disharmony

68. **integrity**

A. completeness B. deceitfulness
C. honesty D. negligence

69. **feedback loop**

A. reaction that affects itself B. end to the problem
C. termination of extra activity D. new set of conditions

70. **exacerbate**

A. exterminate B. lessen
C. mollify D. worsen

Ⅷ. Fill in each of the following blanks with the most appropriate of the four alternatives as required by the context.

Widespread hunger, a crippled economy and a population in desperate need of assistance. Afghanistan is **(71)** _________ a worsening humanitarian crisis.

Most international assistance was cut off after the Taliban took over in August. Hospitals and schools cannot afford to pay their staff, and many people cannot afford to buy food, adding **(72)** _________ an already dire hunger crisis.

"It's the sheer levels of desperation that we're seeing in people," said Vicki Aken, Afghanistan director of the International Rescue Committee. "The humanitarian situation seems to be going from bad to worse."

Over 22 million people, more than half the country's population, are facing crisis-levels of hunger, the majority of them unable to guarantee when their next meal is going to be, according to the U.N. World Food Program. This marks a dramatic increase since September, when more than 14 million people were at risk of going hungry. The organization also estimated that in December, 95 percent of the population had insufficient food consumption, adopting measures to cope with their situation by skipping a meal, for example. Since October 2020, **(73)** _________ drought struck Afghanistan, the situation has continued to get worse.

U.N. officials said the situation is intensifying at an unprecedented rate.

"I've never experienced how quickly it's deteriorated," said Mary-Ellen McGroarty, the Afghanistan director of WFP. "The malnutrition rates are doubling week on week. **(74)** _________ children are coming into the hospitals."

The country was already facing its worst drought in 30 years, leaving many in the countryside desperate. Now with the failing economy, farmers are unable to find work elsewhere.

"The economic **(75)** _________ of food and fuel prices, the impact of the drought and the devastating legacy of the conflict all collide, creating a tsunami of hunger and malnutrition across the country," McGroarty said.

Since the fall of Kabul in August and the withdrawal of U.S. troops, the Taliban-controlled government has been choked off from the international economy, resulting in a currency crisis, extensive poverty and the collapse of key public services such as health care.

"Yes, it was terrible prior to August," Aken said. ″ But when the development funding was cut off on Aug. 15 and the sanctions were imposed and the assets frozen, that really took the situation from very bad to an extreme."

The United Nations estimated that 97 percent of the population could **(76)** _________ into poverty by the middle of this year. In September the poverty rate was at 72 percent. The economic collapse has touched nearly every part of life in the country, from the ability to purchase food to the hopes of finding employment, or keeping warm, or accessing health care.

"It is becoming a vicious circle we are witnessing right now in Afghanistan," said Ingy Sedky, a communication manager at the International Committee of the Red Cross in Afghanistan. "The lack of cash and nonpayment of salaries lead to inability to get proper food and nutrition. And now with the harsh winter conditions, it exposes many to additional health risks."

She described nurses in maternity hospitals only having the money for one small portable heater in a big ward. They would "**(77)** ________ three babies in one incubator as they don't have the heating system, or enough equipment to care for them," Sedky said.

The dire crisis has pushed aid organizations and the United Nations to **(78)** ________ renewed calls for funding. In mid-January, the U.N. and its partners appealed for more than $5 billion for the year, more than the organization has ever requested for a single nation. Most of the aid, $4.4 billion, would be directed to helping Afghans inside the country. The rest would go toward the millions of Afghan refugees in neighboring countries like Iran and Pakistan.

U.N. Emergency Relief Coordinator Martin Griffiths said without those funds, "there won't be a future" for the people of Afghanistan. But in the past the organization has not been able to meet its funding needs.

The United States, which froze much of its Afghanistan funding when the Taliban came into power, has since recommitted to some of its aid, announcing $308 million in additional assistance this month, which will provide shelter, health care, food, water and other basic services.

(79) ________, the U.N., aid groups and donor countries have been working to find ways to bring money to Afghanistan without cash ending up in the hands of the Taliban. Last fall, the U.N. Development Program began to use commercial banks to send direct payments to health workers through cellphones. Those with no phones received cash in person.

Aid workers said it is important that countries continue to support the **(80)** ________ country.

"States must invest in Afghanistan," Sedky said. "This is the only way to prevent a total collapse of the banking system and essential services like health care and education."

71. A. on the pretext of　　B. on the merits of
C. in the midst of　　D. for fear of

72. A. to　　B. that
C. on　　D. in

73. A. because B. when
C. while D. which

74. A. Acquiescent B. Emaciated
C. Endearing D. Fractious

75. A. adversary B. alteration
C. implosion D. opulence

76. A. loom B. abate
C. wreck D. plunge

77. A. disseminate B. surmise
C. squeeze D. wean

78. A. ramp up B. afflict
C. transfigure D. spurn

79. A. Nonetheless B. In the meantime
C. To be sure D. In contrast

80. A. landlocked B. abutting
C. pertinent D. ailing

IX.　Write a short essay in English of 150-200 words as your answer to the following.

How does United Nations support for refugees help all of the world's nations?

マークシート記入例

東京の本会場でA級を受験する、国連 太郎さん、受験番号が「東京01-20001」、生年月日が「1980年10月24日」の場合の記入例です。

【受験番号/氏名】
それぞれ受験票の記載通りに記入してください。

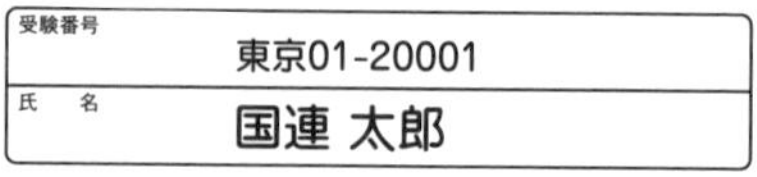

【受験地区】
下段の都道府県部分を塗りつぶしてください。

【会場番号】
都道府県部分に続く２桁の数字を塗りつぶしてください。

【受験番号】
ハイフン（－）以降の５桁の数字を塗りつぶしてください。

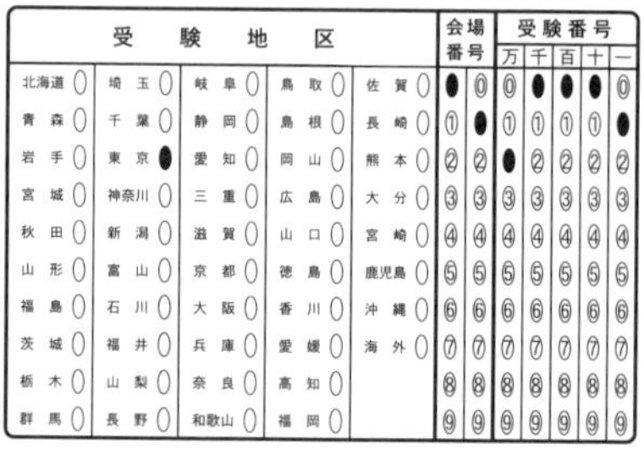

【受験級】
「A」と記入し、下段のA級部分を塗りつぶしてください。

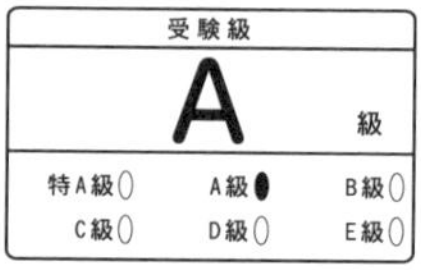

【生年月日】
４桁の西暦・月・日を塗りつぶしてください。
10未満の月・日の十の位は、「０」を塗りつぶしてください。

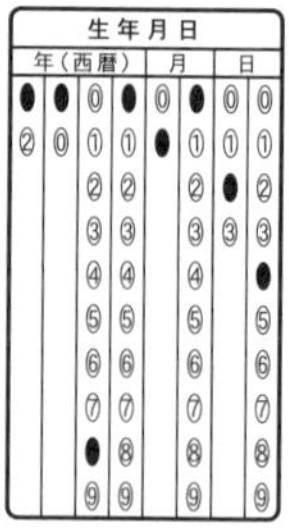

※HB以上の鉛筆を用いてマークをしてください。

※他の地区から会場を変更して受験する場合でも、受験票に記載されている受験地区・会場番号をマークしてください。

2022年
第1回試験

解答・解説

2022年　国連英検A級第1回試験
解答・解説

＊〔　〕内は訳出上の補足や説明

I　『新 わかりやすい国連の活動と世界』に基づき，
空所を埋めるのに最も適切なものを4つの選択肢の中から1つ選びなさい。

1.　解答：D

訳例　個人の権利は，アフガニスタンの女性やアフリカの子供たちにとってそれが重要であるのと同じくらい，ヨーロッパおよび南・北・中央アメリカへの移民や少数民族にとっても重要です（『新 わかりやすい国連の活動と世界』p.12。以下，書名略）。

2.　解答：C

訳例　グローバルなテロの脅威があります。テロを正当化するものなどありません。どのような大義があっても，どのような不満があっても同じことです（同 p.25）。

3.　解答：B

訳例　〔6主要機関の〕ほかに国連の関連機関・専門機関が23あり，保健衛生，放射線防護の規準設置，国際郵便規則や気象観測など様々な分野で活動している（同 p.42）。

4.　解答：A

訳例　国連の目的は，国連憲章第1条に記されて〔いる〕。(同 p.44)。

5.　解答：B

訳例　総会の権限のもとで機能する経済社会理事会（ECOSOC）は，国連およびその専門機関の経済社会活動を調整するための機関である（同 p.56)。

6.　解答：A

訳例　国際司法裁判所の管轄権は，国が裁判所に付託するすべての問題，国連憲章または現行の条約や協定に定められたすべての事項に及ぶ（同 p.60)。

7. 解答：B

訳例　総会は安全保障理事会の勧告に基づき，5 年の任期で事務総長を任命する（同 p.61）。

8. 解答：A

訳例　国連教育科学文化機関（ユネスコ）が発足したのは，〔……中略……〕1946 年 11 月 4 日である（同 p.78）。

9. 解答：D

訳例　1944 年のブレトンウッズ会議では，為替管理や差別的関税を繰り返さないよう，大戦後の国際経済秩序を形成することが議論され，国際通貨基金協定が起草された（同 p.81）。

10. 解答：C

訳例　第 1 次世界大戦終戦後に設立された国際連盟の場合と違い，日本は第 2 次世界大戦末期に創設された国際連合の原加盟国ではなかった（同 p.164）

II

下線を引いた動詞の最も適切な変化形を 4 つの選択肢の中から 1 つ選びなさい。

11. 解答：A

解説　下線部前の whom に導かれる関係節内の定動詞となる。全体の時制を考えると過去形 placed または過去完了形 had placed が適切。

12. 解答：B

解説　下線部 tell 以下は，下線部前の Mr Schshkevitch was phoning ... という部分の目的を表す副詞節となっている。

13. 解答：B

解説　下線部 lead 以下が前の peaceful resistance を形容詞句として修飾していると考えるとつじつまが合う。

14. 解答：B

解説　下線部に先行する Yegor Gaidar 氏が後年書いた内容を述べるセンテン

ス。be＋to 不定詞の形で，自動詞 be が置かれた時から見た未来（予定あるいは運命）を示す。

15. 解答：D

解説 下線部の前に定動詞 meant があるので，下線部以下はその動詞の目的語として名詞句 / 節であるべき。ただ，C のように mean to 不定詞の形では「(主語が) 〜するつもりだった」という別の意味になってしまう。

16. 解答：A

解説 下線部後の them はガスと電気を指す。その冬（過去）の供給がどうなるはずだったかを話題としているので，その時点までを表す過去完了 C や現在から未来を表す B と D は不可。A は仮定法で，過去の非事実 (without them) を仮定して，考えられる帰結を示している。

17. 解答：C

解説 下線部前の entertained themselves の付帯状況を示す現在分詞形が適切。

18. 解答：C

解説 下線部の上行にある定動詞 suggested ＜ suggest の目的格となる名詞節内の定動詞は，(should＋) 原形となる。

19. 解答：A

解説 下線部の上行に ratify the declaration of independence ... とあるので，下線部以下がこの declaration of independence を修飾する句 / 節となる。時制については末尾の immediately after the August coup により判断できる。

20. 解答：B

解説 下線部の上行の precedent ... to の後に不定詞句が 2 つ並行する構造を見抜く。

訳例　1991 年 12 月 8 日（日曜日)，夜 8 時ごろ，ソ連のミハイル・ゴルバチョフ大統領は最高機密回線につながれた電話を取った。電話の主はスタニスラフ・シュシケヴィッチという物理学の教授で，ゴルバチョフ氏の改革によって数カ月前にベラルーシ共和国の国家元首に就任していた。シュシケヴィッチ氏は広大なビャウォヴィエジャ（ベロヴェーシ）の森にある狩猟小屋から電話をかけてきて，大改革者〔ゴルバチョフ〕にこう告げた。「あなたは失職しました。ソ連は終わったのです」。

いまにしてみれば，8月にKGBや強硬派の共産主義者，軍がゴルバチョフ氏を自宅軟禁し，クーデターを起こしたのが，ソ連の最後のあがきであった。ロシアソビエト共和国のボリス・エリツィン大統領率いる3日間の平和的抵抗の後，〔クーデター派〕は引き下がった。これによって，昔のソビエト時代に後戻りする道は絶たれたのである。しかし，ゴルバチョフ氏は，少なくともいくつかの共和国のまとまりを保つ手段として，ある種のソビエト後の自由主義的後継国家〔を作る〕という希望に，いまだすがりついていた。シュシケヴィッチ氏からの電話は，その願いを打ち砕いたのである。

その引き金の1つとなったのが，ロシアの経済破綻だ。エリツィン氏の経済改革の最高責任者であったエゴール・ガイダル氏が後年書き記したとおり，その秋は「並んで食料を待つ人の悲惨な光景……きれいに空っぽになった店舗……何か食べ物はないか，何でもいいからと駆けずり回る女性たち……平均月給7ドル」の秋であった。エリツィン氏は，ガイダル氏が策定を進めていた抜本的な改革を成功させるため，自国の通貨をきちんと管理できるようなロシアを必要としていたが，それはソ連邦からの離脱を意味していた。

シュシケヴィッチ氏の動機もまた，経済の悪化だった。同氏はエリツィン氏を森の別荘に招待し，酒食でもてなすことで，ロシアのガスと電力がベラルーシへ継続して供給されるようにしたいと考えたのだ。その供給がなければ厳しい冬になるところだった。同氏が選んだ場所はヴィスクリという名のロッジで，レオニード・ブレジネフやニキタ・フルシチョフがヨーロッパバイソンなどの狩猟に興じた場所であった（モスクワとの間に電話回線が引かれていたのはそのためである）。

エリツィン氏は，ウクライナ共和国のレオニード・クラフチュク大統領にも来ないかと勧めた。ウクライナはその前の日曜日，8月のクーデター直後に議会（ラーダ）で可決されたソ連からの独立宣言を圧倒的多数で批准していた。

クラクチュフ氏がウクライナで果たしたこの成果をエリツィン氏が望んだのは，経済的な理由からだけではない。独立することが，自らの権力強化と自由民主政の追求のために不可欠と考えた〔からだ〕。そして，19世紀まで，明確に定められた領土を持たず，さまざまな民族の飛び地や深い文化的分断を抱えていたウクライナが，ソ連邦〔時代〕の国境内で独立した単一国家となったことは，ロシアが同じように自らを定義し，チェチェンのような不安定な地域に対して独立を拒む前例となったのである。ロシア共和国が世界で最初にウクライナを独立国家として承認した3カ国に名を連ねたのは，そのためであった。

III

空所を埋めるのに文法的・論理的に最もふさわしいものを4つの選択肢の中から1つ選びなさい。

21. 解答：D

解説 空所前の The とのつながり，空所後の of State and Government of the AU との接続を考える。

22. 解答：B

解説 空所直後に times higher than があるので，空所末尾は数詞 seven が来ると予測し，始まりは空所前の定動詞 remembered とうまくつながるか確認する。

23. 解答：C

解説 空所前に tens of があり，空所内にはどこかに millions が入るので，tens of millions と続く C を第1候補として検討すればよい。

24. 解答：C

解説 空所前の the benefits が上行の定動詞 highlighted の目的語であることを見れば，空所（以下）は benefits を修飾する関係節だと推測できる。空所後の will generate に着目し，空所内がその主語となるものを選ぶ。

25. 解答：B

解説 空所前に I urge you to とあるので，空所頭は不定詞句が続くと予測できる。これには C も当てはまるが，中ほどの for create が文法に反する。

26. 解答：B

解説 空所前に need to があるので空所は不定詞から始まると予測できる。A の最初の語 engine にも動詞用法はあるが engine ignite という続きは文法に反する。

27. 解答：D

解説 空所直前に The があるので，空所頭は名詞（句 / 節）に続いて定動詞が置かれているものと予想できる。

28. 解答：D

解説 空所直前の we から空所頭は定動詞または助動詞（類）と考えられる。B の初めの boost も動詞用法はあるが，文脈に合う「強化する」の意味では他動詞。

29. 解答：A

解説 空所前の called on から〈call on＋O＋to 不定詞〉の構文を取るものが第 1 の候補となる。

30. 解答：D

解説 空所直前の定動詞 need より，名詞（句）または to 不定詞が続くことが予想される。A は文法的には認められるとしても，意味的に前後と合わない。

訳例　国連の〔アントニオ・グテーレス〕事務総長は土曜日，アフリカ大陸自由貿易圏や「アフリカ女性のための金融・経済的包摂の 10 年」の例を特に取り上げ，アフリカが世界にとって「希望の源」であると語った。また，アフリカ連合（AU）が過去 20 年にわたり，「〔アフリカ〕大陸が巨大な潜在力を発揮できるよう，この希望を実現する支援をしてきた」と強調した。今週末エチオピアの首都，アディスアベバで開催中の第 35 回 AU 首脳会議でビデオメッセージを通じて演説を行ったもの。なお，アディスアベバでの会議には，アミナ・モハメド副事務総長が事務総長の代理として参加している。

グテーレス事務総長によると，国連と AU の協力関係は，「持続可能な開発のための 2030 アジェンダ」と「アジェンダ 2063」（平和で統合された，より豊かな大陸を目指すアフリカの青写真）を主な柱に，「これまで以上に強固なものとなっている」。

事務総長は，「さまざまなグローバル・システムに不正が深く根を張っている」が，「最も大きな代償を払っているのはアフリカの人々である」と主張。高所得国のワクチン接種率がアフリカの 7 倍であることを再び指摘するとともに，「道徳的に破綻した世界金融システムは，南の国々を見捨てた」と述べた。

さらに，「アフリカを窒息させている非倫理的な不平等は，武力紛争や政治的，経済的，民族的，社会的な緊張，人権侵害，女性に対する暴力，テロ，軍事クーデター，それに〔何をしても〕罰せられないという心情をあおる〔結果をもたらしている〕」。〔そして〕このために，アフリカ大陸全体で数千万人が避難生活を送っており，民主的な制度が危機に瀕《ひん》している，と述べた。

事務総長は次に，「復興に向けた4つのエンジン」を始動させるべく，国連から支援を提供すると述べた。まず，すべての人にワクチン接種が必要だとして，アフリカ・ワクチン調達・接種タスクチーム（AVATT）を特に紹介するとともに，南アフリカおよびアフリカの他の国々におけるワクチン生産の拡大が生み出す利益について強調した。

「みなさんにお願いしたいのは，知的財産権の問題解決や必要な技術や資金の提供などを通じて，検査，ワクチン，治療法を生み出す能力を備えたアフリカ諸国の数を増やす条件を整備していただきたい，ということだ」（同）。

2番目にグテーレス氏は，加盟国はグローバル金融システムを改革することで，経済回復のエンジンに点火する必要がある，と述べた。「ただし，状況はアフリカに不利となっており，サハラ以南のアフリカは，今後5年間の1人当たりの累積経済成長率が，世界の他の地域に比べて75%も低くなる〔と予測されている〕」（同）。

また，現在支援を必要としている国々に対する特別引出権（IMFが創設した準備通貨資産）の活用や，国際債務構造の改革，それに，より譲許的な形の融資を呼びかけた。

3番目の〔エンジン〕として国連事務総長は，〔アフリカ〕大陸全体にわたるグリーンリカバリー〔環境重視の経済回復〕を取り上げた。この広大な大陸は温室ガス排出量こそ世界全体のわずか3%にすぎないのに，気候変動による影響の中でも最悪のケースが多く及んできている。グテーレス氏は「今日の痛ましい現実に対処するには，アフリカ大陸における適応と緩和に向けた資金供与を根本から増強する必要がある」と述べるとともに，適応資金を200億ドルから倍増するとしたグラスゴーCOP26の公約は実行されなければならないが，それだけでは十分ではない〔と指摘した〕。

同氏は豊かな国々に対し，今年以降，途上国に対して1,000億ドルの気候変動資金を供与する約束を実行するとともに，同じく約束をした民間部門の提携先にも責任を持たせるよう求めた。また，「我々は緊急事態にあり，すべての人の協力が必要だ」と述べ，年内にエジプトで開催される次の国連気候変動会議（COP27）について「アフリカと世界にとってきわめて重要な機会〔となるものだ〕」と指摘した。

最後に，同事務総長は，アフリカ大陸の平和は復興の原動力としても働くものだ，と述べた。アフリカ各地の多民族・多宗教・多文化国家においては，アフリカ連合のような組織は「人々が協力することで共存できること，さらに言えば，繁栄も可能になることを示すもの」だという。

同氏によれば，そのためには「包括的で参加型の構造」が求められることから，加盟国はよい統治を通じてそうした構造を実現する必要がある。これは，アフリカの若者に対して特に重要な〔課題だ〕と同氏は付言した。若者は情報を収集するため接続性の向上を必要としており，また，より高速な通信や，よりよい教育，仕事がメリットとなるからだ。

IV 以下の文章に最も適切に当てはまる語句のペアを４つの選択肢の中から１つ選びなさい。

31. 解答：B

解説 第 1 空所は前後から B. weighing = considering carefully と C. calling for が残るが，C の場合は要求している相手が欠けた形になるのが難点。また，第 2 空所も C. delegates（代表者）の到着で軍の撤退を云々《うんぬん》するのは不自然。

訳例 フランスが西アフリカのマリから軍を全面撤退させることを検討しており，マリの軍事政権との関係悪化とロシア人傭兵の到着を槍玉に上げている〔という〕。フランスの外交トップと，計画を知る西側政府高官 2 人が述べた。

32. 解答：C

解説 第 1 空所は直後の findings の内容がコロン以下に述べられているのでそこから findings を修飾する形容詞として適切なものを選ぶ。第 2 空所も C. infiltrated = enter a place で文意整合する。

訳例 世界自然保護基金（WWF）が委託してまとめた新たな報告書が，厳しい調査結果を示した。海洋汚染の60％を占めるプラスチックが，〔人間の居住地から〕最も離れた海域まで達している〔という〕。プラスチックはマイクロメートル，ナノメートル〔サイズの粒子〕まで分解されるため，ほとんどの海洋生物が摂取している可能性が高く，〔人間にとっても〕消費する食品を介して食卓に戻ってきている恐れがある。

33. 解答：C

解説 第 1 空所は後に続く of weeks of a military buildup に着目すれば，事実関係から C. culmination = something occurring at the end of a long period of development が適切。第 2 空所も C. deploy で周知の事実と合致する。

訳例 ロシアは現地時間の木曜日早朝，ウクライナに対して大規模な攻撃を開始した。ロシアはこれまで数週間にわたって兵力を増強。これに対して NATO 諸国は東欧に部隊を配備し，キーウの〔ウクライナ〕政府に対して武器その他の援助を送っていた。

34.　解答：B

解説　第1空所は文脈から，話題とする事象の背景となる状況を導く前置詞句 B. against the backdrop of が適切。第2空所の過去分詞は上行の community violence を説明するものであり，B. fueled で文意に合う。なお，第2空所だけを考えれば A. exasperated も可能。

訳例　南スーダンの国民統一〔暫定〕政府は，憲法制定作業が遅れ，地域社会における暴力（政治団体や武装民兵によるものが多い）が繰り返される中で，成立2周年の節目を迎えた。現地駐在の国連高官が月曜日，安保理で述べた。

35.　解答：A

解説　第1空所は，冒頭の Bodies are piling up（遺体が積み上がっている）に着目すれば，A. mortuaries が選べる。第2空所も A. stripped で文意に合う。D は原形 ebb が自動詞ということからだけで排除できる。

訳例　香港の病院では死体がますます増えており，霊安室がいっぱいになると廊下にそのまま放置されている。食料品店からは食料品が姿を消した。街が全面ロックダウンされるという噂《うわさ》が流れたことで住民はパニックに陥り，出国者が再び急増した。

36.　解答：C

解説　第1空所は C. invoked < invoke が use something as an authority to achieve something の意味で適切。第2空所も，emergency powers の発動によってどのような措置を行うか示す箇所の先頭にあるから C. outlining がよい。

訳例　ジャスティン・トルドー首相は月曜日，コロナウィルス感染防止規制に怒るトラック運転手らによって〔物流が〕滞るなど〔の影響が出ている〕抗議行動を鎮圧するため緊急権限を発動し，デモ参加者の車両などを撤去した上で，参加者の銀行口座や生計手段を狙いうちする計画の概要を示した。

37.　解答：D

解説　第1空所は cast a shadow over という慣用表現から D が正解。第2空所も，close to being achieved の意味をもつ D. in sight が文脈に最もよく当てはまる。

訳例　ロシアのウクライナ侵攻がイラン核合意の立て直しに向けた協議に影を落としている。新たな合意の見通しについての疑念が深まる中，火曜日には期限と見られていた日付を過ぎる事態となった。

38.　解答：A

解説　第1空所は文意から A. wean (= withdraw from a practice) または B. sever が候補となるが，第2空所を見ると B. exonerate が free from guilt or blame の意で不適。

訳例　〔2021年11月1日，2日に開催された〕国連気候サミット〔世界リーダーズ・サミット〕で世界の首脳らは火曜日，破滅的な地球温暖化の回避を目指す一連の取り決めの一環として，地球の森林の保護やメタンガス排出の削減，南アフリカの石炭依存脱却支援を約束した。

39.　解答：B

解説　第1空所は「経済低迷を逆転させて回復させる」という意味で，A. upend と B. reverse が候補となるが，upend は文字どおり set something on its end の意味なので不適。第2空所も B. roiling＜roil は cause something to be disturbed で文意に合う。

訳例　中国は土曜日，年間経済成長率の目標を過去数十年で最低の水準に引き下げた。ロシアのウクライナに対する戦争によって原油価格が高騰し，世界経済が混乱する中，中国政府は景気の低迷を反転させようと躍起になっている。

40.　解答：D

解説　第1空所は文意より C. capitulation と D. fall が候補となるが，第2空所は D. irreversible の方が適切。

訳例　アフガニスタンがタリバンの手に落ちて半年がたったいま，関係国は同国の新政権との関与を深め，取り返しのつかないような経済破綻が発生しないよう行動を起こすべき時だ――カブール駐在の国連高官が水曜日，安保理で述べた。

V

文法的，語法的にふさわしくないものを下線の中から１つ選びなさい。

41.　解答：B

解説　waited → (should) wait。下線部 B の前に要求を表す動詞 requested があることに注意。要求内容を表す that 節内の定動詞は「(should)＋原形」となる。

訳例　西側情報機関の報告によると，中国当局が2月初旬，ロシア高官に対し，ウクライナ侵攻の開始を北京オリンピックの閉幕後とするよう要請したという。米当局者はこの報告を大筋で信用できると見ているが，その詳細についてはさまざまな解釈が可能だ。

42. 解答：C

解説　to → with。contrastと共起する正しい前置詞に変更する。cf. in contrast with。

訳例　鉄道がなければ，インドが今日のような経済大国に発展していたとは考えられない。ただ，従来の〔鉄道〕システムは，インドにとって大いに役立ちはしただろうが，しだいに時代遅れになってしまった。特に，インドの隣人で地域覇権を争う中国の急速な進歩と対比した場合は〔それが顕著となる〕。

43. 解答：A

解説　growing → growth。この箇所に続くsteadyに注目するとともに，文意を考えれば，keep＋Cでなく，keep＋O＋Cの文型が使われるべきであることが分かる。

訳例　中国は不動産危機と政府のゼロコロナ方針アプローチに対応しているが，その中で政策立案者は，成長をゆるぎないものとして維持するため，山積する課題を抱えている。また，ウクライナ危機の副次的な影響で商品価格が高騰し，成長が鈍化する可能性もある。

44. 解答：D

解説　northern coast of → the northern coast of。名詞句の後のofに続く前置詞句によって名詞句の意味が限定されている。

訳例　南極大陸沖で沈没した極地探検家アーネスト・シャクルトンの〔探検〕船HMSエンデュランス号が，100年以上の歳月を経て発見された。〔船体は〕無傷で状態良好と見られる。同船は1915年に沈没。現在はフォークランド諸島の南方，南極大陸北岸にある南極海〔に開いた〕湾，ウェッデル海の水深3,008mに横たわっている。

45. 解答：D

解説　underwent → undergone。hasに続くのは現在完了形であるから，動詞は過去形underwentでなく過去分詞を組み合わせるのが正しい。

訳例　アフリカでは過去1年余りの間にクーデター3件が成功したほか，ニジェールでクーデター1件が失敗，また，チャドでは専制的な軍政移行が起きた。これらの権力争いは，アフリカが過去20年間経験してきた民主化のプロセスを逆行させ，クーデターが常態化していた時代への逆戻りを危惧させるものだ。

46.　解答：B

解説　be in placed → be placed。主語が An honorary plaque であることに注意すると，B の上記の箇所は単純な受け身の未来形でよいことが分かる。

訳例　2021年1月6日の米国連邦議会議事堂襲撃事件で対応に当った警察官全員の名前を刻んだ記念銘板が，議事堂の西側正面に設置されることになった。〔費用〕は今週議会で審議中の大規模予算案により〔賄われる〕。死に物狂いの反乱に対峙した人々の英雄的行為を記念する〔措置に関する〕条項は，政府機関の閉鎖を回避するため議会が土曜日午前0時までに可決を急いでいる法案の中に盛り込まれた。

47.　解答：D

解説　was → were。上行の show 以下が that 節で，節内の主語が the earliest known Covid-19 cases（複数）。

訳例　コロナウィルスは動物に由来するもので，2019年末に中国武漢の華南海鮮市場でヒトに広がった――そのことを示す新たな証拠が，土曜日に公表された2件の査読前研究で示された。一方の研究（2件とも査読前で専門誌にも未掲載）は，空間分析〔の手法〕を用いて，知られるかぎり最初期のコロナウィルス感染者（2019年12月に確認）が同市場を中心に発生していたことを示している。

48.　解答：B

解説　to → on。「～に対する攻撃」の意味で assault と共起する前置詞は on。

訳例　インドのナレンドラ・モディ首相はその人を「親愛なる友人」と呼んだ。中国の習近平主席はさらに一歩踏み込んで，「最高の親友」と呼んだ。だが，ロシアの強権的指導者ウラジミル・プーチンが，挑発も受けないままウクライナに対して加えた攻撃は，これまでロシアがアジアの両大国との間に築いてきた友好関係に疑問を投げかけるものとなった。にもかかわらず，中国，インドとも，ロシアの残虐な侵略をあえて真っ向から批判しない。

49. 解答：B

解説 that → what。動詞 support に名詞節が続くが，その節内の定動詞 suspected は他動詞。that 節では suspected の目的語が欠けた不完全なセンテンスとなってしまう。

訳例 緊急治療室で身体の痛みに苦しむ患者にとっては，犬と 10 分間だけいっしょに過ごすことが，痛みの緩和に役立つ場合がある。水曜日に発表された研究で明らかになった。世界中の愛犬家が長い間うすうす感じてきたことを裏付ける結果だ。犬の愛情深さは多くの病気を治すだけでなく，病院の人材や設備不足にしばしば悩む患者や医療従事者にとってもちょっとした明るい材料となった。

50. 解答：A

解説 for → of。the tech giant の前の定動詞 accuse に注目すると，共起する前置詞 for が間違っていることが分かる。

訳例 ハイテク企業アマゾンについて独占禁止法違反の疑いで調査を進めている米下院議員らは，同社が議会で虚偽〔証言〕を行ったと非難するに至った。議員らは司法省に対し，同社と同社の一部の幹部による「犯罪行為の可能性」について調査を求めている。議員らは，第三者の販売者から収集したデータの用途について「アマゾンは 1 人の幹部の宣誓証言を通じて虚偽を述べた」としている。

VI

以下の文章の中に含まれる太字の語句および空所の意味として文脈上最も近いものを 4 つの選択肢の中から 1 つ選びなさい。

51. 解答：B

解説 文脈から空所は「〜を受け継いだ」の意味と推測できる。これに最も近いのは，B. inherited ＜ inherit = receive a situation, object, etc. from a predecessor である。

52. 解答：B

解説 下線部 catastrophic は causing very great harm の意。これに最も近いのは，B. disastrous = ending in failure である。

53. 解答：D

解説 下線部 autonomy はこの場合，(a political unit's) right of governing or controlling itself の意。

54. 解答：C

解説 空所より２行上から A win-win situation についての説明が続いている。下線部から続く causing a direct political and organizational collision はその状況では**起きない**はずであったことに着目する。

55. 解答：D

解説 下線部 ambiguity は the quality of being open to more than one possible interpretation の意。これに最も近いのは，D. vagueness = the quality of not being clearly expressed である。

56. 解答：C

解説 空所を含む香港基本法からの引用に続いて，Nevertheless 以下に，引用で言われる nominating committee を NPCSC が a heavy pro-Beijing bias を持つものと解釈したとある。したがって，基本法では行政長官の選出を民主的手続き**によって**行うと定めているのに対して，現実にはそれがゆがめられているという文脈だと推測できる。

57. 解答：D

解説 下線部 legitimacy は conformity to the law の意。これに最も近いのは，D. validity = the quality of being able to be accepted である。

58. 解答：C

解説 空所以下の内容を見ると，まず their freedom is being existentially threatened とあり，続いて their way of life that ... is also under siege とあるので，この２つが並列の関係となる語句を選べばよい。not only A, but also B の変形的な構文となる。

59. 解答：D

解説 下線部 demonstrates ＜ demonstrate は make something clear の意。これに最も近いのは，D. reveals ＜ reveal = make known something that was previously unknown である。

60. 解答：A

解説 下線部 treason は the crime of being **disloyal** to one's country の意。

訳例 「一国二制度」は，大きく異なる 2 つの政治単位間の衝突を防ぐ解決策となるものである。香港の繁栄は 156 年にわたるイギリス統治時代に受け継いだ資本主義体制によるものだが，一方〔中国本土〕では 1949 年以降，中華人民共和国（中国）が中国的な特色を持つ社会主義に基づく国づくりを進めてきた。両者は，政治やイデオロギーの違いに加え，言語，通貨，自由度，法体系も共通ではない。その結果，両政治単位を強硬なやり方で統合することは政治的に無責任な行為となろう――それは香港にも中国本土にも破滅的な政治的不安定をもたらすであろう。

香港のコンパクトな基本法には，「一国二制度」の原則を反映したさまざまな条文が定められている。例えば，第 2 条は，香港に「高度の自治を実施し，行政管理権，立法権，独立した司法権を享有する」権利を認めている。さらに第 9 条では，英語を公用語の 1 つと認めている。〔こうして〕双方に利益をもたらす状況が生み出された。すなわち，香港は思いのままに活動するが，北京も「一国二制度」の傘の下，政治的，組織的な直接の衝突を引き起こすことなく香港を取り戻し，しかも「東洋の真珠」〔香港〕から経済的繁栄を得るというものである。

しかし，この政治バランスは基本法の曖昧さによって損なわれつつある。第 45 条は，「行政長官の選出方法は〔……中略……〕最終的には広汎な代表性をもつ指名委員会が民主的手続きによって指名〔……中略……〕するのが目標である」と規定して，香港の民主化を約束している。にもかかわらず，2014 年 8 月 31 日，全国人民代表大会常務委員会は，「広汎な代表性をもつ指名委員会」の意味を，親中傾向の強い定員 1,200 名の委員会と解釈した。

2014 年の大規模な占拠運動を引き起こしたのは，中国政府のそうした解釈であった。全人代常務委の決定は，香港人のアイデンティティーや自治権，民主化に対する最大級の政治的脅威である。香港と中国双方の国内的・対外的正統性が蝕《むしば》まれたが，それは全人代常務委の決定だけによるものではなく，平和的な抗議者の弾圧において警察が催涙弾を 87 発も発射したり，ある抗議者に手錠をかけ，隠れて殴打したりするなど，数々の不正行為を犯したことも要因となった。

「一国二制度」の弱体化は，関係するすべての政治単位の組織的安定と市民の幸福を打ち壊してしまう。香港人によれば，香港の自由が実存的に脅かされているだけでなく，「一国二制度」の原則によって保証されてきた香港の生活様式もまた，包囲された状態にあるという。占拠運動の中心的な概念に数えられる「我要真普選（真の普通選挙を求める）」は，「共同宣言」と「基本法」が約束した民主化を取り戻すことを目的としていた。警察の不正行為が絡む一連の事件も，香港の法執行システムが政治的理由によって腐敗していることを実証している。こうした言説はいずれも，香港の自治が「一国二制度」の原則を損なう別の政治単位からの影響によって政治的に脅かされているというレトリックを中心に据えている。

こうした安全保障の試みの中で，議論は自治，自己決定，さらには独立へと向かうようになってきた。親中派の政治家や香港政府は，第 23 条の立法化によって中国への反逆を禁止することを含め，さまざまな緊急措置を提起している。本章の結論は，今後，香港の政治的安全保障をいずれの側が成功させるかは問題ではなく，両政治単位にとって不利な状況となる，というものである。なぜなら，「一国二制度」によって確立された政治的均衡は，〔今後は〕不可避的に損なわれるだろうから。

Ⅶ

下線部の単語や句の意味を最もよく表しているものを
４つの選択肢の中から１つ選びなさい。

61.　解答：C

解説　下線部loomingは (something unwanted) being about to happenの意。これに最も近いのは，C. ominous = suggesting that something bad is going to happen. なお，D. providential = happening at a favorable time の意。

62.　解答：D

解説　下線部 wreak havoc は cause great confusion or damage の意。これに最も近いのは D. inflict chaos であるが，inflict = cause (something unpleasant) to be experienced の意。

63.　解答：A

解説　下線部chronicは (of something bad) continuing for a long timeの意。これに最も近いのは，A. habitual = done constantly である。

64.　解答：D

解説　下線部 harnessed ＜ harness は control and make use of の意。これに最も近いのは，D. utilized ＜ utilize である。

65. 解答：A

解説 下線部 terrestrial はこの場合生物について living on or in the ground の意。これに最も近いのは，A. earthly である。

66. 解答：C

解説 下線部 bear は，植物について **produce** fruit or flowers の意。

67. 解答：D

解説 下線部 out of synch は通常２つのものについて，reaching the same or related stage different times の意。これに最も近いのは，D. into disharmony であるが，disharmony = lack of harmony or agreement である。

68. 解答：A

解説 下線部 integrity はこの場合 the quality of being **whole and complete** の意。

69. 解答：A

解説 下線部 feedback loop は an effect where the some portion (or all) of a process's output **affects the output of the same process** at a later time の意。これに最も近いのは，A. reaction that affects itself である。

70. 解答：D

解説 下線部 exacerbate は make even worse の意。これに最も近いのは，D. worsen である。なお，C. mollify は make someone less angry の意。

訳例　国連環境計画（UNEP）は，木曜日に発表した新たな報告書の中で，死者を伴う山火事や騒音など，迫り来る環境面の脅威によって生態系に広範な損害が生じる可能性があり，緊急に対処する必要があると指摘した。

UNEP のインガー・アンダーセン事務局長は，「今回の『フロンティアレポート』では，各国政府や一般市民が注目し，行動を起こすべき３つの環境問題を取り上げ，その解決策を提示している」と述べている。

2022 年版の『騒音，火災，ミスマッチ：環境問題の新たな課題』は，早期に対処しなければ地域的あるいは世界的に大惨事を引き起こす恐れのある新たな環境問題に注意を喚起するもの。

この最新報告書は，国連環境総会（UNEA）再開〔セッション開催〕の数日前に発表されたもので，自然のライフサイクルを乱し，全世界で生態系に深刻な影響を及ぼす公衆衛生上の脅威が拡大していることに注目している。

アンダーセン氏は次のように述べている。「都市の騒音公害と山火事，生物季節学的変化という今回のフロンティアレポートの３つのテーマは，気候変動，公害，生物多様性の損失という地球が抱える３つの危機に対処する緊急の必要性を顕著に示すものだ」。

報告書によると，道路交通，鉄道，レジャーなどで発生する迷惑な長時間にわたる高いレベルの騒音は，人間の健康と幸福を害する。

交通による慢性的な不快感や睡眠妨害は，ごく若い人たちには深刻な心臓病や代謝障害をもたらすほか，高齢者や交通量の多い道路の近くの疎外されたコミュニティーに最も大きな影響を及ぼす。

騒音公害は動物にも脅威を与えている。〔それは〕鳥や昆虫，両生類などさまざまな〔生物〕種のコミュニケーションや行動を変化させることによるものだ。

この報告書では都市計画の担当者に対し，騒音の削減を優先するための手段として，都市内部における林帯の設置や壁面緑化，緑地の拡大など，良好なサウンドスケープを形成する都市インフラ整備に投資することを推奨している。これらの対策はさまざまな健康上の利点をもたらすものだ。

ロンドンの超低排出ガスゾーンや，ベルリンの広い道路に新たに設けられた自転車専用車線，エジプトの騒音対策を目指す国家計画などは，世界がコロナ禍からよりよい形で復興するに当たって活用できる好事例である。

また，気候や動植物のリズムとの相互作用も考慮しなければならない。生物季節学は，環境の力に起因してライフサイクル段階が反復するタイミングや，生態系内で互いに関わり合うさまざまな種が，変化する条件に対してどのように反応するかということ〔を研究対象とする〕。

陸上，水中，海洋の生態系に棲《す》む動植物は，気温や日照時間，降水量などを手がかりに，結実，移動その他の変化に適した時期を判断している。

しかし，気候変動はこうした自然のリズムを乱してしまう。〔具体的には〕植物や動物が自身の自然のリズムを逸脱し，植物がライフサイクル段階を移していくペースが草食動物の行動に対して早まってしまうなど，ミスマッチを引き起こすことを報告書は指摘している。

一方，渡り鳥の渡りのきっかけとなるその地方の気候の変化が，目的地や渡り経路上の休息地の〔飛来時点での〕状況をもはや正確に示すものではなくなっている可能性がある。また，農作物においては，季節変化に生じた生物季節学的シフトによって食料生産が困難となっている。

報告書は，適切な生息地や生態学的接続性の維持，生物学的多様性の健全性の強化，移動経路上における国際的取り組みの調整といった保全目標がきわめて重要であるとして警鐘を鳴らす。

特に，温暖化ペースを抑える上で CO_2 排出量削減が重要である点を強調している。

さらに，山火事防止の必要性もまた，関心が持たれる分野の1つである。報告書によると，2002年から2016年にかけての地球全体の地表焼失面積は，〔年〕平均で欧州連合（EU）の面積にほぼ匹敵する4億2,300万ヘクタールとなっており，今後は，これまで被害を受けていなかった地域を含め，危険な山火事がより頻繁に，激しく，より長く続くようになることが予想されるという。

気候変動は非常に大きな山火事を引き起こすが，それによって雷が発生し，それが火災前線のはるかかなたで新たな火災をもたらし，いわゆる危険なフィードバックループを生み出す恐れがある。

人間の健康に対する長期的な影響は，山火事の消火隊や避難者，家を失った人々にとどまらず，持病のある人や女性，子ども，高齢者，それに貧困層の間で被害が悪化する。

同時に，山火事で発生する黒色炭素やその他の汚染物質は，水源を汚染する，氷河融解を加速させる，地滑りを誘発する，熱帯雨林を炭素吸収源に変えてしまう〔といった問題を引き起こす〕可能性がある。

これに対処する手立てとして報告書では，山火事リスクの低減や予防および対応管理手法の開発，衛星やレーダーなどの遠隔検知機能の強化に向けた資金補充を行うよう求めている。

Ⅷ 文脈上，空所を埋めるのに最もふさわしいものを4つの選択肢の中から1つ選びなさい。

71. 解答：C

解説 空所がある前のセンテンスにアフガニスタンの状況が例示されている。問題のセンンテンスはそれをまとめて表すものと考えられるから C. in the midst of が最も適切。

72. 解答：A

解説 add to (= be joined to something so as to increase its extent) は頻出する句動詞。

73. 解答：B

解説 空所以下 drought struck Afghanistan が空所前 October 2020 の説明になっていることを見抜き，非限定の関係副詞節を導く B. when を選ぶ。

74.　解答：B

解説　空所のあるセンテンスの前に malnutrition とあることに着目すると，B. Emaciated = weak and thin が最適。

75.　解答：C

解説　前後から空所には経済の劣悪な状態を指す語が入るものと考えられる。よって，C. implosion = a sudden collapse of a system が最適。

76.　解答：D

解説　前後から空所以下は「貧困に**陥る**」の意だと推測できる。

77.　解答：C

解説　前後から空所以下は「赤ちゃん 3 人を保育器 1 台に**押し込む**」意だと分かる。

78.　解答：A

解説　前後から空所以下は「呼びかけを**強める**」という意味だと考えられる。なお，D. spurn は reject with contempt の意。

79.　解答：B

解説　空所の前のパラグラフは米国の行動について，空所に続くパラグラフは国連や援助団体，援助国の取り組みについて，それぞれ述べている。よって，この場合 on the other hand の意味を表す B. In the meantime で接続するのがよい。

80.　解答：D

解説　問題文全体はアフガニスタンの窮状を記述しているので，それを表す形容詞としては，D. ailing = experiencing difficulty が最適。

訳例　広がる飢餓，機能不全に陥った経済，切実に支援を必要とする人々。アフガニスタンの人道危機は悪化の一途をたどっている。

8月にタリバンが政権を掌握してから，国際支援のほとんどが打ち切られた。病院や学校は職員に給与を支給する余裕がなく，国民の多くは食料を買う余裕もない〔状況〕にあり，そうでなくとも悲惨な飢餓の危機に拍車をかけている。
国際救済委員会のアフガニスタン事務所長を務めるヴィッキー・アケン氏は，「人々が絶望のどん底にあるのが我々には分かる。人道状況は悪化するばかりのようだ」と述べた。
国連世界食糧計画〔WFP〕によると，アフガニスタンの人口の半分以上に当たる 2,200 万人以上が危機レベルの飢餓に見舞われており，その大半は次の食事がいつになるか不確かな状態だという。これは，飢餓に陥る恐れのある人が 1,400 万人余りだった 9 月から急激に増加したことを示している。また WFP の推定によると，12 月には食べるものが十分に得られず，食事を抜くなどして対処する人が人口の 95%に達したという。アフガニスタンでは，干ばつに襲われた 2020 年 10 月以降，状況が悪化の一途をたどっている。
国連関係者によると，状況は前例のない速さで激化しているという。
WFP アフガニスタン事務所長のメアリ・エレン・マクグローティー氏は次のように話している。「こんなに急速な悪化は経験がない。栄養不良率が毎週毎週倍増し，ガリガリに痩せた子どもたちが病院に運ばれてくる」。
アフガニスタンは以前から過去 30 年間で最悪の干ばつに見舞われ，農村地帯では多くの人が絶望的な状況に陥っていた。今，景気の悪化に伴い，農民たちは出稼ぎ先を見つけられなくなってしまった。
「食料価格，燃料価格面での経済崩壊や干ばつの影響，それに紛争がもたらした悲惨な結果が全部ぶつかりあって，国中に津波にも似た飢餓と栄養不良の被害を生み出している」(同)。
8 月のカブール陥落と米軍撤退以来，タリバンが実権を握る政府は国際経済から締め出され，通貨危機や貧困の拡大，医療など主要な公共サービスの崩壊を引き起こしている。
アケン氏は言う。「そう，8 月以前はひどかった。しかし，8 月 15 日に開発資金が打ち切られ，そして制裁発動，資産凍結となると，事態はひどいどころではなく〔悲惨の〕極みに達した」。
国連の予測では，アフガニスタンでは人口の 97%が今年半ばまでに貧困に陥るとしていたが，9 月の貧困率は 72%となった。経済崩壊の影響は，食料の購買力や就労の見通し，そして身体を暖かく保つことや医療を受けることなど，国民生活のほぼすべての面に及んでいる。
アフガニスタン赤十字国際委員会のインギ・セドキ コミュニケーション部長は次のように話している。「アフガニスタンでいままさに起きていることは，悪循環になりつつある。「現金が不足している上，給与が支払われないために，食料と栄養を適切に取ることができなくなっている。そしていま，厳冬を迎え，多くの人がさらなる健康リスクにさらされている」。
同氏の話によると，産婦人科病院の看護師らには大部屋の病室に小さな携帯型ヒーターを 1 台置く金額しか与えられていないという。「暖房システムもなければ，赤ちゃんを世話するのに十分な設備もないため，1台の保育器に赤ん坊を3人も押し込む始末だ」(同)。

この悲惨な危機によって，援助団体や国連には資金提供の新たな呼びかけを強めることが求められている。国連と国連の提携団体は1月中旬，今年分の資金として50億ドル以上を提供するよう訴えた。国連の1カ国に対する要請額としてはかつてない規模で，その大半を占める44億ドルをアフガニスタン国内での支援に，残りをイランやパキスタンなどの近隣諸国にいる数百万人のアフガニスタン難民に回すというもの。国連のマーティン・グリフィス緊急援助調整官は，その資金がなければアフガニスタン国民に「未来はない」と述べた。しかし，国連はこれまでその資金ニーズに応えることができていない。

米国はタリバンが政権を掌握した際，アフガニスタンへ提供する資金の多くを凍結したが，その後は援助の一部を再開，3億800万ドルの追加援助を今月発表した。住居，医療，食料，水，その他の基本サービスを提供するものだ。

一方，国連や各援助団体，各援助国は，現金がタリバンの手に渡らない方法で，アフガニスタンに資金を送る方法を模索してきた。国連開発計画は昨秋，商業銀行を利用して，医療従事者に対して携帯電話を介して直接支払金を送る取り組みを開始した。携帯電話を持たない人は，直接現金を受け取った。

援助関係者らは，この病める国を各国が支援し続けることが重要であると語った。

セドキ氏は次のように述べている。「各国はアフガニスタンに投資してほしい。それこそが，銀行システムや，医療・教育といった生活に必要な基本サービスが全面崩壊するのを防ぐ唯一の方法だ」。

IX

以下の質問に対し，150～200語の短いエッセイを英語で書きなさい。

質問文：国連の難民支援はいかにして，世界のすべての国に対する支援となっているか？

解答例 I will focus on how the United Nations High Commissioner for Refugees' (UNHCR) purpose and expanded role helps nations.

The UNHCR, established December 1949 by the UN General Assembly, as an "Other Entity" to provide refugees—individuals outside their places of origin to escape violence, conflict, and persecution—with international protection. Its mandate, initially enlarged to include returnees and stateless persons, has expanded over 12 times since 1950. Although not generally mandated to protect internally displaced people, UNHCR may be involved in security and humanitarian assistance operations.

Currently, UNHCR supports over 82 million people who have been displaced forcibly worldwide; one in every 95 people in the world has had to flee her or his home because of conflict or persecution. UNHCR's present central role supports States to fulfill their international commitments to care for refugees, stateless persons, and asylum- seekers. Start-of-March 2022 UNHCR reports say over a million people fled Ukraine to escape the Russian invasion. General UNHCR-mandated functions—relief distribution, emergency humanitarian activities, determination of status, registration, issuance of documentation—support Ukrainian refugees and their host nations.

Ultimately, the UNHCR helps world nations two ways: overseeing international obligations toward refugees and partnering with nations in fulfilling these commitments.

解説　全体を通して，国連システム（この場合 UNHCR は国連の補助機関）と現在の状況についての正確な知識を織り交ぜつつ，文章を展開するとよい。

第 1 パラグラフは，テーマを絞り込み，国連において難民支援を司る難民高等弁務官事務所（UNHCR）に注目する。

第 2 パラグラフは，UNHCR の設立時期や目的，活動を概観している。

第 3 パラグラフは，難民などの保護を行う上で UNHCR が各国をどのように支援しているかを詳しく提示している。

第 4 パラグラフは，以上を受けての結論として，UNHCR（国連）の難民支援がいかにして各国に対する支援となるかをまとめて示している。

訳例　国連難民高等弁務官事務所（UNHCR）の目的と拡大された役割が，どのように各国のために役立っているかを中心に考えてみたい。

UNHCR は，難民（暴力や紛争，迫害から逃れるために出身地を離れた人々）に対して国際的な保護を提供する「補助機関」として 1949 年 12 月，国連総会〔の決議〕によって設立された。その仕事の範囲は，帰国子女や無国籍者を対象に含めるよう広げられたのを皮切りに，1950 年以降 12 回以上拡大されている。UNHCR は，国内避難民の保護は一般的には対象としていないものの，安全保障や人道支援の活動に関わることがある。

現在，UNHCR は世界中で 8,200 万人以上の強制避難民を支援している。つまり，世界には，紛争や迫害のために故郷を離れることを余儀なくされた人が95人に1人いるという計算になる。UNHCRの現在の中心的な役割は，各国が国際公約として表明している難民，無国籍者，亡命希望者の保護をきちんと実行できるよう，各国を支援することである。2022年3月初めのUNHCRの報告によると，ロシアの侵攻から逃れるためにウクライナから国外へ避難した人が100万人以上に達しているという。救援物資の配給や緊急人道支援活動，〔難民〕認定，登録，文書の発行といったUNHCRの一般的な業務は，ウクライナ難民やその受け入れ国を支援するものである。

結論としては，UNHCRは，各国の難民に対する義務〔履行状況〕を監視する，そしてその公約が果たされるよう各国と連携して取り組むという2つの方法で世界各国を支援している〔と言える〕。

2022年A級第1回試験　正解一覧

Ⅰ

1. D	2. C	3. B	4. A	5. B	6. A	7. B	8. A	9. D	10. C

Ⅱ

11. A	12. B	13. B	14. B	15. D	16. A	17. C	18. C	19. A	20. B

Ⅲ

21. D	22. B	23. C	24. C	25. B	26. B	27. D	28. D	29. A	30. D

Ⅳ

31. B	32. C	33. C	34. B	35. A	36. C	37. D	38. A	39. B	40. D

Ⅴ

41. B	42. C	43. A	44. D	45. D	46. B	47. D	48. B	49. B	50. A

Ⅵ

51. B	52. B	53. D	54. C	55. D	56. C	57. D	58. C	59. D	60. A

Ⅶ

61. C	62. D	63. A	64. D	65. A	66. C	67. D	68. A	69. A	70. D

Ⅷ

71. C	72. A	73. B	74. B	75. C	76. D	77. C	78. A	79. B	80. D

2022年

第2回試験

問題

A級第１次試験問題用紙

A級

外務省後援

２０２２年度第２回国際連合公用語

英語検定試験（120分）

受験上の注意

1．問題用紙は試験開始の合図があるまで開いてはいけません。その間に、この**受験上の注意を熟読しておいてください**。

2．**受験番号と氏名を解答用紙（マークシートと作文用紙）**に記入してください。

3．解答用紙の配布は１人１部のみです。複数の配布は致しません。

4．試験開始前は、答案への解答記入は禁止です。

5．マークシートの記入は、１～100までの記入箇所がありますが、この級では１～80までを使います。

6．マークシートの記入は、必ずＨＢ以上の濃い鉛筆を使って該当箇所を黒く塗りつぶしてください。書き間違いの場合は「アト」が残らないように消してください。マークシートは絶対に折ったり曲げたりしないでください。

7．受験級、受験地区、会場番号、受験番号のマークシートへの記入は監督者の指示に従い、間違いなく記入してください。**（裏表紙の「マークシート記入例」参照）**

8．作文は、⑴読みやすい文字をペン、ボールペンまたはＨＢ以上の濃い鉛筆で書いてください。⑵使用語数の150～200語を目安にしてください。

9．試験問題についての質問は、印刷が不鮮明な場合を除き、一切受けつけません。

10．中途退室の際は、マークシートと作文用紙を持って監督者に渡し、他の受験者の迷惑にならないように静かに退室してください。中途退室後の再入室はできません。

11．試験中は他の受験者の妨げとなる行動は慎んでください。また携帯電話等の電源はお切りください。

12．マークシートと作文用紙は監督者に提出し、問題用紙はご自由にお持ち帰りください。

＊試験問題の複製や転載、インターネットへのアップロード等、いかなる媒体への転用を禁止します。

試験結果について

1．第１次試験の結果は2022年11月24日㈭頃に受験申込書に記載された住所に郵送で通知します。

2．その間に住所変更をされた方は、郵便局へ住所変更の届け出を忘れずに行ってください。

3．発表前の試験結果のお問合せには応じられません。

第２次試験について

1．第１次試験合格者には、試験結果発表と同時に試験日時、会場を指定して通知します。（第１次試験を特別会場で受験した合格者には最寄りの２次試験会場が指定されます。）

2．第２次試験は2022年12月11日㈰です。Ａ級の試験地は札幌・仙台・東京・名古屋・大阪・福岡・鹿児島・沖縄のいずれかになります。（特Ａ級との併願で特Ａ級の第１次試験に合格された方の試験地は東京と大阪になります。）あらかじめご了承願います。

UNA-JAPAN
公益財団法人 日本国際連合協会
http://www.unaj.or.jp/

I. Fill in each of the following blanks with the most appropriate of the four alternatives according to the knowledge and information gained from *New Today's Guide to the United Nations.*

1. Foreword

From this vision of the role of the United Nations in the next century flow three key priorities for the future: eradicating poverty, preventing conflict, and promoting ________.

A. democracy B. multilateralism
C. human rights D. peace

2. Address to the General Assembly

Third, unresolved conflicts and systematic violations of international humanitarian law. We are all shocked by the dramatic escalation of sectarian tensions in ________ Rakhine State.

A. Rwanda's B. Myanmar's
C. Afghanistan's D. Syria's

3. Forerunner of the United Nations

The original members of the League were the victorious allies of the war (with the exception of the United States, which never ratified the Treaty of ________), and other neutral States.

A. Paris B. Ghent
C. Washington D. Versailles

4. Official Seal, Emblem and Flag

The official seal and emblem of the United Nations is a map of the world, as seen from the North Pole, surrounded by a wreath of ________ branches.

A. laurel B. oak
C. olive D. maple

5. Security Council

Each member of the Security Council has one vote. Decisions on matters of procedure require the approval of at least nine of the ________ members.

A. 7 B. 10
C. 12 D. 15

6. **Secretariat**

The Secretariat, an international staff of approximately ________ men and women, carries out the day-to-day work of the United Nations both at Headquarters in New York and in offices and centers around the world.

A. 10,000 B. 40,000

C. 80,000 D. 120,000

7. **Budget of the United Nations**

The main source of funds for the regular budget is the contributions of Member States, who are assessed on a scale specified by the ________ on the recommendation of the 18-member Committee on Contributions.

A. Security Counsel B. Assembly

C. Secretary-General D. Secretariat

8. **International Atomic Energy Agency (IAEA)**

The Statute of the International Atomic Energy Agency (IAEA) was approved on 26 October 1956, at an international conference held at United Nations Headquarters, and the Agency came into existence in ________ on 29 July 1957.

A. Geneva B. The Hague

C. Vienna D. Turin

9. **World Health Organization (WHO)**

The World Health Organization (WHO) came into being on 7 April ________, when 26 United Nations member States had its Constitution ratified.

A. 1945 B. 1946

C. 1947 D. 1948

10. **Overview of Japan and the United Nations**

Starting in 1978 when ________ was appointed to the position of Under-Secretary-General for Public Information, a Japanese candidate has been routinely serving as one of the Under-Secretary-Generals in the UN.

A. Genichi Akatani B. Hiroshi Nakajima

C. Koichiro Matsuura D. Sadako Ogata

Ⅱ. Choose from among the four alternatives the one that is the most appropriate form of each of the underlined verbs.

It seems the moral imperative for climate action just isn't computing. In Europe, hope for the ambitious climate action we need was whittled away this summer, with the G-7 reneging on its earlier promises to stop funding fossil fuel projects **(11)** **decide** in late June to keep developing natural gas overseas, while the European Union passed a proposal in early July that would categorize natural gas projects as sustainable investments. And while a surprise climate deal with Senator Joe Manchin (D., W.Va) was a relief for many **(12)** **value** the future of the planet, the twists and turns of working it out, including last week's apparent breakdown of negotiations, showed that emissions cuts were far from the highest concern for many of the politicians involved.

In Europe and the U.S., politicians made enormous compromises to short term interests—choosing energy security and inflation worries, for instance, over immediate emissions cuts—but they are likely to reverberate through the decades **(13)** **come**: more greenhouse gasses in the atmosphere ultimately mean more disastrous climate impacts on people around the world, especially in the poorest and most vulnerable nations. Yet we are still putting off the toughest necessary action, even though every delay worsens what we and our descendants will have to endure.

In the burgeoning field of climate ethics, there's a couple different explanations for what's going on. In one view, part of the challenge is that climate change is just a difficult moral problem for people **(14)** **wrap** their minds around. Dale Jamieson, a professor of environmental studies and philosophy at New York University, gives the example of someone stealing a bike today—which most people would say is wrong—versus one group of unacquainted people **(15)** **take** a set of actions that means, years down the road, somewhere in the world, other people don't get to have bikes—a scenario that separates the perpetrators from the consequences in both time and space. "Even though we can produce exactly the same outcomes—somebody gets harmed, and other people benefit—it doesn't have the logic that really speaks to our moral emotions," he says. "Evolution didn't build us to respond to those kinds of problems."

Jamieson says that means trying to persuade people **(16)** **act** on climate change based purely on what's right and wrong just isn't going to get much traction. Instead, we're better to dispense with the outrage and focus on the practical side: how to craft rules and economic incentives that will lead to lower emissions.

But not everyone **(17)** **agree**. Stephen Gardiner, a professor of philosophy and environmental studies at the University of Washington, says that our moral intuitions can grasp the abstract and immense challenge of climate change just fine. Instead of the bicycle example, he likens our continued burning of fossil fuels more to a group of friends **(18)** **shoot** fireworks over a poor section of a city, even though they know it'll risk setting fire to people's houses there. For most of us, the moral dimensions are pretty clear here—

as they are with the problem of rich nations shooting off emissions into the atmosphere, which disproportionately affect people in poorer parts of the world, like Bangladesh, **(19) be** incredibly vulnerable to devastating flooding.

The problem, he says, comes down to the fact that our institutions might not be capable of properly dealing with issues **(20) affect** people across the world and through multiple generations. That's a moral problem too. "There's too much of a tendency to think that if the government's not solved it, then it's nobody's problem," he says. "Whereas I think... we have a responsibility as citizens to get together and create better institutions."

11. A. to decide B. and deciding
C. deciding D. and decided

12. A. valued B. who value
C. value D. to value

13. A. coming B. to come
C. came D. will come

14. A. wrapped B. that wrap
C. wrapping D. to wrap

15. A. taking B. takes
C. taken D. to take

16. A. to act B. acting
C. are acting D. that act

17. A. agreeing B. who agrees
C. to agree D. agrees

18. A. to shoot B. shoot
C. shooting D. has shot

19. A. being B. to be
C. which is D. is

20. A. affected B. that affect
C. by affecting D. to affect

Ⅲ. Fill in each of the following blanks with the best and most grammatically and logically appropriate of the four alternatives <u>in the context</u> of the article below.

It is totally unacceptable for states in possession of nuclear weapons to admit the possibility of a nuclear war, António Guterres underscored early on Saturday in Japan at a ceremony marking the 77th anniversary of the atomic bombing of Hiroshima.

"Nuclear weapons are nonsense. Three-quarters of a century later, we must ask what we've learned from the mushroom cloud that swelled above this city in 1945", he urged **(21)** ________________ attended by dozens of people, including hibakusha, young peace activists, Japan's Prime Minister and other local authorities.

The UN Secretary-General warned that a new arms race is picking up **(22)** ________________ cost of hundreds of billions of dollars with almost 13,000 nuclear weapons currently held in arsenals around the world. "...Crises with grave nuclear undertones are spreading fast — from the Middle East to the Korean peninsula, to Russia's invasion of Ukraine... Humanity is playing with a loaded gun", he cautioned.

Mr. Guterres called the current Review Conference of the Treaty on the Non-Proliferation of Nuclear Weapons in New York a 'sign of hope'. "Today, from this sacred space, I call on this Treaty's members to work urgently to eliminate the stockpiles that threaten our future, to strengthen dialogue, diplomacy and negotiation, and **(23)** ________________ of destruction", he emphasized.

He underscored that countries with nuclear weapons must commit to the "no first use" of them, and assure other states that they will not use—or threaten to use—nuclear weapons against them. "We must **(24)** ________________ times, recognizing there is only one solution to the nuclear threat: not to have nuclear weapons at all", the UN chief stated.

Guterres stressed that leaders cannot hide from their responsibilities. "Take the nuclear option off the table—for good. It's time to proliferate peace. Heed the message of the hibakusha: 'No more Hiroshimas! No more Nagasakis!'", he said, recognizing that in 1945, **(25)** ________________ Japan—first in Hiroshima on 6 August, and Nagasaki three days later, on 9 August.

Mr. Guterres also sent a message to **(26)** ________________ hibakusha have begun. "The world must never forget what happened here. The memory of those who died—and the legacy of those who survived—will never be extinguished", he concluded.

Later in the day, the Secretary-General met five surviving victims of the atomic bombs in Hiroshima and Nagasaki, known as Hibakusha, and heard their stories. He expressed his admiration for them, acknowledging that they have suffered enormously but have overcome trauma with ‘enormous courage and resilience’. Mr. Guterres also called them an example for the world, and told the three women and two men reunited with him **(27)** ______________________________ that ‘nuclear weapons are nonsense’. “The UN is committed to keeping the memory of what happened alive, and to make sure that your stories echo forever”, he said.

The hibakusha told the UN chief how they have remained engaged in issues of peace and disarmament for most of their lives: for example, one of them wrote a song to raise awareness and another illustrated her experiences in pictures. They all expressed **(28)** ______________________________ reality of nuclear weapons.

António Guterres was also part of an informal dialogue session with young Japanese activists currently leading initiatives on nuclear disarmament, non-proliferation and other global issues. “I would like to apologize **(29)** ______________________________ the world we are leaving to your generation”, he said, reiterating an apology he’s made before to the youth worldwide. “Our generations need to work together ... and then you will assume the responsibilities, and you need to be prepared and be in very good shape”, he told the young participants.

The UN chief also met with the mayor of Hiroshima, and the deputy mayor of Nagasaki, and was granted honorary citizenship of Hiroshima. “I accept this great honor on behalf of all the women and men of the United Nations who are working for peace around the world. I accept it on behalf of the diplomats and negotiators who — this very week—are **(30)** ______________________________ nuclear weapons”, he expressed.

21. A. at the Hiroshima Peace Memorial Park solemn event during
B. during the solemn event at Hiroshima Peace Memorial Park
C. Hiroshima Peace Memorial Park event during at the solemn
D. Memorial solemn during Hiroshima the event at Peace Park

22. A. at a speed and stockpiles leaders are enhancing world
B. enhancing world speed and at stockpiles leaders are a
C. speed and world leaders are enhancing stockpiles at a
D. world leaders and are enhancing stockpiles at a speed

23. A. by eliminating my disarmament agenda to support these devices
B. devices eliminating my disarmament by these agenda to support
C. eliminating disarmament devices by these support to my agenda
D. to support my disarmament agenda by eliminating these devices

24. A. all keep in view at Hiroshima of the horrors
B. in all keep Hiroshima at the horrors of view
C. keep the horrors of Hiroshima in view at all
D. view all the horrors in Hiroshima of keep at

25. A. atomic bombs over the skies detonated of two were
B. bombs were atomic over the two skies of detonated
C. skies detonated over the two atomic bombs were of
D. two atomic bombs were detonated over the skies of

26. A. young people urging them to finish the work the
B. work urging the people to finish the young them
C. people urging to finish them the work the young
D. finish people to them young urging the work the

27. A. leaders that have the moral authority tell to they
B. that they have the moral authority to tell leaders
C. the moral authority to tell leaders that they have
D. to have leaders that tell they the moral authority

28. A. that the crude young people also understand their desire
B. the crude desire understand that young people also their
C. their desire that young people also understand the crude
D. understand their desire that the young people also crude

29. A. for generation on my behalf of the state of
B. of behalf on my generation of the state for
C. on behalf of my generation for the state of
D. of the generation state for on behalf of my

30. A. meeting in New York to stop the spread of
B. of the spread in New York to stop meeting
C. spread in New York to stop the meeting of
D. stop the meeting in New York of spread to

Ⅳ. Choose from among the four alternatives the one that best completes the following sentence.

31. The scale of the ________ in Mali, as the last French troops exited after nine years, shows how the central zone of Islamist-related violence has ________ away from the Middle East and South Asia.

A. havoc − taken
B. demolition − put
C. carnage − shifted
D. obliteration −carried

32. The commander of a militia unit resisting Russian forces in the ________ Ukrainian city of Mariupol said his soldiers will fight until the end despite constant bombardments and ________ supplies of food and water.

A. beset − surging
B. pounded − enduring
C. grumpy − ebbing
D. besieged − dwindling

33. The ________, to take effect in two weeks, will allow Ottawa to stop imports without waiting for Parliament to pass legislation. But critics say it doesn't get ________ the real problem: Firearms smuggled illegally from the United States.

A. statute − by
B. ban − at
C. acquiescence − around
D. decree − through

34. The international community must dramatically increase efforts to urge the ________ authorities in Afghanistan to ________ basic human rights principles, a group of UN independent rights experts said on Friday.

A. interim − eschew
B. scrupulous − forfeit
C. provincial − heed
D. de facto − adhere to

35. Putin's trip comes days after Biden visited Israel and Saudi Arabia — a hint at Moscow's plans to ________ closer ties with Tehran ________ Western sanctions.

A. forge − in the face of
B. sever − at the discretion of
C. sap − on the verge of
D. buttress − under the pretext of

36. The Russian military's ________ of the Black Sea has prevented Ukraine from exporting wheat and soybeans, putting Ukrainian farmers in a ________ situation as the domestic price of surplus grain has plummeted.

A. fortification − implausible
B. vindication − calamitous
C. blockade − dire
D. beleaguerment − ignominious

37. **U.S. House Speaker Nancy Pelosi arrived in Taiwan late Tuesday, becoming the highest-ranking American official in 25 years to visit the ________ island claimed by China, which quickly announced that it would conduct military ________ in retaliation for her presence.**

A. sovereign − alliance　B. non-aligned − amalgamation
C. self-ruled − maneuvers　D. hapless − reinforcement

38. **U.N. Secretary General Antonio Guterres called for "massive" international support for flood-________ Pakistan while visiting the country on Friday, while Islamabad ________ the cost of flood-related damage at $30 billion.**

A. ravaged − put　B. inebriated − reckoned
C. nagged − approximate　D. devastating − recouped

39. **Russia on Thursday ________ travel bans on U.S. Vice President Kamala Harris, Facebook chief Mark Zuckerberg and dozens of ________ Americans and Canadians in retaliation for sanctions imposed over Ukraine.**

A. ameliorated − adept　B. slapped − prominent
C. defied − pertinent　D. rebuked − hallowed

40. **The ________ shutdown of hundreds of civil society organizations in Nicaragua is deeply concerning and will have a ________ effect on activists and human rights defenders across the country, UN-appointed independent human rights experts said on Friday.**

A. draconian − buoyant　B. despotic − unequivocal
C. benign − wrenched　D. arbitrary − chilling

V. Choose from among the underlined phrases the one that is grammatically or idiomatically incorrect.

41. **(A)** London got so warm this summer that newspapers splashed with headlines saying temperatures in the city had **(B)** exceeded those of scorching hot Dubai. But experts say that temperature alone isn't an adequate measure of the livability **(C)** of a city — a combination of heat and humidity are. And that's why as the climate crisis unfolds, the Middle East **(D)** will be far less livable than Europe even at the same temperatures.

42. The former attorney general of Mexico **(A)** was arrested on Friday in relation to the 2014 disappearance of 43 students. **(B)** The prosecutor's office said in a statement that it considers him a suspect in "the crimes of forced disappearance, torture and against the administration of justice." **(C)** The case ignited international outrage, and then-President Enrique Peña Nieto **(D)** was criticized for his lack transparency in investigating the matter.

43. As the US attempts to wean itself off **(A)** its heavy reliant on fossil fuels and shift to cleaner energy sources, **(B)** many experts are eyeing a promising solution. The rooftops and parking lot space available at major retail outlets **(C)** is massive. And these largely empty spaces are being touted as untapped potential for **(D)** solar power that could help the US reduce its dependence on foreign energy, slash planet-warming emissions and save companies millions of dollars in the process.

44. North Korea has rejected South Korea's **(A)** offer of economic support in exchange for denuclearization. A top North Korean official **(B)** disparaged at the offer by President Yoon as "pipedream-like remarks." Yoon **(C)** first proposed what he called an "audacious plan" to swap economic cooperation **(D)** for an end to North Korea's nuclear program during his inauguration speech in May.

45. **(A)** A local entrepreneur in the Japanese tourist destination of Nara **(B)** has developed alternative to plastic shopping bags to protect the town's sacred deer. Hidetoshi Matsukawa, who works for Nara-ism, a souvenir wholesale agent, said he heard last year that **(C)** the deer, which roam the city's park, were dying after ingesting plastic bags. The city is home to around 1,000 sacred **(D)** deer, which are officially designated as a natural treasure in Japan.

46. Saudi women's rights campaigner Salma al-Shehab **(A)** was sentenced for 34 years in prison on Monday because of her activity on Twitter. The PhD student at Leeds University in the United Kingdom **(B)** had been arrested in January 2021 and **(C)** was subjected to questioning over a period of 265 days. She **(D)** was initially given a six-year sentence which was increased to 34 years after al-Shehab filed an appeal.

47. **(A)** The United Kingdom is enduring a summer of misery as its beloved health service descends into crisis, **(B)** inflation soars, taps run dry and strikes halting trains. Meanwhile, the government is nowhere to be seen. **(C)** The sense of collapse is only mounting; health leaders on Friday **(D)** issued the grim warning of a "humanitarian crisis" without action to stop energy prices increasing over the winter.

48. **(A)** Estimating just how catastrophic climate change will be for the global economy has historically proven challenging. But this summer, **(B)** it's increasingly evident how quickly costs can pile up. Extreme heat and drought conditions **(C)** are battering the United States, Europe and China, compounding problems for workers and businesses at a time when economic growth **(D)** is already slowed sharply and adding to upward pressure on prices.

49. There's a shortage of truck drivers worldwide, **(A)** exacerbated by the e-commerce boom brought on by the pandemic. One solution to the problem is autonomous trucks, **(B)** and several companies are in a race to be the first to launch one. One company's latest road test involved hauling fresh produce 951 miles, **(C)** from Nogales, Arizona to Oklahoma City. Almost of the trip was autonomous; **(D)** only the pickup and the dropoff were handled by a human driver.

50. Across the African continent, innovative transport systems, telecoms operations **(A)** and smart cities are being developed to boost economies and increase trade opportunities. **(B)** One example is the Kazungula Bridge. The 923-meter long bridge over **(C)** the Zambezi River connecting Botswana and Zambia. Opened in May 2021, it **(D)** replaces a ferry and was built to speed up truck traffic along a key north-south trade artery.

Ⅵ. Choose from among the four alternatives the one that most closely corresponds to the meaning of words in bold type and blanks in the following passage.

Fifteen years ago, it was necessary to argue that international relations (IR) as a discipline ignored popular culture (Weldes 1999, p. 117). Happily, this is no longer the case. Some corners of what might be called 'mainstream IR' (but only quite narrowly **(51) construed** and mostly North American) still implicitly or explicitly insist that popular culture is not worthy of scholarly IR attention, perhaps because it is seen as 'low' politics, domestic politics, or not political at all. However, scholars from assorted perspectives and disciplines are eagerly and productively investigating **(52) myriad** forms of popular culture in relation to every conceivable aspect of IR and world politics. One might even argue that there now exists a sub-(inter-)discipline of Popular Culture and World Politics (PCWP).

In teaching a unit entitled 'Popular Culture and World Politics'—which Jutta first taught in the US in the 1990s and Christina and Jutta have taught/teach at the University of Bristol—we have been genuinely **(53) flummoxed** by one thing. Some students invariably complain, well into or even at the end of the unit, 'But I don't understand—how *does* popular culture relate to world politics?' Asking this question, given that the entire unit is organised around addressing it head on, indicates a 'stuckness' in a narrow understanding of IR (as discipline) or international relations (as state practice) or world politics (as a wider, but still conventional, set of trans-border practices). At the same time, this question reflects a further **(54)** _________, sometimes surprisingly difficult to shift, that there is/ought to be a simple, perhaps even singular, way to grasp how one 'thing'—popular culture—'relates' (preferably causally) to another 'thing'—world politics. In typical positivist fashion, students often expect to find that popular culture 'does' something 'to' world politics (or, less often, that world politics 'does' something 'to' popular culture).

But these assumptions misunderstand. Analytically, both 'popular culture' and 'world politics' are complex and **(55)** _________ concepts, so there can be no singular understanding of either. Empirically, the objects and practices to which the terms refer, and the 'relations' between and among them, are varied, complex and dynamic. In this paper we **(56) take a stab at** categorising analytically the relations that obtain between 'popular culture' and 'world politics'—and at suggesting why they matter. We present six types of relations between PC and WP, viewing each, in turn, as multifaceted and not unrelated to the others. We then use the 'diamond engagement ring' to **(57) underscore** the interconnections among these various relations.

A **(58) caveat** is in order here: we are emphatically *not* precluding arguments about other possible relationships between popular culture and world politics. We wish to open up analytical spaces, not close them down. We want to show that there are already at least these very diverse (ways of understanding the) ways in which these 'things' relate to one another. To paraphrase Robert Cox (1981, p. 128), these PCWP relationships matter to different audiences for diverse and sometimes competing reasons.

This article **(59)** __________ highlights diverse ways in which these relationships matter (to us) in order to highlight how they should matter to more people, especially scholars and practitioners of world politics, in which we include the general public (Rowley and Weldes 2012). In so doing, we deliberately raise more questions than we can possibly answer. In drawing attention to the **(60) sheer** breadth of what can be explored, we view this article as, in part, contributing to a very broad, but not definitive, PCWP research agenda.

51. In this context, "construed" is best replaced by

A. asserted　　B. constructed
C. interpreted　　D. missed

52. In this context, "myriad" is best replaced by

A. indefinable　　B. innumerable
C. multi-layered　　D. multinational

53. In this context, "flummoxed" is best replaced by

A. awed　　B. overwhelmed
C. perplexed　　D. stunned

54. From the context, the underlined blank could best be filled with

A. apprehension　　B. assumption
C. miscalculation　　D. undertaking

55. From the context, the underlined blank could best be filled with

A. contested　　B. esteemed
C. invalid　　D. flawed

56. From the context, "take a stab at" is closest in meaning to

A. attempt　　B. decipher
C. eliminate　　D. resolve

57. In this context, "underscore" is best replaced by

A. downplay　　B. highlight
C. reiterate　　D. underemphasize

58. **From the context, "caveat" is closest in meaning to**

A. clause
B. deterrent
C. mandate
D. proviso

59. **From the context, the underlined blank could best be filled with**

A. albeit
B. nonetheless
C. not only
D. thus

60. **In this context, "sheer" is best replaced by**

A. entire
B. frank
C. outright
D. severe

VII. Choose from among the four alternatives the one that best explains each of the underlined words or phrases in the context of the article below.

"I do not for a moment suggest that Japan should be unmindful of acquiring modern weapons of self-protection. But this should never be allowed to go beyond her instinct of self-preservation. She must know that the real power is not in the weapons themselves, but in the man who **(61) wields** those weapons; and when he, in his eagerness for power, multiplies his weapons at the cost of his own soul, then it is he who is in even greater danger than his enemies.

Things that are living are so easily hurt; therefore they require protection. In nature, life protects itself within its coverings, which are built with life's own material. Therefore they are in harmony with life's growth, or else when the time comes they easily **(62) give way** and are forgotten. The living man has his true protection in his spiritual ideals, which have their vital connection with his life and grow with his growth. But, unfortunately, all his armor is not living,—some of it is made of steel, inert and mechanical. Therefore, while making use of it, man has to be careful to protect himself from its tyranny. If he is weak enough to grow smaller to fit himself to his covering, then it becomes a process of gradual suicide by shrinkage of the soul. And Japan must have a firm faith in the moral law of existence to be able to assert to herself that the Western nations are following that path of suicide, where they are smothering their humanity under the immense weight of organizations in order to keep themselves in power and **(63) hold** others in subjection.

What is dangerous for Japan is, not the imitation of the outer features of the West, but the acceptance of the **(64) motive force** of the Western nationalism as her own. Her social ideals are already showing signs of defeat at the hands of politics. I can see her motto, taken from science, "Survival of the Fittest," writ large at the entrance of her present-day history—the motto whose meaning is, "Help yourself, and never **(65) heed** what it costs to others"; the motto of the blind man who only believes in what he can touch, because he cannot see. But those who can see know that men are so closely knit that when you **(66) strike** others the blow comes back to yourself. [···]

Never think for a moment that the hurts you inflict upon other races will not infect you, or that the **(67) enmities** you sow around your homes will be a wall of protection to you for all time to come. To **(68) imbue** the minds of a whole people with an abnormal vanity of its own superiority, to teach it to take pride in its moral callousness and ill-begotten wealth, to perpetuate humiliation of defeated nations by exhibiting trophies won from war, and using these in schools in order to breed in children's minds contempt for others, is imitating the West where she has a festering sore, whose swelling is a swelling of disease eating into its vitality.

Our food crops, which are necessary for our **(69) sustenance**, are products of centuries of selection and care. But the vegetation, which we have not to transform into our lives, does not require the patient thoughts of generations. It is not easy to get rid of weeds; but it is easy, by process of neglect, to ruin your food crops and let them **(70)** **revert to** their primitive state of wildness.

Likewise the culture, which has so kindly adapted itself to your soil—so intimate with life, so human—not only needed tilling and weeding in past ages, but still needs anxious work and watching. What is merely modern—as science and methods of organization—can be transplanted; but what is vitally human has fibers so delicate, and roots so numerous and far-reaching, that it dies when moved from its soil. Therefore I am afraid of the rude pressure of the political ideals of the West upon your own."

61. **wields**

A. brandishes　　B. concedes

C. eschews　　D. shares

62. **give way**

A. become dominant　　B. gain weight

C. lose importance　　D. take precedence

63. **hold**

A. imprison　　B. liberate

C. release　　D. emancipate

64. **motive force**

A. negation　　B. rationale

C. rejection　　D. skepticism

65. **heed**

A. overlook　　B. neglect

C. forget　　D. care

66. **strike**

A. assault　　B. discover

C. elevate　　D. surprise

67. **enmities**

A. amenities　　B. amities

C. harmonies　　D. hostilities

68. **imbue**

A. deprive
B. empty
C. enlighten
D. fill

69. **sustenance**

A. deprivation
B. nourishment
C. profusion
D. scarcity

70. **revert to**

A. depart from
B. never revisit
C. return to
D. stay at

Ⅷ. Fill in each of the following blanks with the most appropriate of the four alternatives as required by the context.

Russia's state-controlled gas provider, Gazprom, has announced that it is cutting down to 20 percent of capacity the amount of natural gas it delivers to Germany through the main pipeline connecting both countries. Whatever pretext Moscow might offer for the move, the real reason is clear to all: Russia is retaliating for E.U. sanctions **(71)** _________ because of its war against Ukraine. "Russia is blackmailing us," European Commission President Ursula von der Leyen complained. "Russia is using energy as a weapon."

Von der Leyen made her announcement **(72)** _________ it were news. But it's not—not to anyone who's been paying attention over the past two decades. Using energy as a political weapon is hardly a novel tactic for Russian President Vladimir Putin. That Europe faces an energy crisis because of Russian energy blackmail, then, is just as predictable as Russia's atrocious conduct in its war on Ukraine.

It did not have to be this way. Led by the continent's biggest and richest power, Germany, Europe had plenty of time to avoid the unenviable **(73)** _________ in which it now finds itself. The European energy dilemma is the result of three interrelated illusions: that dependence on Russian gas was worth whatever (minor) risks it entailed, that the supplier of that gas was a partner rather than an adversary, and that conventional war on the continent was a thing of the past.

For years, German politicians routinely **(74)** _________ criticism of Nord Stream by stating that their hands were tied. The pipeline was a "commercial project," they insisted, over which the German government exercised no control. But increasing European dependence on Russian gas **(75)** _________ other sources has always entailed a political dimension, especially in Germany. No one forced Berlin to shutter its nuclear energy sector in a fit of characteristically German panic in the aftermath of the 2011 Fukushima disaster. Unlike the island nation of Japan, Germany sits in the middle of a continent, safe from the earthquake-induced tsunamis of the sort that destroyed the Fukushima plant. **(76)** _________ then-Chancellor Angela Merkel's hasty decision to phase out nuclear energy by the end of 2022, by the time Putin decided to wage energy war against Europe, Germany was even more addicted to Russian gas.

Belying their excuse that Nord Stream 2 exists beyond the reach of politics, the German political establishment fell under the spell of another illusion, which was that the project represented the apotheosis of Russia's integration with the West. A mere week after Russia annexed the Crimean Peninsula in 2014, the chief executive of German industrial giant Siemens visited Moscow, where he spoke of the first armed seizure of territory on European soil since World War II as mere "short-term turbulence" in an otherwise constructive relationship. A few months later, then-foreign minister Frank-Walter Steinmeier traveled to Yekaterinburg, Russia, to endorse an "economic-political" partnership between Moscow and the European Union.

Plans for a second Nord Stream pipeline **(77)** ________ despite the threat of sanctions from the Trump administration. Last February, nearly 80 years after his country's invasion of the Soviet Union, Steinmeier (now Germany's president) defended Nord Stream 2 as "one of the last bridges between Russia and Europe," **(78)** ________ the enterprise with the moral gravity Germany usually reserves for initiatives related to postwar reconciliation. Only after Russia's invasion of Ukraine was the pipeline put on hold.

Europe would not be facing an energy crisis today had more of its leaders seen through the third and final illusion, that of a continent blessed with perpetual peace. Putin's belief that he could subjugate Ukraine—the precipitating cause of the imminent energy crisis—owes a great deal to Western Europe's lackluster military support for its embattled neighbor as well as its own anemic defense **(79)** ________. NATO's refusal, at the behest of France and Germany, to provide Georgia and Ukraine with pathways to membership in 2008 sent Putin a greenlight to invade both countries. The decrepit state of European militaries, Germany's in particular, similarly signaled a lack of seriousness about defending the continent from Russian predation.

Western European leaders were warned repeatedly as to the nature of their illusions, no more forcefully than by Eastern Europeans. As early as 2006, Poland's defense minister compared Nord Stream to the 1939 Molotov-Ribbentrop Pact, which infamously divided the nations of Eastern Europe between Nazi Germany and the Soviet Union. Three years later, in response to the Obama administration's **(80)** ________ "reset" with Moscow, a group of distinguished Central and Eastern European statesmen issued an open letter, declaring that "Russia is back as a revisionist power pursuing a 19th-century agenda with 21st-century tactics and methods." Their admonitions went unheeded.

If Germans find themselves shivering more than usual this winter, they have no one to blame but themselves.

71. A. annulled B. levied
C. lifted D. imperiled

72. A. while B. as if
C. since D. that

73. A. rout B. renunciation
C. predicament D. tussle

74. A. addressed B. divulged
C. merited D. deflected

75. A. at the expense of B. in light of

	C. in arrears with	D. according to
76.	A. Despite	B. Amid
	C. Thanks to	D. Until
77.	A. necessitated	B. proceeded
	C. aborted	D. stalled
78.	A. imbuing	B. undertaking
	C. forgoing	D. subsidizing
79.	A. blueprint	B. lesion
	C. curtailment	D. outlays
80.	A. auspicious	B. equitable
	C. ill-fated	D. nefarious

Ⅸ. Write a short essay in English of 150-200 words as your answer to the following.

Discuss one UN initiative and an example of action on this initiative that gives us reason for hope in the world.

マークシート記入例

東京の本会場でA級を受験する、国連 太郎さん、受験番号が「東京01-20001」、生年月日が「1980年10月24日」の場合の記入例です。

【受験番号/氏名】
それぞれ受験票の記載通りに記入してください。

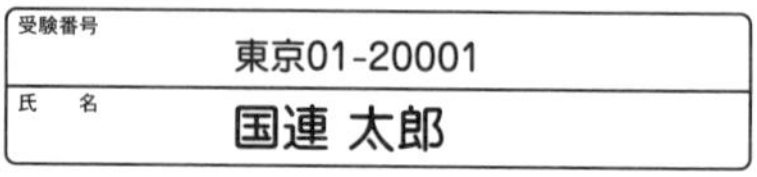

【受験地区】
下段の都道府県部分を塗りつぶしてください。

【会場番号】
都道府県部分に続く２桁の数字を塗りつぶしてください。

【受験番号】
ハイフン（−）以降の５桁の数字を塗りつぶしてください。

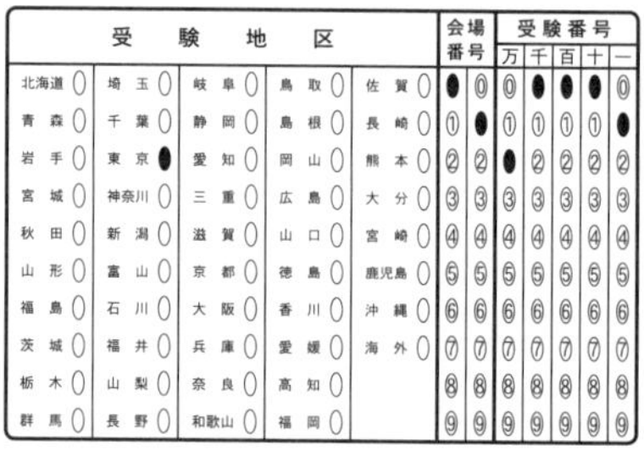

【受験級】
「A」と記入し、下段のA級部分を塗りつぶしてください。

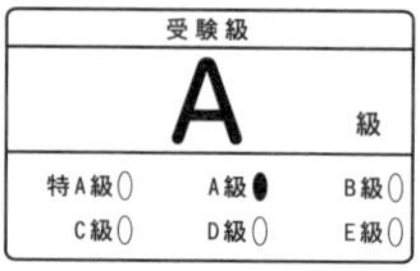

【生年月日】
４桁の西暦・月・日を塗りつぶしてください。
10未満の月・日の十の位は、「０」を塗りつぶしてください。

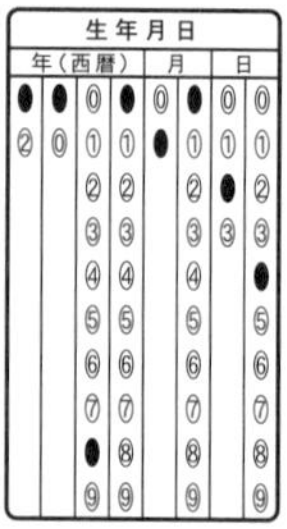

※HB以上の鉛筆を用いてマークをしてください。

※他の地区から会場を変更して受験する場合でも、受験票に記載されている受験地区・会場番号をマークしてください。

2022年

第2回試験

解答・解説

UNA-JAPAN

2022年　国連英検A級第2回試験
解答・解説

＊〔　〕内は訳出上の補足や説明

I　『新 わかりやすい国連の活動と世界』に基づき，
空所を埋めるのに最も適切なものを4つの選択肢の中から1つ選びなさい。

1.　解答：A

訳例　21世紀の国連の役割に関するこのようなビジョンから，未来に向けての最も重要な課題が3つ生まれます。貧困の根絶，紛争の防止，そして民主主義の促進です（『新 わかりやすい国連の活動と世界』p.12。以下，書名略）。

2.　解答：B

訳例　第3に，未解決の紛争や，国際人道法の組織的違反の問題が挙げられます。ミャンマーのラカイン州で宗派間の緊張が劇的に悪化したことについては，私たち全員がショックを覚えました（同 p.25）。

3.　解答：D

訳例　創設時のメンバーは，第1次世界大戦の戦勝国（ヴェルサイユ条約を批准しなかったアメリカ合衆国を除く）と他の中立国であった（同 p.42）。

4.　解答：C

訳例　国連の公式の印章および標章は北極の上から見た世界地図で，輪状になったオリーブの枝で囲まれている（同 p.45）。

5.　解答：D

訳例　安全保障理事国は，それぞれ1票の投票権を持つ。手続き事項の決定には，15理事国のうち少なくとも9理事国の賛成を必要とする（p.55）。

6.　解答：B

訳例　約4万人の男女国際職員から成る事務局は，ニューヨークの国連本部および世界各地の事務所やセンターで，国連の日常業務を行っている（同 p.61）。

7. 解答：B

訳例　通常予算の主な財源は，各加盟国の分担金であり，それは18人から成る分担金委員会の勧告に基づき総会が定めた分担率に従って割り当てられる（同 p.62)。

8. 解答：C

訳例　国際原子力機関（IAEA）の憲章が 1956 年 10 月 26 日，国連本部で開かれた国際会議で承認され，機関は 1957 年 7 月 29 日にウィーンで発足した（同 p.76)。

9. 解答：D

訳例　世界保健機関（WHO）は，国連加盟国 26 カ国が同機関の憲章を批准した 1948 年 4 月 7 日に発足した（同 p.79)。

10. 解答：A

訳例　1978 年に任命された赤谷源一事務次長（広報担当）を皮切りに，日本人候補者が恒例的に複数ある国連事務次長職の 1 つに登用されてきた（同 p.165)。

II

下線を引いた動詞の最も適切な変化形を 4 つの選択肢の中から 1 つ選びなさい。

11. 解答：B

解説　with the G-7 reneging ... 以下は，付帯状況を表す with＋A（目的語）＋現在分詞：-ing（A が〜している状況で）の形式になっており，reneging と並列関係になるように and deciding とすると意味が通る。

12. 解答：B

解説　後に続く語句から，この value は動詞であり，a relief for many が「多く（の人）にとっての救い」であると考えれば，主格の関係代名詞 who でつなぐのが適当である。

13. 解答：B

解説　「この先数十年（にわたり）」という意味になるには，未来を含意する不定詞 to come（来たるべき）が最もふさわしい。同様の用法で for years/weeks/days to come などのコロケーションは頻繁に見られる。

14. 解答：D

解説 wrap one's mind around は「理解する」という意味で，to wrap ... とすれば，for people を意味上の主語とした不定詞として「人々が理解するには（難しい道徳問題)」という意味を成す。

15. 解答：A

解説 the example of ... に続く語句として，someone stealing ... と versus を挟んで並列していると考えれば，同様に現在分詞の後置修飾の形で，one group of unacquainted people taking ... とすると意味が通る。

16. 解答：A

解説 persuade＋A（目的語）＋to ...（不定詞）（A を説得して～させる）の形にすると意味が通る。

17. 解答：D

解説 主語 everyone は単数扱いの代名詞であり，続く述語動詞は 3 人称単数現在形になる。

18. 解答：C

解説 liken A to B（A を B になぞらえる」の B の部分を名詞句にするには a group of people shooting ...（～を打っている人々）とするのが最もふさわしい。

19. 解答：C

解説 (be) incredibly vulnerable to devastating flooding の部分は先行する Bangladesh の追加説明になっており，関係代名詞の継続用法として ...Bangladesh, which is ～ のようにするのが適当である。

20. 解答：B

解説 affect 以下の部分は，先行する issues を修飾して「世界中の，複数世代の人々に影響を及ぼす（問題)」となると考えれば意味が通るため，that を用いて関係節にする。

訳例　気候変動対策を行う道徳的責務というものが，意味を成していないようだ。欧州では今夏，我々が必要としている野心的な気候変動対策への希望が削がれてしまった。G7が化石燃料事業への資金提供を停止するという以前の約束を破り，6月末には海外での天然ガス開発の継続を決定する一方，EUは7月初旬，〔EUタクソノミーにおいて〕天然ガス事業を持続可能投資に分類する提案を可決した。また，ジョー・マンチン上院議員（民主党，ウェストバージニア州選出）との間で成立した気候対策に関する突然の合意は，地球の将来を大切に考える多くの人にとっては救いであったが，合意に至る紆《う》余《よ》曲《きょく》折《せつ》は，先週の交渉決裂と思われた事態も含め，排出削減〔という課題〕が，関係する多くの政治家の最大の関心事では決してないことを示した。

欧州や米国の政治家たちは，短期的な利益のために大きな妥協をした（たとえば，即時の排出量削減よりエネルギー安全保障やインフレ懸念を優先するなど）が，そうした妥協は今後数十年にわたってマイナスの影響を及ぼすだろう。大気中の温室効果ガスが増えれば，最終的には世界中の人々，特に最も貧しく弱い国々の人々に対する気候による影響がより悲惨なものになる〔からだ〕。しかし，遅れが出るたびに，自分たちや子孫が将来被ることになる事態を悪化させているのに，我々は，必要とされる最も厳しい措置をいまも先送りしているのが現状だ。

急成長している気候倫理の分野では，どのような事態が進んでいるかに関して2つの異なる説明がなされている。その1つは，困難さの一部として，気候変動が人にとって理解しづらい道徳問題であること〔を指摘する〕。ニューヨーク大学のデール・ジェイミーソン教授（環境学・哲学）は例として，2つの〔ケースの比較〕を提示する。すなわち，現時点で何者かが自転車を盗む〔場合〕（これについては大半の人が悪いことだと言うだろう）と，ある面識のない人の集団が一連の行動を起こした結果，何年も経ってから世界のどこかで他の人々が自転車を持てなくなるという〔場合〕（このシナリオでは時間と空間の両方の意味で，加害者と加害の結果が切り離されている）である。同教授は言う，「誰かが被害を受け，他の人が利益を得るという，まったく同じ結果が生み出されうるのに，我々の道徳感情を本当に揺さぶる論理がない。人間はこのような種類の問題に対応できるように進化してこなかった〔からだ〕」。つまり，何が正しくて何が間違っているか〔という考え〕だけに基づいて気候変動に対して行動するよう人を説得しようとしても，あまりうまくいかないということになる，と同教授は言う。むしろ，怒りの感情を捨てて，現実的な側面を重視した方がよい。つまり，排出量の削減につながるルールや経済的インセンティブをどう作るか〔という課題に着目するということだ〕。

しかし，すべての人の意見が一致するわけではない。米ワシントン大学のステファン・ガーディナー教授（哲学・環境学）によると，人間の道徳的直観は，気候変動という抽象的で巨大な課題をうまく把握できるという。人類が化石燃料を燃やし続けることの喩えとして教授が自転車の例に代えて持ち出すのは，街の貧しい地区に集まって，人家が火事になる危険があると知りながら花火を打ち上げて遊んでいる友人どうしのグループである。この例では，我々の多くにとって道徳的次元がかなり明らかとなる。それは，豊かな国々が大気中に排出ガスを放出し，それがバングラデシュのような，破壊的な洪水に対して非常に脆弱《ぜいじゃく》な世界の貧しい地域の人々に対して過度に大きな影響を与える問題の場合と同様である。

この問題は煎じ詰めれば，我々の制度が世界中の人々や複数の世代に影響を及ぼす問題に適切に対処できない可能性があるという事実に行き当たる，と同教授は言う。それは道徳的な問題でもある。同教授は次のように話している。「政府で未解決なら誰の問題でもない，と考える傾向が強すぎる。しかし，我々には市民として，力を合わせてよりよい制度を作り上げる責任があると思う」。

III

空所を埋めるのに文法的・論理的に最もふさわしいものを
４つの選択肢の中から１つ選びなさい。

21.　解答：B

解説　後に続く attended by dozens of people が修飾する語句として the solemn event がまとまり，それに場所を表す修飾語句として at Hiroshima Peace Memorial Park が付き，前置詞 during「その event の最中に」と全体をまとめている。

22.　解答：C

解説　まず pick up speed（スピードを上げる）のコロケーションが来て，次に新たな文「世界の指導者たちは…備蓄を強化している」の文が続く。最後の部分は at a cost of ...（…を費やして）が成り立つ。

23.　解答：D

解説　全体の文構造が，下線部の上行から call on＋A＋ to ...（不定詞）（A に～するように求める）になっており，to work ..., to strengthen に続いて，to support ... の形になる。by eliminating ...（…を除去することによって）のまとまりも文意に沿っている。

24.　解答：C

解説　keep ... in view（…を心に留めておく），at all times（つねに）の慣用

句を考え合わせるとこの語順になる。

25. 解答：D

解説 two atomic bombs を主語とした受動態の文になる。最後の部分は直後の Japan につながる形として over the skies of (Japan) がふさわしい。

26. 解答：A

解説 先行する sent a message to に続くものとしてまず young people が来る。それを urge＋A＋to ...（不定詞）（A に〜するよう促す）が現在分詞になって修飾する。最後に後に続く hibakusha に付く the が来る。

27. 解答：B

解説 先行する部分を含め全体として，tell＋A＋that ...（A に…ということを告げる）の文構造になる。moral authority（道徳的権威）には不定詞句 to tell leaders ...（指導者たちに…を教えるための）が続く。

28. 解答：C

解説 先行する expressed の目的語として their desire が続き，その同格として that 節がつながる。最後は後に続く語句とともに the crude reality（ありのままの現実）となる。

29. 解答：C

解説 まず on behalf of ...（〜を代表して）がまとまるが，全体として先行する apologize を含め apologize for ...（〜について謝罪する）の形になる。

30. 解答：A

解説 先行する who ... are には meeting がつながり現在進行形にするのが適当である。最後は後に続く語句とともに the spread of nuclear weapon（核兵器の拡散）となり意味が通る。

訳例　核兵器を保有する国が核戦争の可能性を認めることは，まったく容認できない──訪日中のアントニオ・グテーレス〔国連事務総長〕は土曜朝，広島への原爆投下77周年を記念する式典で，そう強調した。

「核兵器は愚かなものです。4分の3世紀を経たいま，私たちは1945年にこの街の上空に立ち上ったキノコ雲から何を学んだかを問わねばなりません」。事務総長は，被爆者や若い平和活動家，日本の首相，自治体関係者ら数十人が参列し，広島平和記念公園で行われた厳粛な式典で訴えた。

事務総長はまた，新たな軍拡競争が加速しており，世界の指導者たちが数千億ドルをかけて，世界中の兵器庫に現在貯蔵されている核兵器約1万3,000発の備蓄を強化しているとして，警鐘を鳴らした。同氏は「中東から朝鮮半島，ロシアのウクライナ侵攻に至るまで，核〔使用の可能性〕が仄《ほの》めかされる重大な危機が急速に広がっています〔……中略……〕人類は実弾が込められた銃で遊んでいるのです」と警告を発した。

グテーレス氏は，ニューヨークで現在開催中の核兵器不拡散条約運用検討会議を「希望の光」と呼んだ。

同氏は次のように力強く述べた。「本日，この神聖な場所から，私はこの条約の締約国に対し，私たちの未来を脅かす〔核兵器〕備蓄の廃絶に緊急に取り組み，対話，外交，交渉を強化するとともに，これらの破壊兵器の廃絶によって私の軍縮提案を支持するよう呼びかけます。

同氏はまた，核兵器保有国は核兵器の「先制不使用」を約束し，他の国に対して核兵器を使用したり，使用の脅しをかけたりしないと保証する必要がある，と強調した。「我々は広島〔原爆〕の恐ろしさを常に心に留め，核の脅威に対する解決策はただ1つ，核兵器を持たないことだと認識しなければなりません」(同)。

グテーレス事務総長は，指導者は責任を逃れることはできないと強調するとともに，次のように述べた。「核兵器という選択肢を取り下げてください——永遠に。いまこそ，平和を広める時です。被爆者のメッセージを聞き入れてください：『もう二度と，広島の悲劇を引き起こさないでください。もう二度と，長崎の惨禍を繰り返さないでください』」。1945年，日本の上空——8月6日に広島，3日後の8月9日に長崎——で2つの原子爆弾が炸裂したことを銘記して〔の発言だ〕。

また，グテーレス氏は若者に対して，被爆者が始めた仕事をやり遂げるよう呼びかけるメッセージを送った。〔そして次のように〕締めくくった。「世界はこの地〔広島で〕起こったことを決して忘れてはなりません。犠牲者の皆様の記憶，そして生き残った方々が残してくださった遺産は決して消滅することはありません」。

事務総長は同日式典後，広島と長崎の被爆者5人と面会し，話を聞いた。事務総長は，被爆者が大いに苦しみながらも「多大な勇気と回復力」をもってトラウマを克服してきたことを知り，敬服の意を表した。グテーレス氏はまた，再会したこの女性3人と男性2人を世界の模範と呼び，「皆様には指導者たちに『核兵器は愚かなものだ』と教える道徳的権威があります」と声をかけた。「国連は，〔原爆の惨禍〕の記憶を受け継ぎ，皆様の物語が永遠に広く伝えられるよう取り組みます」(同)。

5人の被爆者は国連事務総長に対し，平和と軍縮の問題に生涯の大半を費やして関わり続けてきたと語った。1人は〔一般の人の〕意識を高めるために歌を作り，別の1人は自分の体験を絵に描いた〔という〕。5人は口をそろえて，若い人たちにも核兵器のありのままの現実を理解してほしいと述べた。

グテーレス氏は，核軍縮や核不拡散といった地球規模の課題に関する取り組みをいま引っ張っている日本の若手活動家たちとの非公式な対話集会にも参加した。「私は自分の世代を代表して，私たちが皆さんの世代に残すことになる世界の現状についてお詫びしたいと思います」と述べた。かつて世界の若者に対して行った謝罪を繰り返したものだ。「私たちの各世代が協力する必要があります〔……中略……〕そのあとで皆さんがその責任を負うことになるのですから，準備万端，万全の態勢で臨んでいただきたいのです」。同氏は若い参加者にそう呼びかけた。

事務総長はまた，広島市長および長崎副市長と会談し，広島市〔特別〕名誉市民の称号を授与された。同氏は次のように述べた。「私は，世界中で平和のために働いている国連のすべての職員を代表して，この偉大な称号を授かりたいと思います。ちょうど今週，核兵器拡散阻止のためにニューヨークに集まっている外交官や交渉官を代表してお受けします」。

Ⅳ 以下の文章に最も適切に当てはまる語句のペアを4つの選択肢の中から1つ選びなさい。

31. 解答：C

解説 Cは，「マリでの『大虐殺』の規模」，「(イスラム教主義者に関連する暴力の中心地帯が) ～から (遠く離れたところに)『変わった』」となり意味が通る。A，Bについては，第1空所は可だが，第2空所については，Aのtake awayには目的語が必要，Bのput wayには「出航する」(自動詞) の用法があるが意味的に合わないため不適。Dのobliteration (抹消) は文意に合わない。

訳例 9年ぶりにフランス軍が撤退するマリで〔発生している〕殺戮《さつりく》の規模〔の大きさ〕は，イスラム教主義者に関連する暴力の中心地帯が移動して中東や南アジアを離れたことを示している。

32. 解答：D

解説 Dは，「『包囲された』ウクライナの都市マリウポリ」，「絶え間ない砲撃」

と並んで,「『減少する』食料と水の供給」という意味を成し，文意に合う。A, B については，第 1 空所候補の beset（包囲された), pounded (猛撃されている）は可だが，第 2 空所候補の surging（大きく増加する), enduring（永久的な）がどちらも不適である。C は，第 2 空所候補 ebbing（衰退する）は可だが，第 1 空所候補の grumpy は「(人が）気難しい」などの意味であるため不適。

訳例　ウクライナのマリウポリで同市を包囲するロシア軍に抵抗を続ける民兵部隊の司令官は，砲撃は絶え間なく，食料と水の供給は減ってきているものの，兵士たちは最後まで戦うだろうと述べた。

33. 解答：B

解説　B は,「(2 週間後に発効する)『禁止令』」,「～に届く，及ぶ」となり意味が通る。A, D については，第 1 空所候補 statute（成文法), decree（法令）は可だが，第 2 空所候補 get by（～を通過する）は意味的に不適，through は「get＋人＋through（困難などを乗り切らせる)」の形ではないので当てはまらない。C については，第 1 空所候補の acquiescence (黙認，承諾) が take effect に呼応せず，第 2 空補候補が作る get around は「～を避けて通る」となり不適。

訳例　〔カナダの拳銃輸入〕禁止措置は 2 週間後に実施予定で，カナダ政府は議会の法案可決を待たずに輸入を止めることが可能となる。ただ，それでは米国からの密輸銃器という本来の問題には手がつけられないという批判の声もある。

34. 解答：D

解説　D は「事実上の」,「～を固守する」となり意味が通る。A, C については，第 1 空所候補 interim（暫定的な), provincial（州・省の）は現在のタリバン政権の状況の事実に反し，第 2 空所候補 eschew (〈基本的人権を〉避ける), heed（心に留める）は不適（後者は文意からすると意味が弱い)。B. scrupulous（節操のある), forfeit（～を犠牲にする）はともに文意に合わない。

訳例　国際社会はアフガニスタンの事実上の政権に対して，基本的な人権原則を順守するよう促す取り組みを大幅に強化する必要がある――国連の独立人権専門家グループが金曜日，述べた。

35. 解答：A

解説 Aは「～を築く」,「～に直面して」となり意味が通る。Bは「西側の制裁の『裁量により』イランとの緊密な関係を『断つ』」となるため全体の文意に合わない。Cについては，第2空所候補 on the verge of（～の寸前で）は可だが，sap（～を弱める）は不適。Dについては，第1空所候補 buttress（～を強化する）は可だが，under the pretext of（～を口実に）は文意に合わない。

訳例 プーチン氏の〔イラン〕訪問は，バイデン氏がイスラエルとサウジアラビアを訪問した数日後に行われ，西側の制裁に対してイラン政府との関係をより緊密にしようとするロシア政府の意向を示唆するものとなった。

36. 解答：C

解説 Cは「封鎖」,「悲惨な」となり意味が通る。Aについては，fortification（要塞化）は事実に反し implausible（信じがたい）は「主張・意見」などについて使われるため不適。Bの第2空所候補 calamitous（悲惨な）は可だが，第1空所候補 vindication（弁護）は合わない。Dの第1空所候補 beleaguerment（包囲）は事実に反し，第2空所候補 ignominious（恥ずべき）は意味的に不適。

訳例 ロシア軍の黒海封鎖により，ウクライナは小麦と大豆の輸出ができなくなった。そのため余剰穀物の国内価格が急落し，ウクライナの農家は悲惨な状況に陥っている。

37. 解答：C

解説 Cは「自治の（島国)」,「(軍事）演習」となり意味が通る。A, B, Dの第2空所候補 alliance（同盟），amalgamation（併合），reinforcement（強化）はいずれも事実に反し，第1空所候補 sovereign（独立した），non-aligned（中立の），hapless（不運な：通常人の形容に使われる）がいずれも「中国の主張（claimed by China)」としては適当でない。

訳例 ナンシー・ペロシ米下院議長は火曜夜，台湾に到着，中国が〔領土と〕主張する〔中で〕自治を続けるこの島国を過去25年間で訪問した最高位の米高官となった。中国はただちにペロシ氏の訪台に対する報復として軍事演習の実施を発表した。

38. 解答：A

解説 Aはravage(d)（破壊する）がflood-ravaged「洪水に見舞われた」を，putがput ... at ...「〜を〜と見積もる」を作り，意味が通る。B，Cについては，第2空所候補reckon（計算する），approximate（概算する）は可だが，第1空所候補inebriated（酒に酔った，高揚した）は不適で，nagged（心配事にいつも悩まされた）は文意に合わない。Dについては，第1空所候補devastating（壊滅的な）がfloodとの組み合わせでは文意に合う複合形容詞を作れない，第2空所候補のrecoup(ed)（取り戻す）が文意に合わないことから不適。

訳例 アントニオ・グテーレス国連事務総長は金曜日，洪水に見舞われたパキスタンを訪問し，「大規模な」国際支援を呼びかけた。なお，パキスタン政府は洪水関連の被害額を300億ドルと推定している。

39. 解答：B

解説 Bは「〜を〜に（on ...）課す」，「有名な〜」となり意味が通る。A，C，Dの第2空所候補adept（熟練した），pertinent（関連する），hallowed（神格化された）はいずれも事実に反し，第1空所候補ameliorated（改良した），defied（抵抗した），rebuked（強く非難した）がいずれもRussiaがアメリカ副大統領らへのtravel banに対して行うこととしてふさわしくない。

訳例 ロシアは木曜日，ウクライナをめぐる制裁に対する報復として，カマラ・ハリス米副大統領やマーク・ザッカーバーグ米フェイスブックCEOら，米国とカナダの著名人数十人を入国禁止とした。

40. 解答：D

解説 Dは，「独裁的な」，「恐ろしい」となり意味が通る。A，Bの第1空所候補draconian（厳格な），despotic（専制的な）はいずれも可だが，第2空所候補buoyant（楽天的な），unequivocal（明白な）がそれぞれ不適。Cはbenign（慈悲深い），wrenched（ねじれた）がいずれも文意に合わない。

訳例 ニカラグアの数百の市民社会団体が独裁的に閉鎖されたことは，深刻な懸念をもたらすもので，国内各地の活動家や人権擁護者に萎縮効果をもたらすだろう。国連に任命された独立人権専門家らが金曜日，述べた。

V 文法的，語法的にふさわしくないものを下線の中から1つ選びなさい。

41. 解答：C

解説 are → is。a combination（単数）に呼応するbe動詞なのでareではなくisになる。

訳例 ロンドンはこの夏非常に暑く，新聞には同市の気温が灼熱のドバイを上回ったという見出しが躍った。しかし専門家によれば，都市の住みやすさを示す指標としては気温だけでは不十分で，気温と湿度の組み合わせが〔重要なのだという〕。このことから，気候危機が進行すると，同じ気温でも中東は欧州に比べてはるかに住みにくくなると考えられる。

42. 解答：D

解説 lack → lack of。hisがついていることからこのlackは名詞で，名詞のtransparencyと連続して使えないため，ここではofを加えた，(a) lack of ～（～の欠乏）の熟語を適用する。

訳例 〔メキシコで〕2014年に学生ら43人が失踪した事件で，金曜日，元検事総長が逮捕された。検察庁は声明を発表し，元検事総長を「強制失踪罪，拷問罪，司法行政に反する犯罪」の容疑者と考えると述べた。この事件は国際的に激しい憤りを買い，当時のエンリケ・ペニャ・ニエト大統領はこの問題の調査で透明性を欠いているとして批判された。

43. 解答：A

解説 reliant → reliance。its heavyの後はそれが修飾する名詞（～への依存）になる。

訳例 米国が化石燃料への大きな依存から脱却し，よりクリーンなエネルギー源へシフトする中，多くの専門家が注目している有望な解決策がある。大手小売店の屋上や駐車場のスペース〔だ。〕広さがある上，多くが空いていることから，太陽光発電に利用できる未開発資源としてもてはやされている。太陽光発電は，米国が外国産エネルギーへの依存を減らして地球温暖化の原因となる排出物を削減し，その中で企業に対して何百万ドルもの節約を実現する上で役立ちうる〔からだ〕。

44. 解答：B

解説 disparaged at → disparaged。disparage（～をけなす）は他動詞なので，直後に目的語が来る。

訳例　北朝鮮は，非核化と引き換えに経済支援を行うとする韓国の提案を拒否した。北朝鮮のある高官は，尹大統領の提案を「現実離れした〔愚かさの極み〕」とこき下ろした。北朝鮮の核開発計画の中止と引き換えに経済協力を行うという「大胆な計画」は，尹氏が5月の就任演説で初めて提案したもの。

45. 解答：B

解説　alternative → an alternative。alternative は可算名詞なので，前に不定冠詞が必要である。

訳例　日本の観光名所，奈良の地元企業家が，街中〔に生息する〕神〔の使いとされる〕鹿を守ろうと，プラスチック製レジ袋の代替品を開発した。土産物の卸売業を手掛ける「ならイズム」の松川英朗氏は〔取材に応じ〕，昨年，奈良公園を歩き回る鹿がプラスチックの袋を食べて死ぬケースが発生しているという話を聞いたと話す。奈良市には神鹿が約1,000頭生息しており，国の天然記念物にも指定されている。

46. 解答：A

解説　for → to。「～を…の刑に処する」は sentence ～ to ... である。

訳例　サウジアラビアの女性権利運動家サルマ・アルシェハブ氏が月曜日，ツイッターでの活動を理由に34年の禁錮刑を言い渡された。〔同氏は〕英リーズ大学の博士課程の学生で，2021年1月に逮捕され，265日間にわたって尋問を受けていた。当初は6年の判決を受けたが，控訴審で34年に増刑された。

47. 解答：B

解説　halting → halt。「主語＋動詞」の形で列挙している部分で，strikes 以下もその形になるのが適当である。

訳例　英国が悲惨な夏に耐えている。国民に好評の医療サービスが危機に陥った上，インフレの高騰，水道の枯渇〔使用制限〕，ストライキによる鉄道の運行停止などが発生する一方，政府の姿はどこにも見えない。崩壊の予感は増すばかりだ。金曜日には医療の指導者らが，冬の間のエネルギー価格の上昇を食い止める対策を講じなければ「人道危機」に陥るとして厳しい警告を発した。

48. 解答：D

解説　slowed → slowing。文意から主語 economic growth の動詞部分は and 以降と同様に「is＋現在分詞（現在進行形）」の形になる。

訳例　気候変動が世界経済に及ぼす壊滅的な打撃の大きさについては，予測困難であることが歴史的に分かってきた。ただこの夏は，代償がいかに速いペースで積み重なりうるのかが，ますます明らかになりつつある。異常な高温と干ばつが米国，欧州，中国を襲いつつある中，経済成長がすでに急減速を始め，物価上昇の圧力を強めているだけに，労働者と企業双方にとって事態は悪化の一途をたどっている。

49. 解答：C

解説 Almost → Almost all。almost（ほとんど～）は副詞で，単独で名詞化（× ほとんどのもの）されない。

訳例　世界的にトラック運転手が不足しているが，事態はコロナ禍に伴う電子商取引の急成長によって悪化している。問題の解決策の 1 つとして自律運転トラックがあり，企業数社が発売一番手となるべく競争を繰り広げている。1 社が最近実施した路上走行試験では，米アリゾナ州ノガレスから〔同オクラホマ州〕オクラホマシティーまでの 951 マイル（約 1,530km）を走行し，生鮮食品を運んだ。輸送作業はほぼすべて自律的に行われ，積み下ろしだけ人間の運転手が担当した。

50. 解答：C

解説 connecting → connects。The 923-meter long bridge 以下の部分が文として成り立つために，connecting を述語動詞にする必要がある。

訳例　アフリカ大陸全域で，各国経済の活性化と貿易機会の拡大に向けて，革新的な交通システムや通信事業，スマートシティーの開発が進められている。その一例となるのが，カズングラ橋だ。全長 923m。ザンベジ川に架かり，ボツワナとザンビアを結ぶ。2021 年 5 月に開通し，フェリーの代替となったもので，南北の貿易の大動脈〔を行き交う〕トラック輸送の高速化のため建設された。

VI

以下の文章の中に含まれる太字の語句および空所の意味として文脈上最も近いものを 4 つの選択肢の中から 1 つ選びなさい。

51. 解答：C

解説 construe(d) は「解釈する」の意味で，C.「解釈する」に最も近い。A は「断言する」，B は「構成する」，D は「し損なう」の意味。

52. 解答：B

解説 myriad は「無数の」の意味で，B.「数えきれない」に最も近い。A は「言葉に表せない」，C は「重層的な」，D は「多国籍の」の意味。

53. 解答：C

解説 flummoxedは「困惑して」の意味で，C.「当惑して」に最も近い。Aは「恐れて」，Bは「圧倒されて」，Dは「あぜんとして」の意味。

54. 解答：B

解説 A.「懸念」，B.「仮定」，C.「見込み違い」，D.「請け負い仕事」の中で，同格になるthat節（～がある／あるはずだ）に合うのはBである。

55. 解答：A

解説 A.「争われる／争点となる」，B.「尊重される」，C.「説得力のない」，D.「欠点のある」の中で，同じ文の中で述べられているcomplex, no singular understandingと矛盾しない主張を表すのはAである。

56. 解答：A

解説 take a stab atは「～をやってみる」の意味で，A.「～を試みる」に最も近い。Bは「～を解読する」，Cは「～を除く」，Dは「～を決心する」の意味。

57. 解答：B

解説 underscoreは「～を強調する」の意味で，B.「～を強調する」に最も近い。Aは「～を控えめに扱う」，Cは「～を繰り返して言う」，Dは「～を十分に強調しない」の意味。

58. 解答：D

解説 caveatは「但し書き」の意味で，D.「但し書き」に最も近い。Aは「条項」，Bは「抑止力」，Cは「選挙民から与えられる権限，命令」の意味。

59. 解答：D

解説 A.「～にもかかわらず」，B.「それにもかかわらず」，C.「～だけでなく」，D.「したがって」の中で，語順に影響しないこと，意味的にまとめの文であることを考え合わせると，Dになる。

60. 解答：A

解説 sheerは「(後の名詞を強調して) 全部の，莫大な」などの意味で，A.「全体」に最も近い。Bは「率直な」，Cは「完全な，あからさまの」，Dは「厳しい」の意味。

訳例　15年前は，国際関係論（IR）が学問として大衆文化を無視していると主張する必要があった（Weldes 1999）。幸いにも，それはもはや事実ではない。いわゆる「主流派IR」（ただし，かなり狭く解釈したもの。また，大半が北米の流派）の一部は相も変わらず，大衆文化を「低俗な」政治，国内政治，あるいはまったく政治とは無関係と見て，IRが学問的に注目するには値しないと明に暗に主張しているけれども，〔今では〕観点や学問分野がさまざまに異なる研究者が無数の形態の大衆文化を取り上げ，IRや世界政治の考えうるあらゆる側面との関連において熱心に，そして生産的に研究するようになった。いまや「大衆文化と世界政治」（PCWP）という下位（学際）分野が存在する，とも言えるかもしれない。

「大衆文化と世界政治」と銘打つ単位――ジュッタ〔・ウェルデス〕が1990年代に米国で初めて教え，クリスティーナ〔・ローリー〕とジュッタがブリストル大学で教えてきた/教えている単位であるが――を教える中で，我々が本当に困惑していることが1つある。開講後かなり経ってから，また，単位が終わるころになっても「でも，大衆文化は世界政治とどう関係しているのですか？　私には理解できません」と，不満を漏らす学生が必ずいるのである。この問いを問うということは，この単位全体がそれを正面から扱うよう組み立てられていることを考えれば，〔問う者が〕IR（学問としての）や国際関係（国家の活動としての），世界政治（より広い，しかしまだ従来型の国境にまたがる活動の集合としての）に対する狭い理解に「縛られている」ことを示す。同時に，この問いはもう1つの仮定があることを示している。時に驚くほど動かしがたいその仮定とは，ある「もの」（大衆文化）が別の「もの」（世界政治）とどのように（なるべくなら因果的に）「関係」しているかを把握するための単純な，おそらく唯一の方法がある（はずだ），というものである。典型的な実証主義者の流儀で，学生はしばしば，大衆文化が世界政治「に対して」何事かを「なす」ということ（あるいは，数はあまり多くないが，世界政治が大衆文化「に対して」何事かを「なす」ということ）が見いだせるだろうと思っているわけである。

しかし，こうした仮定は誤解〔に基づくものである〕。分析的に見れば，「大衆文化」と「世界政治」はともに複雑で，争点となる概念であり，いずれについても唯一の理解というものはありえない。経験面で言えば，これらの術語が指す対象や活動，そして両者の間の「関係」は，多様で複雑かつ動的である。

本稿では，「大衆文化」と「世界政治」の間に生じる諸関係を分析的に分類し，そうした関係がなぜ重要なのかを示唆することを試みる。大衆文化と世界政治の間の６つのタイプの関係を提示し，それぞれを多面的で他と無関係ではないものとして順番に捉えていく。そして，「ダイヤモンドの婚約指輪」を用いて，これらの多様な関係の間の相互の結びつきを強調する。

ここで１つ補足しておきたいのだが，我々は大衆文化と世界政治の間の他の可能な関係についての議論をことさら排除しているわけではない。分析的な場を開拓したいのであって，閉鎖したいのではないからである。これらの「もの」が互いに関係する非常に多様なあり方（を理解する非常に多様な方法）だけは少なくとも，すでに存在することを示したいのである。ロバート・コックス（1981）の言葉を借りれば，こうした大衆文化と世界政治の関係は多様な読者にとって重要である。そしてその理由もまた多様で，時としては相矛盾するものである。

したがって本稿では，これらの関係が（我々にとって）重要となる多様なあり方を際立たせることで，これらの関係がより多くの人，特に世界政治の学者や実務家（一般市民を含む）にとって，いかに重要であるはずのものであるか(Rowley and Weldes 2012）を明らかにするものである。そうすることで，我々は自ら答えうるより多くの問いを意図的に投げかけようとしている。本稿は，探求されうる事柄〔が持つ〕莫大な幅に注目することで，きわめて幅広くはあるが，明確に決まってはいない大衆文化・世界政治の研究課題にいく分かは貢献するものと考える。

Ⅶ

下線部の単語や句の意味を最もよく表しているものを
４つの選択肢の中から１つ選びなさい。

61. 解答：A

解説 wield(s) は「(武器などを) 振り回す」の意味で，A.「(武器などを脅しとして) 振り回す」に最も近い。B は「(権利などを) 与える」，C は「～を控える」，D は「～を共有する」の意味。

62. 解答：C

解説 give way は「壊れる，退く」などの意味で，C.「重大さを失う」に最も近い。A は「優勢になる」，B は「重量が増える」，D は「優位になる」の意味。

63. 解答：A

解説 hold は「～を拘束する」の意味で，A.「～を収監・拘束する」に最も近い。B は「～を釈放する」, C は「～を解放する」, D は「～を自由にする」の意味。

64. 解答：B

解説 motive force は「原動力」の意味で, B.「根本的理由」に最も近い。A は「否定・反駁《はんばく》」, C は「拒絶」, D は「懐疑」の意味。

65. 解答：D

解説 heed は「～に注意を払う」の意味で, D.「～を気にする」に最も近い。A は「～を見逃す」, B は「～を無視する」, C は「～を忘れる」の意味。

66. 解答：A

解説 strike は「～を打つ・たたく」の意味で, A.「～を襲撃する」に最も近い。B は「～を発見する」, C は「～を昇進させる」, D は「～を驚かせる」の意味。

67. 解答：D

解説 enmity(-ies) は「敵意」の意味で, D.「敵意」に最も近い。A は「快適さ」, B は「友好」, C は「調和・平和」の意味。

68. 解答：D

解説 imbue は「(思想・野心などを) 吹き込む・満たす」の意味で, D.「～を満たす」に最も近い (with ... との共起も共通である)。A は「～を奪う」, B は「～をからにする」, C は「～を啓発する」の意味。

69. 解答：B

解説 sustenance は「生存維持」の意味で, B.「栄養 (を与えること)」に最も近い。A は「(権利などの) 剥奪」, C は「豊富」, D は「不足」の意味。

70. 解答：C

解説 revert to は「～に戻る」の意味で, C.「～に戻る」に最も近い。A は「～から出発する」, B は「～に二度と立ち戻らない」, D は「～にとどまる」の意味。

訳例　「日本は自衛のための近代的な兵器の入手に無頓着であるべきだとは，私は決して言う者ではない。ただ，それは決して自衛本能を超えるものであってはならない。本当の力は兵器そのものにあるのではなく，その兵器を使う人間にあることを日本は知らなければならない。また，力を求めるあまり，己《おのれ》の魂を犠牲にして武器を増強すれば，敵よりもさらに大きな危険にさらされるのは己自身なのだということを知らねばならない。

生きているものは大変傷つきやすく，そのため保護が求められる。自然界では，生命は，生命自身の材料でできた己の被覆の内部に自らを守っている。それゆえ，被覆は生命の成長と調和している。あるいは，時が来ればたやすく壊れ，忘れ去られる。生きている人間の場合，本当の保護はその人の精神的理想のうちにある。その理想はその人の生との間に不可欠の関係を持ち，その人の成長とともに成長する。しかしあいにく，その鎧《よろい》はすべてが生きたものではない――一部が鋼鉄でできており，鈍重かつ機械的である。したがって，人間はそれを利用しながらも，その暴虐から己を守るために注意深くあることが必要となる。もしその被覆に己を合わせるために小さくなるような弱さがあるならば，それは魂の縮小による緩慢な自殺の過程となる。そして日本は，存在の道徳法則に対する確固たる信仰を持たなければならない。それは，西洋諸国が己の権力を維持し，他を服従させるために，組織の巨大な重量で押さえつけて人間性を窒息させる自殺の道をたどっていることを，己に対して言い聞かせられるようにするためである。

日本にとって危険なのは，西洋の外面的特徴を模倣することではない。むしろ，西洋ナショナリズムの原動力を日本自身のものとして受け入れることである。日本の社会的理想は，すでに政治の手にかかって敗北の兆しを見せている。私には，日本が科学から採用した座右の銘，すなわち「適者生存」の語が，日本の現代史のとば口に大書されているのが見える。その意味は「自ら助けよ，そして他にかかる代償を決して考えるな」である。〔すなわち〕目が見えないために自分が触れることができるものだけを信じる盲人の座右の銘である。しかし，目が見える人は，人間はお互いにきわめて緊密に結びついており，自分が他者を打てば，その一撃は己自身に返ってくることを承知している。〔……中略……〕

己が他の人種に与えた傷が己に影響しないとか，己の家の回りに撒《ま》いた敵意が，今後ずっと己の防護壁となるなどとは，一瞬たりとも考えてはならない。一民族全体の心に，己の優越性について異常な虚栄心を植え付け，己の道徳的無慈悲と不正に得た富を誇りとするよう教え，戦利品をひけらかすことによって，そしてそれを学校で使って子どもの心に他者への軽蔑を産み付けることによって敗戦国の屈辱を永続させることは，西洋の模倣である。しかも西洋が膿《う》んだ傷を持つ側面で西洋を模倣することになる。その傷の腫れは活力を食い破る病の腫れなのである。

我々の生存維持に必要な食用作物は，何世紀にもわたる選択と栽培の結果である。しかし，我々の生命に変える必要がない植物には，何世代にもわたる忍耐強い考慮を要しない。雑草を除くことは容易ではないが，世話を怠ることで食用作物を駄目にし，原始の野生の状態に戻らせることは容易である。

同様に，非常な思いやりをもって諸君の〔国の〕土壌に適応した栽培植物，つまり生命にとても親密で，とても人間的な栽培植物は，過去の時代に土を耕し，除草する必要があったのみならず，いまも細心の手入れと監視を必要とする。科学や組織の方法など，単に近代的なものは移植しうるが，決定的に人間的なものは，繊維がきわめて繊細で，根が非常に多く，広く張るために，その土壌から動かすと死んでしまう。それゆえに私は，西洋の政治理念が諸君自身の政治理想に無礼な圧力をかけることを恐れるのである。

VIII 文脈上，空所を埋めるのに最も ふさわしいものを 4つの選択肢の中から1つ選びなさい。

71. 解答：B

解説 先行するsanctionを後置修飾し，文意に最もふさわしいのは，B.「課された」である。Aは「無効にされた」，Cは「解除された」，Dは「危険にさらされた」の意味。

72. 解答：B

解説 後に続くit were newsに先行して仮定法の節をつくるB.「まるで～であるかのように」が最もふさわしく意味が通る。Aは「一方～」，Cは「～なので」，Dは「～ということ」の意味。

73. 解答：C

解説 Europeがin which it now finds itself（現在それに陥っている）の状況として文意から最もふさわしいのは，C.「苦境」である。Aは「暴動」，Bは「断念」，Dは「乱闘」の意味。

74. 解答：D

解説 ドイツの政治家たちがロシアからのパイプラインに政治的責任を負おうとしていないという文意から，D.「(批判などを) かわしてきた」が最もふさわしい。Aは「～に取り組んできた」，Bは「～をあばいてきた」，Cは「～に値してきた」の意味。

75. 解答：A

解説 Russian gasとother sourcesが対比されており，前者がincreasingのとき，それに伴う（後者の）状況として，A.「～を犠牲にして」が最もふさわしい。Bは「～の観点から」，Cは「～が滞って」，Dは「～にしたがって」の意味。

76. 解答：C

解説 原子力発電の廃止決定が原因となって，ロシアのガスへの依存を高めた，という文意から，C.「～の結果」が最もふさわしい。Aは「～にもかかわらず」，Bは「～の最中に」，Dは「～までずっと」の意味。

77. 解答：B

解説 後に続く「制裁の恐れがあるにもかかわらず」に呼応して意味を成すのは，B.「進んだ」である。Aは「～を必要とした」，Cは「未完に終わった」，Dは「止まった」の意味。

78. 解答：A

解説 Steinmeierがこの事業を擁護しているという文脈，with ... との共起から，A.「～に…を与えた」が最もふさわしい。Bは「～を引き受けた」，Cは「～を見捨てた」，Dは「～を買収した」の意味。

79. 解答：D

解説 as well asを挟んで，先行するlackluster military supportと意味的にも並列の関係になっていることから，D.「経費」（defense outlays：防衛費）が最も文意に合う。Aは「詳細な計画」，Bは「損害」，Cは「抑制」の意味。

80. 解答：C

解説 “reset” with Moscowの結果として“Russia is back ...”と後述されていることから，“reset”がうまくいかなかったことがわかるので，C.「不運な」が最もふさわしい。Aは「幸先のよい」，Bは「正当な」，Dは「極悪非道な」の意味。

訳例　ロシアの国営ガス会社ガスプロムは，ドイツと結ぶ主要パイプライン〔ノルドストリーム1〕を通じてドイツに送る天然ガスの供給量を容量の20％まで減らすと発表した。ロシア政府がどのような口実を述べようと，真の理由は誰の目にも明らかだ。ウクライナに対する戦争で受けたEUの制裁への報復である。欧州委員会のウルズラ・フォン・デア・ライエン委員長は「ロシアは我々を脅迫している。ロシアはエネルギーを武器として使っているのだ」と不満を口にした。

フォン・デア・ライエン氏は，あたかもそれがニュースであるかのように発表したが，それは違う――過去20年以上も注意を向けてきた人にとっては違うのだ。エネルギーを政治の武器として利用することは，プーチン露大統領にとっては別に新奇な戦術ではない。だから，ロシアのエネルギーによる恐喝のために欧州がエネルギー危機に直面することは，ロシアのウクライナ戦争における非道な行為とまったく同じく予測可能なことである。

このようになる必然性はなかったのだ。大陸で最大にして最も豊かな大国ドイツが指導的役割を果たす欧州には，現在陥っているような迷惑な苦境を回避するための時間が十分にあった。欧州のエネルギーのジレンマは，相互に関連する次の3つの幻想の結果である。①ロシアのガスへの依存は，それに伴うどんな（小さな）リスクにも見合うものである。②そのガスの供給者は，敵対者ではなくパートナーである。③大陸での通常戦争は過去のものである。

これまで何年もの間，ドイツの政治家はノルドストリームへの批判を，「自分たちは両手を縛られている」という決まり文句でかわし続けてきた。同パイプラインは「商業プロジェクト」であり，ドイツ政府の統制を受けない，というのだ。しかし，他の供給源を犠牲にして欧州のロシア産ガスへの依存を高めることは，常に政治的な次元に関わる問題だった。特にドイツではそうだった。2011年の福島原発事故の後にいかにもドイツらしいパニックに陥った際，ドイツ政府は誰に強いられるでもなく原子力エネルギー部門を封印した。島国の日本とは異なり，ドイツは大陸の真ん中に位置しており，福島原発を破壊したような地震による津波の被害を受ける恐れはない。当時のアンゲラ・メルケル首相が2022年末までに原子力発電を廃止するという性急な決断をしたせいで，プーチンが欧州に対してエネルギー戦争を仕掛ける決断をするころには，ドイツはロシアのガスに対していっそう依存することになったのだった。

ノルドストリーム2が政治の手の届かないところにあるという言い訳とは裏腹に，ドイツ政治の権力層は別の幻想の呪縛に陥った。同事業がロシアの西側への統合の模範となっているという〔思い込み〕である。2014年，ロシアのクリミア半島併合からわずか1週間後，ドイツの大手企業シーメンス社の最高経営責任者がモスクワを訪問し，第２次世界大戦後初となった欧州の領土の武力占領について，全般的には建設的な関係の中〔に生じた〕「短期的な混乱」だと述べた。数カ月後には，フランク＝ヴァルター・シュタインマイヤー外相（当時）がロシアのエカテリンブルクを訪れ，ロシアとEUの「経済・政治的」パートナーシップを承認した。

２本目のノルドストリーム・パイプラインの計画は，トランプ政権による制裁の恐れがある中でも進められた。シュタインマイヤー（現ドイツ大統領）は，ソ連によるドイツ侵攻から80年近くを経た昨年２月，ノルドストリーム2〔事業〕を「ロシアとヨーロッパを結ぶ最後の架け橋の１つ」として擁護し，ドイツが通常，戦後和解に関わる取り組みに対して示す道徳的重みをこの事業に与える形となった。ロシアのウクライナ侵攻後になってようやく同パイプラインは保留となった。

〔上述の〕最後第３の幻想，すなわち恒久的な平和に恵まれた大陸という幻想を見破る指導者がもっとあったなら，欧州は今日エネルギー危機に見舞われることはなかっただろう。ウクライナを征服できるというプーチンの信念は，〔欧州に〕差し迫ったエネルギー危機をもたらした直接の原因であるが，その〔信念が生まれた〕要因としては，西欧が窮状に立つ隣国に対する軍事支援を渋り，自らも防衛費を低く抑えてきたことが大きい。NATOが2008年，グルジア〔現在ジョージア〕とウクライナに加盟の道を開くことをフランスとドイツの要請で拒否したことが，プーチンに対して両国への侵攻のゴーサインを送ることになったのだ。欧州の軍備，特にドイツ軍が老朽化していることも，大陸をロシアによる略奪から防衛することへの真剣さの欠如を示していた。

西欧の指導者たちは，その幻想がどういう性質のものであるかについて繰り返し警告を受けた。中でも最も強く警告したのが東欧の人々だ。ポーランドの国防相はすでに2006年の時点で，ノルドストリームを1939年のモロトフ・リッベントロップ協定になぞらえていた。東欧諸国〔とフィンランド〕をナチスドイツとソビエト連邦〔の勢力範囲〕に分割した悪名高き〔独ソ不可侵条約である〕。その３年後，オバマ政権によるロシア政府との「リセット」が失敗したことを受けて，中欧と東欧の著名な政治家のグループが公開書簡を発表し，「ロシアは21世紀の戦術と方法で19世紀の課題を追求する修正主義の大国として復活した」と断じた。その忠告は聞き入れられなかった。

この冬〔2022～23年〕，ドイツ人が例年以上に〔寒さに〕震えることになるとすれば，それは身から出た錆以外の何物でもない。

IX

以下の質問に対し，150～200語の短いエッセイを英語で書きなさい。

質問文：国連のイニシアチブを１つ取り上げ，そのイニシアチブに対する取り組みで世界に希望を与えている例を１つ示して論じよ。

解答例 UN ocean restoration initiatives, based on SDG14, Life Below Water, give us hope for how we may improve the world.

At the UN Ocean Conference, hosted at the end of July 2022 in Lisbon by the governments of Portugal and Kenya, UN Secretary-General Guterres powerfully advocated for increased efforts in four areas of action: 1) investing in sustainable ocean economies, 2) replicating ocean restoration successes, 3) protecting people whose food sources and jobs depend on fishing and fisheries, and 4) developing more science and innovation.

As an example of science and innovation-based action and a best-practices model (items 4) and 2) above), the Colombian Government's 'One Million Corals for Colombia' project—a UN Decade of Ocean Science for Sustainable Development 2021–2030 commitment—is the largest ocean reef restoration undertaking in the Americas. Supporting over a thousand square miles of coral reefs, it aims to reestablish—in such places as Seaflower UNESCO Biosphere Reserve oceanic archipelago and Corales del Rosario and San Bernardo National Park—200 hectares of reefs by 2023.

Certainly, this example does not achieve all the SDG14 goals immediately; however, it is an inspiring "proof of concept" demonstrating forward-looking and hopeful ways ocean restoration is being accomplished.

解説 国連のイニシアチブとして，SDGs（2015年国連サミットにて採択）はトピックとして現在最もふさわしいと思われるため，そのうちの１つを取り上げて詳しく論じるとよいだろう。

第１パラグラフでは主題を提示し，SDG 14「海の豊かさを守ろう」について，「世界に希望を与える」という視点で，国連の働きを論じることを宣言している。

第２パラグラフでは，国連海洋会議においてグテーレス国連事務総長によって提唱された４つの行動分野を紹介している。

第３パラグラフでは，「科学と革新のいっそうの推進」により「海洋修復の成功例」となった，コロンビア政府のサンゴ再生事業について説明している。

第 4 パラグラフでは，前のパラグラフで挙げた例について，希望につながる大きなきっかけになると述べることで，国連のイニシアチブを肯定的なものとして結論付けている。

訳例　SDG 14「海の豊かさを守ろう」に基づく国連の海洋再生イニシアチブは，私たちがどのように世界をよくしていけるかという点について希望を与えてくれる。

2022 年 7 月末にポルトガルとケニアの両国政府が共催してリスボンで開かれた国連海洋会議において，グテーレス国連事務総長は，次の 4 つの行動分野における取り組みの強化を力強く提唱した。1）持続可能な海洋経済国への投資，2）海洋修復の成功例に倣うこと，3）食料源と雇用で漁業・水産業に依存する人々の保護，4）科学と革新のいっそうの推進。

科学と革新に基づく取り組み例として，またベストプラクティスモデル（上記 4）と 2)）として，コロンビア政府の「コロンビアに 100 万株のサンゴを」プロジェクト（「持続可能な開発のための国連海洋科学の 10 年」＝ 2021 ～ 2030 年の約束の 1 つ）は，米州最大の海洋サンゴ礁再生事業である。1,000 平方マイル以上のサンゴ礁を支援対象とする同事業は，ユネスコのシーフラワー生物圏保全地域に指定されている〔サン・アンドレス〕諸島〕とコラレス・デル・ロサリオおよびサン・ベルナルド国立公園などにおいて，2023 年までに 200 ヘクタールのサンゴ礁再生を目指している。

なるほど，この例は SDG 14 のすべての目標を直ちに達成できるものではないけれども，海洋再生が前向きで希望に満ちたしかたで実現に向かっていることを示す，刺激的な「概念実証」となっている。

2022年A級第2回試験　正解一覧

Ⅰ

1. A　2. B　3. D　4. C　5. D　6. B　7. B　8. C　9. D　10. A

Ⅱ

11. B　12. B　13. B　14. D　15. A　16. A　17. D　18. C　19. C　20. B

Ⅲ

21. B　22. C　23. D　24. C　25. D　26. A　27. B　28. C　29. C　30. A

Ⅳ

31. C　32. D　33. B　34. D　35. A　36. C　37. C　38. A　39. B　40. D

Ⅴ

41. C　42. D　43. A　44. B　45. B　46. A　47. B　48. D　49. C　50. C

Ⅵ

51. C　52. B　53. C　54. B　55. A　56. A　57. B　58. D　59. D　60. A

Ⅶ

61. A　62. C　63. A　64. B　65. D　66. A　67. D　68. D　69. B　70. C

Ⅷ

71. B　72. B　73. C　74. D　75. A　76. C　77. B　78. A　79. D　80. C

2次試験（面接テスト）について

2次試験は，特A級およびA級の1次試験合格者を対象に，第1回目は7月中旬の日曜日，第2回目は12月中旬の日曜日に実施されます。

特A級は外国人面接官1名，日本人面接官1名との2対1でのインタビュー，A級は外国人面接官と1対1でのインタビューです。面接時間は，特A級が15分，A級が10分です。A級については会場によりSkype等によるオンライン面接となる場合もあります。また面接テストの内容は公正な評価を行うため，すべて録音（オンライン面接の場合は録画）され，一定期間試験記録として保管されます。

外国人面接官は，インタビュアーとしての研修を受け，最終審査に合格した英語のネイティブスピーカーです。外国人面接官の選抜には，国籍や人種のバランスも考慮されています。日本人面接官は，外務省大使OBなど外交実務経験者，または大学教授です。大使経験者は英語を駆使し，なおかつ世界で活躍した人々であり，大学教授はTOEIC® 満点，国連英検特A級合格，通訳案内業国家試験合格など，公的に英語力を証明できる資格を持ち，なおかつ国際舞台で活躍している人々です。

2次試験では，まず面接シート（INTERVIEW SHEET）に事前に必要事項を英語で書き，入室と同時に面接シートを面接官に渡します。受験者が記入したくないと思う事項については書く必要はありません。面接シートは次ページのとおりです。面接シートの目的の1つは，受験者にとって身近な話題からインタビューを始め，リラックスした雰囲気で試験を行うことですから，面接の話題にしてほしいような内容はぜひ記入しておきましょう。受験者が着席すると面接が始まります。国連英検の面接官はインタビュアーとしての訓練を受けた専門家ですから，受験者が落ち着いて面接を受けられるように配慮しています。多くの場合，受験者にとって話のしやすい身近な話題から会話が始まり，質問は徐々に国際事情へと発展します。特定のトピックについて数分間のスピ−チをするといったことはないため，自分にとって興味があり，得意とする分野に話題を導くことができれば有利となるでしょう。ただ，面接官は国際事情に詳しいので，日頃から海外のニュース（CNN, BBC など）や UN News に親しみ，幅広い知識を身につけておくことが必要不可欠です。

面接シート
INTERVIEW SHEET

受験級 Class	受験記号・番号

Name	
氏名	

【記入上の注意 Notes】
1．下記の各項目を英語で記入して下さい。ただし、答えたくない項目は記入しなくて構いません。
2．記入された内容や記入量によって、試験の採点が影響されることはありません。

a. Family 家族（例：Father,Mother,Two brothers,One Daughter）

b. Home Address 現住所（区、市、郡まで。例：Nerima-ku,Tokyo）

c. Occupation 職業（例：Student,Office worker,Housewife,Bank clerk）

d. Special Qualifications 特技（例：Computer）

e. Education 教育（専攻のみ。例：Western History,Economics）

f. Hobbies,Interests,Special Concerns 趣味・興味を持っていること（例：Tennis,World Peace）

g. Your Favorite Authors 好きな作家・愛読書（例：Dickens,B.Russell）

h. Persons You Respect 尊敬する人物（例：My Father,Lincoln）

i. Foreign Countries Visited 海外経験（なければ None,あれば場所、時期、期間、目的）

j. Foreign Countries You Want to Visit 訪れたい国（例：India,Ireland）

国連英検の面接では，ただ単に国際事情の知識があるだけでは不十分です。日本人として，日本が国際社会でどのように行動したらよいか，どのようにすれば国際貢献できるのかといった視点から，理路整然かつ論理的に話ができる必要があります。付け焼刃の国際事情の知識ではとても太刀打ちできません。広く浅く議論を無難にこなせる分野だけではなく，深い議論が可能な分野もいくつか持っていることが必要です。

面接において，日本との関係が希薄な国際事情について詳しく問われることはあまりありません。たとえ面接官が外交実務経験の豊富な大使経験者であっても，世界中の国際会議などで講演を常に行っている大学教授であっても，あくまで日本と日本人という視点からの質問が中心となります。

２次試験の評価方法は，以下の４分野（合計７項目，括弧内は配点の割合）についてそれぞれ10段階で採点され，配点の割合に準じた得点の総合点＝総合評価で合否が判定されます。

特Ａ級は総合評価で８点以上，Ａ級は７点以上が合格です。

Examiner' s analysis of candidate' s strengths and weaknesses
(Circle on number between 1 and 10 for each area of ability, adding "+" if desired.)

Level of Strength / Area of Ability	Weak	Middle Range	Strong	Weight	Office Use
1) Comprehension	1 2 3	4 5 6 7	8 9 10	25.00%	
2) Speaking: Pronunciation	1 2 3	4 5 6 7	8 9 10	25.00% (6.25%)	
Fluency	1 2 3	4 5 6 7	8 9 10	(6.25%)	
Structure	1 2 3	4 5 6 7	8 9 10	(6.25%)	
Vocabulary	1 2 3	4 5 6 7	8 9 10	(6.25%)	
3) Communication	1 2 3	4 5 6 7	8 9 10	25.00%	
4) Knowledge (International Affairs)	1 2 3	4 5 6 7	8 9 10	25.00%	

なお，２次試験の受験対策教材として『国連英検 特Ａ級・Ａ級 面談対策』（三修社）が刊行されています。また，特Ａ級・Ａ級で実施される２次試験（面接テスト）の様子を紹介した動画が国連英検のホームページ上に公開されています。

http://www.kokureneiken.jp/about/interviewmodel

国連英検実施要項

（2023 年度時点）

主　催	公益財団法人 日本国際連合協会 国連英検事務局
問い合わせ先	〒 104-0031　東京都中央区京橋 3-12-4 MAOビル 4 階 TEL 03-6228-6831 ／ FAX 03-6228-6832 http://www.kokureneiken.jp/

※国連英検 D 級・E 級は 2023 年度より開催を休止中。最新の実施情報は国連英検ホームページ http://www.kokureneiken.jp/ で必ず確認すること。

<table>
<tr><td>試験日</td><td>
<table>
<tr><th></th><th>１次試験</th><th>２次試験</th></tr>
<tr><td>第 1 回</td><td>毎年 5 月下旬の日曜日</td><td>毎年 7 月中旬の日曜日</td></tr>
<tr><td>第 2 回</td><td>毎年 10 月下旬の日曜日</td><td>毎年 12 月中旬の日曜日</td></tr>
</table>
※ 2 次試験は特 A 級・A 級のみ。
</td></tr>
<tr><td>試験地</td><td>■ 1 次試験…札幌・仙台・さいたま・千葉・東京・神奈川・名古屋・神戸・京都・大阪・広島・福岡・鹿児島・那覇の予定
■ 2 次試験…特 A 級：東京・大阪
※特 A 級・A 級の併願者の 2 次試験はすべて東京・大阪で行なわれる。
A 級：札幌・仙台・東京・名古屋・大阪・福岡・那覇の予定
受験会場名，所在地は受験票に明示される。受験地の変更はできない。なお，1 次試験を特別会場で受験した受験者の 2 次試験は，最寄りの試験会場となる。
※開催最小人数に満たない会場は開催を中止する場合がある（1 次・2 次共）。</td></tr>
<tr><td>検定料
（税込）</td><td>特 A 級…13,200 円　A 級…11,000 円
B 級…8,800 円　C 級…5,500 円
※一度納入された検定料は返却できない。申し込み後の変更もできない。
※事務局が申込書を検定料の受領後，受付完了。</td></tr>
<tr><td>併願受験
検定料
（税込）</td><td>特 A 級＋ A 級＝ 22,000 円　A 級＋ B 級＝ 17,600 円
B 級＋ C 級＝ 13,200 円
※一度納入された検定料は返却できない。申し込み後の変更もできない。
※事務局が申込書を検定料の受領後，受付完了。</td></tr>
<tr><td>1 次試験の
開始時間</td><td>A 級　C 級……午前 10 時 30 分（集合時間午前 10 時）
特 A 級　B 級……午後 2 時（集合時間午後 1 時 30 分）</td></tr>
</table>

試験内容

■ 1 次試験

級	試験方法	試験時間
特A・A	リーディング・英作文	120 分
B	リスニング・リーディング・英作文	120 分
C	リスニング・リーディング	100 分

■ 2 次試験

※特 A 級・A 級の 1 次試験合格者および 1 次試験免除者が対象。

※面接シートに事前に所要事項を英語で書き込み，外国人面接官などの質問事項に答える。

※ A 級については会場により Skype 等によるオンライン面接になる場合もある。

※面接の内容は試験実施の品質向上と厳正さを担保することを目的に録音（オンラインの場合は録画）される。

合格発表

合格者には合格カードを発行

試験結果は郵送にて通知。

	1 次試験	2 次試験
第 1 回	毎年 6 月下旬	毎年 8 月中旬
第 2 回	毎年 11 月下旬	毎年 1 月中旬

受験申し込み要項

●併願の場合

午前午後で隣接する 2 つの級を同日に受験することができる。併願を希望する場合は「受験申込書」の併願欄に記入して申し込むこと。

● 1 次試験免除

前回または前々回の 1 次試験に合格し，2 次試験に不合格または欠席した場合，申請により 1 次試験が免除され，2 次試験のみ受験できる。申込書の所定欄にその旨を記入し申し込むこと。検定料は同じ。

受験票

申込書と検定料金の受理後，受験地の会場・所在地が記載された受験票が 1 次試験日の 1 週間前までに送付される。届かない場合は，必ず試験日の 3 日前までに国連英検事務局（03-6228-6831〈代表〉）へ問い合わせること。顔写真 1 枚（4 センチ× 3 センチ）を試験日までに用意し受験票に貼り付けておくこと。試験当日は，受験票とともに身分証明書を持参すること。

受験申し込み方法

書店，郵送，インターネット（PC・スマートフォン）で申し込みができる。
詳細は国連英検ホームページ http://www.kokureneiken.jp/ で確認する。

申込受付期間

第 1 回　3 月初旬～ 4 月下旬　※翌日消印有効
第 2 回　8 月初旬～ 9 月下旬　※翌日消印有効

検定料のお支払い方法

電話で申し込む場合	国連英検事務局へ電話・FAXにて申し込みができる。申し込み受付後「コンビニ支払用紙」が郵送される。
郵送で申し込む場合	国連英検事務局に受験申込書を請求する。 ●支払方法：必ず受験者氏名で銀行または郵便局から振り込む。
インターネット (PC・スマートフォン) で申し込む場合	国連英検のホームページから申し込みができる。 (PC・スマートフォン) http://www.kokureneiken.jp/ ●支払方法：クレジットカード支払い，コンビニエンスストア支払い，銀行または郵便局から振り込む。

検定料の各種支払詳細

振込の場合	●銀行からの振込 銀行名：　三菱UFJ銀行　日本橋支店 口座名：　(公財) 日本国際連合協会　国連英検事務局 口座番号：普通口座 0010400 金額：　　該当級の受験料 ※振込手数料は受験者負担。 ※現金・為替は取り扱い不可。 ※いずれも事務局が申込書と検定料の受領を確認後，受付完了。 ※インターネット（PC・スマートフォン）で申し込んだ受験者は，ご依頼人の前に「受付番号」（メールにて通知される）を記入する。
	●郵便局からの払込 郵便局設置の払込書（青票）にて以下の内容を記入の上，払い込む。 加入者名：(公財) 日本国際連合協会 口座番号：00130-7-24670 金額：　　該当級の受験料 ※振込手数料は受験者負担。 ※ご依頼人欄に受験者名，住所，電話番号を必ず記入する。インターネット（PC・スマートフォン）で申し込んだ受験者は，ご依頼人の前に「受付番号」（メールにて通知される）を記入する。 ※払込金受領書は必ず保管する。
クレジットカードの場合	●インターネット（PC・スマートフォン）からの申し込みのみ可能 入力フォームにて「クレジットカード払い」を選択し，カード番号，有効期限などを入力する。 ※利用可能クレジットカードは国連英検のホームページで確認のこと。
コンビニエンスストアの場合	●インターネット（PC・スマートフォン）からの申し込みの場合 入力フォームにて「コンビニ払い」を選択すると，払込票が送付される。 ●電話・FAXで申し込みの場合 申し込み受付完了後事務局より「コンビニ支払用紙」が郵送される。 ※全国の主要なコンビニエンスストアにて受験料を支払う。

著者・執筆協力者プロフィール

著　者

髙橋信道（たかはし・のぶみち）
翻訳家。京都大学理学部および文学部卒。国連英検指導検討委員会委員。著書に『国連英検過去問題集特A級・A級』（共著，三修社）他。

長　和重（ちょう・かずしげ）
高崎経済大学講師。敬和学園大学講師。国連英検指導検討委員会委員。著書に『国連ニュースで読む世界』（共著，三修社），『国連英検過去問題集特A級・A級』（共著，三修社）他。

村越亮治（むらこし・りょうじ）
玉川大学准教授。学術博士。国連英検指導検討委員会委員。

Lawrence Karn（ローレンス・カーン）
大妻女子大学特任教授。成城大学講師。学術博士。国連英検指導検討委員会委員長。論文に「Developing English Skills by Reporting on Current Events and World News」（OJSIS），著書に『国連英検過去問題集特A級・A級』（共著，三修社）他。

執筆協力者

服部孝彦（はっとり・たかひこ）
大妻女子大学・同大学院教授。言語学博士。国連英検統括監修官。著書に『国連英検ベーシック・トライアル』（三修社）など多数。

武藤克彦（むとう・かつひこ）
東洋英和女学院大学准教授。国連英検指導検討委員会委員。著書に『国連英検特A級・A級対策［改訂版］』（共著，三修社），『上級時事英文法』（三修社）など多数。

Paul Underwood（ポール・アンダーウッド）
東洋英和女学院大学教授。言語学博士。国連英検指導検討委員会委員。著書に『CLIL Writing about Global Relations』（三修社）他，英語教育関係の論文多数。

Gordon Myskow（ゴードン・ミスコウ）
神田外語大学大学院准教授。応用言語学博士。国連英検指導検討委員会委員。著書に『EFL Writing in Japan: Theory, Policy, and Practice』（メディアイランド）他，英語教育関係の論文多数。

国連英検過去問題集《こくれんえいけんかこもんだいしゅう》［A級《えーきゅう》］〈2021-2022年度実施《ねんどじっし》〉

2023年8月31日　第1刷発行

編　者　公益財団法人　日本国際連合協会

著　者　髙橋信道　長和重　村越亮治　ローレンス・カーン

執筆協力　服部孝彦　武藤克彦　ポール・アンダーウッド　ゴードン・ミスコウ

発行者　前田俊秀

発行所　株式会社三修社
〒150-0001 東京都渋谷区神宮前2-2-22
TEL 03-3405-4511　FAX 03-3405-4522
振替 00190-9-72758
https://www.sanshusha.co.jp

印刷・製本　日経印刷株式会社
編集協力／大嶋晶代
装丁デザイン／仁井谷伴子

ISBN978-4-384-06074-4 C2082